The Resistant Writer

SUNY series,
Literacy, Culture, and Learning: Theory and Practice

Alan C. Purves, editor

The Resistant Writer

Rhetoric as Immunity, 1850 to the Present

Charles Paine

State University of New York Press

Production by Ruth Fisher
Marketing by Fran Keneston

Published by
State University of New York Press, Albany

For information, address State University of New York Press,
State University Plaza, Albany, NY 12246

Library of Congress Cataloging-in-Publication Data

Paine, Charles, 1957–
    The resistant writer : rhetoric as immunity, 1850 to the present /
Charles Paine.
        p.   cm. — (SUNY series, literacy, culture, and learning)
    Includes bibliographical references (p. 231) and index.
    ISBN 0-7914-4049-4 (hc : alk. paper). — ISBN 0-7914-4050-8 (pb :
alk. paper)
    1. English language—Rhetoric—Study and teaching—United States.
2. English language—Rhetoric—Study and teaching—United States—
History—19th century.   3. English language—Rhetoric—Study and
teaching—Massachusetts—Cambridge.   4. Rhetoric—Political aspects—
United States—History—19th century.   5. Rhetoric—Social aspects—
United States—History—19th century.   6. Language and culture—
United States—History—19th century.   7. Channing, Edward Tyrrel,
1790–1856.   8. Hill, Adams Sherman, 1833–1910.   I. Title.
II. Series.
PE1405.U6P28   1999
808'.042'07073—dc21   98-27341
                                                              CIP

10 9 8 7 6 5 4 3 2 1

Cover illustrations:

(top, left) Edward Tyrrel Channing (1790–1856), c. 1852
by George Peter Alexander Healy (1813–1894)

oil on canvas
76.9 cm. x 64.2 cm. actual
Gift of a large number of the alumni graduated since 1819 to Harvard
College, 1852. Copyright © President and Fellows, Harvard College, Harvard
University Art Museums.

(top, right) Adams Sherman Hill. Courtesy of the Harvard University Archives.

(bottom) Harvard Yard, c. 1890. Courtesy of the Harvard University Archives.

For Susan

and

For my parents

Contents

Preface

This book straddles and integrates two important areas in rhetoric and composition: historical inquiry and contemporary pedagogical theory and practice. I do this by tracing the relationship between two ideas: (1) the idea that rhetorical training reacts to and strives to ameliorate the "current" decline in popular public discourse (as with literacy, public discourse seems always to be in crisis), and (2) the idea that rhetorical training can endow students with the capacity to "resist" (to see through, to refuse to get caught up in, or to be generally unaffected by) the unhealthy and unhealthful discourse of the public sphere. Traditionally, in order to resist public discourse (as one might resist a virus or a sinful temptation), the student-citizen had to be "whole" (as in "sound" and "healthy"), and so the way to resist popular public discourse is to know "who you are and what you stand for." I look, in other words, at the part of rhetorical training that tries to *safeguard* students and citizens from a dangerous world of discourse, rather than trying to *activate* them as responsible, contributing citizens.

Throughout the work, I often return to the central metaphor of public and individual health. Historically, bad rhetoric (whether in form or in substance) is often equated to disease, the spread of bad rhetoric to contagion or epidemic. As Susan Sontag writes: "Illnesses have always been used as metaphors to enliven charges that a society was corrupt or unjust. . . . Disease imagery is used to express concern for social order, and health is something everyone is presumed to know about" (72). In terms of rhetoric and rhetorical training, healthy students or citizens would be those whose constitution ("natural immunity") or training ("acquired immunity") provides them with a kind of immunity against such pernicious cultural forces.

And throughout the work, I try to create a useful resonance between the nineteenth-century decline in public discourse and the current decline in public discourse. In addition to the composition-studies scholars I discuss in the final chapter, mainstream authors such as linguistics professor

Deborah Tannen, media critic Howard Kurtz, *Atlantic Monthly* editor James Fallows, and columnists Haynes Johnson and David S. Broder, to name just a very few, have argued that something is terribly wrong with the dominant norms of public discussion. Of these authors, it is Tannen who, in *Argument Culture,* most explicitly argues that degraded forms of public discussion degrade our personal discussion, our sense of who we are, and our sense of what argument and knowledge are and should be. Of course, rhetorical theorists since Isocrates and Aristotle have recognized that training in rhetoric might help remedy degraded public discussion. In nineteenth-century America, Harvard Boylston Professors E. T. Channing and A. S. Hill reacted in a similar fashion to the journalistic practices that were changing around them, and they tried to make rhetorical training count beyond the walls of academe. Like many contemporary writing teachers, they worried that the arguing self suggested by public discussion had invaded the identities of citizens and students. Even so, I criticize them as well as some contemporary pedagogical practices for the way they ask students to trade their sense of the world and of themselves for our (intellectual, academic) models of self, world, discussion, and knowledge. I do not suggest that these issues are somehow "off limits" to writing teachers but only that we carefully consider *how* we address the problem.

In the first part of the book, I suggest a binary division in the goals for rhetorical training: rhetoric as production and rhetoric as reception. The first seeks to transform students into active rhetors, the other to safeguard them from the dangerous discourse of other active rhetors. The first strives to teach students how to persuade others of the validity of their arguments, the second how to resist persuasion. In this sense, rhetorical training serves as something like an "inoculation" against dangerous discourse. Using the work of medical anthropologist Emily Martin and the "inoculation and resistance" theories of "counterattitudinal resistance" of social psychologists, I look primarily at the modernist metaphor of immunity, which imagines the body striving to keep the outside from getting inside, and when the outside (what is alien, not of the self) does get inside, our immune system must be prepared to exterminate it. This is the model of immunity that is still dominant in our culture, and in fact still dominant in our models for how persuasion occurs and how persuasion is resisted. A postmodern metaphor of immunity is now dominant in scientific discourse of the immune system, and it seems emergent in many other discourses as well. This metaphor sees the immune system not so much as a remorseless border patrol for the body, but as a complex, even intelligent and "flexible" (to use Martin's metaphor), system of give and take between self and nonself.

In the second part of the book, I examine an intentionally limited part of composition history in an effort to illuminate how the tradition of rhetorical training often sees its primary role as safeguarding rather than liberating and activating students. After looking at some of the current issues for composition history (chapter 2), I turn my attention to Edward T. Channing (chapter 3) and Adams Sherman Hill (chapters 4 and 5), the third and fifth Boylston Professors at Harvard (1819–51 and 1876–1904). They have been portrayed simplistically, for the most part, as "villains," as having been up to no good. But I want to show that their cases are not so clear. By looking at their goals and practices, I think we gain insight into our own practices and goals. More specifically, the goals of learning to write as they envisioned them overlap in some interesting and I hope troubling ways with the goals we envision. Like so many of us today, they feared (per the cliché of Emersonian thought) the power of society to dominate the individual—as we might say today, the power of culture to colonize the subject's consciousness. In the nineteenth century, rhetorical education was viewed, as it often is today, as a means for helping students "distance" themselves (gaining "critical distance," gaining "resistance") from the cultural forces that in various ways impinge upon their individuality or that lead them away from their best interests. To put this another way, having achieved such distance, one can discover one's real self and authentic voice— or at least a voice that protects one from a dangerous culture. Such distancing is what I am calling the *inoculation and resistance* model of education, where teaching and civic debate "fortify the immunities" (to use Channing's phrase) of students and citizenry against a culture that often threatens to overwhelm individuality.

Chapter 2, "The Uses of Composition History," examines the fairly young tradition of composition historiography, its polemics and assumptions. Although this historiography is undergoing tremendous and healthful change, historians have concentrated too much on hero-villain dichotomies, have taken on problems of enormous scope, and have employed a rhetoric of victimization. Composition and composition forebears have been portrayed as flat because the concept of "culture" has remained flat. "Culture," that is, has often been portrayed as always and everywhere controlled by "dominant" ideologies, with clean cause-and-effect relationships between ideology and practice. Or "culture" has been limited to academic/intellectual culture, as if that culture were somehow unaffected and unresponsive to the larger aspects of American culture. Cultural composition histories—that is, histories that read compositionists and their theories *through* competing institutions of their eras—may helpfully complicate this historiography.

Chapter 3 examines the rhetorical theory of Edward T. Channing in the context of some of the cultural and political debates of his era. I demonstrate how Channing's theories of rhetorical education responded to some of the political and social issues that dominated public debate around 1817. With the supposedly emerging "era of good feelings," it was believed by many that divisive and embittering discourse would give way to constructive debate. Channing's *Lectures* were intended to provide the blueprint for a fundamentally new kind of civic debate. His teaching was to provide the human agents to carry out these debates. I conclude that while Channing's goal for reformed debate was noble (a goal, in fact, that this work and much of composition studies scholarship endorses), it strived to heal public discourse by quelling the voices of dissent—by discouraging conflict rather than eliciting, pointing up, and trying to resolve it. New technologies had engendered new forms of culture (e.g., "the news," a recent invention), which threatened Channing's hopes for enlightened communication practice and for an enlightened citizenry. It endangered (as we might say today) the "critical-thinking capacities" of the populace by encouraging the "massification" of thought. In this way, my argument historicizes the sentiment, shared by both Channing and his student Emerson, that the thinker must turn his back to society. Like the advocates of the current "cultural studies in composition movement," Channing believed that by learning to write and read well (i.e., "properly"), students were provided with a "critical distance" from or "critical perspective" on social discourse. In this way, such learning might enable students to *resist* the enfeebling and overwhelming onslaughts of a culture. Channing's theory of rhetoric valued arguments that were neat, straightforward, and tidy, rather than arguments that might be less manageable and might lead to untidy, confused prose. The kind of "self" encouraged by Channing's composition philosophy was very much in the Scottish Common Sense tradition: one could construct an authentic self by reading the great works of great men, a self that could resist the onslaughts of other, nonsanctioned arguments.

In chapters 4 and 5 I examine the life and works of Adams Sherman Hill as a test case and object lesson in the way composition studies repudiates its own past and, in doing so, replicates the pattern of polarized thinking so often found in composition students. Hill has long been considered, in the words of Robert J. Connors, American composition's *bête noire*, the figure most responsible for "the rhetoric of mechanical correctness" and for removing rhetoric from the center of the curriculum to a tiny corner of the intellectual and social world. Although there is much truth in this portrait, the whole picture is more complex and more interesting. Whereas Channing conceived his *Lectures* during the "era of good feelings," Hill's rhetorical theory was produced during the period preceding the Progressive Era, when "patrician intellectuals" perceived that they and their arguments had become disenfranchised from the worlds of politics, commerce, and popular culture. (The now-common historical theory that

composition practice was intimately and straightforwardly linked to economic power forgets the intense animosity between the intellectual class
and the economically and politically powerful.) Intellectuals abhorred the
rise of American mass culture. In particular, they contemned the newspaper
industry, which had assumed the communicative and cultural functions
traditionally provided by the pulpit, the bar, and the lectern. Therefore, Hill,
like Channing, wanted the study of writing to endow the student with
certain powers of resistance against an infectious and seemingly omnipres-
ent mass culture. In order to do this, Hill encouraged students to pursue
superficial, easy-to-manage rhetorical arguments, sacrificing complex thinking to tidy, straightforward reading and writing. Hill's conception of critical
thinking and self-construction meant preserving oneself from the infection
of culture for a better time in the future when the world might be ready
to heed intellectuals' designs for the way things ought to be.

In the third part of the book, I take these historical lessons and attempt
to show how they might guide us in thinking through how we teach our
students today. Chapter 6 places these historical analyses into a diachronic
relationship with contemporary concerns and methods in composition studies. It strives to bridge the gap between the cultural predicaments faced by
Channing and Hill and the cultural and institutional predicaments faced by
contemporary writing teachers. That is, I try to clarify some of the problems concerning the relationship between the writing course and students'
worldviews and conceptions of the self. As the historical portion of this
work makes clear, there is nothing new in employing the writing course for
encouraging students to challenge (as we may view them) the pernicious
assumptions implanted by their culture. We share, perhaps to our discomfort, common goals with our forebears, who had very different assumptions
about the nature of identity and the nature of culture.

What *would* be new is entrusting our students with the "responsibility"
to produce their own criticisms of culture. "Responsible pedagogy," as I
advocate, entails neither declared "political neutrality" nor a "decentered
classroom" nor any paradigmatic recipe for critical thinking. Instead, responsible pedagogy encourages students to assume the responsibility to
grapple in complex ways with the culture they produce and with the culture that has produced *them*. The very word "responsibility," I propose,
offers a helpful heuristic for enabling students to conceive and reconceive
their role within a "social constructionist" epistemology—that is, their role
as both learners and producers of knowledge, in the classroom and in the
world. When reading and responding to arguments, students should not—
per popular conceptions of argumentation—regard themselves as entering
a battle zone in which they strive to "preserve" their self, or shield their
position and themselves from arguments. Engaging oppositional positions

should not be viewed as a "battle against the enemy" or "a foray into an infected discourse." The goal of the reading-and-writing act ought to be engagement with and permeability to different ideas, not a preserving of self against the possibility of change. For the teacher, responsible pedagogy also involves such permeability: that is, the teacher, like the student, must be willing to be changed by the teaching experience.

The final chapter offers an historically contextualized reading of the current "cultural studies and composition" movement. Just as I question the nineteenth-century belief that reading great works of literature and sound linguistic training could endow the writing student with the "moral stamina" (Hill's term) to resist the temptations of culture, I question the idea that reading cultural theory in the classroom can provide students with a kind of protective barrier between them and their culture—in order to provide them with "resistance" to culture, so that culture cannot gain so profound a grasp on their consciousness. True, we "expose" students to cultural conflict, but we often do so by importing it into the classroom in small, safe doses, usually with an accompanying essay that would help them understand and thus ward off the power of that conflict. While I agree that mass culture is in many respects dangerous, I do not believe that the royal road to combining cultural studies and composition lies in providing students (per Freire's "banking style") with the critical theory to unmask and thus "master" culture. The "ideal of mechanical correctness" has been rejected by most of composition studies. However, even with its postmodern agenda, cultural-studies pedagogy still clings to the ideal of the autonomous human being behind the pen, who fortifies herself against confusion and against an alien culture *by* writing. I am not suggesting we encourage incoherent meandering, but if we want our students to face and embrace cultural conflict, it should be real conflict, and not just imported, safe conflict ("sanforized conflict," as one of my students put it). With many others, I believe composition studies is unique in its capacity for engaging student response, for addressing students as individuals, and for helping them wrestle with the conflicts *they* bring with them to the classroom. Embracing such conflict leads inevitably to messiness and very often to writerly selves that "fall apart" both mechanically and ethically. Focusing on this sort of conflict may do little to "inoculate" students against dangerous strains of discourse within their culture, but it can do much, I think, toward bringing them to a healthful understanding of the complexity and confusion of their culture as well as the complexity and confusion of their role in that culture.

Channing and Hill, like many of us, saw composition instruction as *countercultural*, as helping students "resist" (again, as they might resist a cold or an infection) cultural domination. It is this distance—this particu-

lar notion of resistance—that I argue we ought to question. The goals of
the writing course should not be *shoring up* the self against a sea of dangerous, chaotic culture, but learning to live in chaos and conflict, living in
and contributing to the dialogue of working out ideas, whether that dialogue takes place in the classroom or the broader public sphere. We need
to avoid the idea of community that stresses above all else the resolution
of conflict (the "peace at any cost" model). Instead, we should be teaching
our students to live *in* conflict, *in* culture, *in* confusion as part of the
human condition. Rather than gaining some sort of Olympian critical distance, we might teach them, to co-opt C. S. Peirce's expression, "contrite
conflictualism." Again, these arguments fall right in line with the kind of
composition theory that views conflict as our most important tool for
knowing, rather than something to overcome. The historical approach,
however, and the turn toward cultural studies are new.

After struggling with this work, I realize that my double perspective (as
one of my anonymous readers put it) is ambitious, perhaps too ambitious,
and in many areas and in many of the details I am sure that my reach has
exceeded my grasp. But I hope, nonetheless, that this perspective on writing instruction might at least hold the interest of my readers and might
even lead them toward asking new questions. I hope too that this work
might provide some historical context for academic intellectuals' current
vexation about becoming public intellectuals. Hill in particular tried to
make composition engage with and countervail an American culture that
had seemed to have slipped out of the control of the patrician-intellectual
class. And today, certainly, one of the attractive aspects of cultural studies
is its engagement with a sphere of influence beyond the academic sphere.
But merely addressing public issues in the classroom or in academic writing does not make us or our students public intellectuals. It remains extremely difficult to make academic knowledge count for something in the
popular public sphere. Although I give no explicit answers, perhaps this
work can provide some ways of talking about this very difficult and important concern.

In all I hope this study might make us aware of the similarities we
share with our forebears, as well as throw into sharper relief our differences. I hope too that it might yield some valuable lessons for the way we
conceive of our students, the way we encourage them to conceive of themselves, and, of course, the way we teach them to write.

Acknowledgments

This work began, really, during my first year of graduate school at Duke University. Although I went there intending to change the world by studying American Literature and literary theory, I soon discovered that the most direct route to my goals lay in teaching. And thank goodness there were people there who took my interests in teaching seriously, people like Jane Tompkins, Terry Eagleton, and Barbara Herrnstein Smith. When these interests quickly led me to composition studies, George D. Gopen, who was director of the writing program and who introduced me to the history of rhetoric, helped me realize that teaching is a worthy and exciting academic endeavor. Van E. Hillard, the current director, deepened my convictions and introduced me to the community of composition studies; the direction of this work owes more to his ideas than I can possibly acknowledge. Cathy N. Davidson agreed to advise me even though my research in composition studies was almost unknown territory on the third floor of the Allen Building. She has been for me a model of an intellectual, a scholar, and a teacher that I will always strive to emulate. And Erika Lindemann, at the University of North Carolina, was always generous with her help.

When this work was still in its dissertation stage, the Spencer Foundation provided generous financial and other assistance.

Many thanks to Priscilla C. Ross at SUNY Press for her patience, perseverance, and generous understanding. Ruth Fisher, also at SUNY Press, was an excellent production editor whose conscientious help was invaluable.

Many others have read portions or early versions of this work and have given me a great deal of help and encouragement, including Andrea Penner, Andy Smith, Bob Affeldt, John Trimbur, S. Michael Halloran, and John Gage. Others who have helped me in various ways were Roland Delyser, Rebecca Aronson, and Vickie Ricks. My colleague at the University of New Mexico Wanda Martin was especially helpful. Another colleague, Rick Johnson-Sheehan, with his uncanny knack for seeing the story behind any argument, was always willing to sit down with me and talk through the latest problem. William Waters was an excellent and helpful proofreader. Jack Ben Ezra and Mikey Weinstein provided the kind of support rarely, if ever, received by an academic. Hank Majestic made it possible for me to get this project off the ground. I extend my special gratitude to Jack Brereton, who read the entire manuscript twice and provided meticulous criticism and ample suggestions. These persons helped me improve my work immeasurably, but the weaknesses that remain, of course, are entirely mine.

As is customary, I thank my family for their patience and understanding, but what my family has done and has put up with goes far beyond the customary. Our son, Kellen, stayed awake many an evening waiting for my return from those late nights at the office. Dana, our daughter, was an inspiration that only those who know her could understand. And most of all I thank Susan, who has made so many things possible, including this.

Part One

Introduction

1

Introduction: On the Idea of Discourse Immunity, or the Public Health of Rhetorical Instruction

Immunity. (L. *immunitas*, exemption) The protection of an organism against infectious agents or toxic antigens afforded by a variety of predominately specific humoral or cellular factors.
acquired immunity. The specific protection against pathogens or toxins afforded by a known prior exposure through infection or immunization.

—Arthur M. Silverstein (immunology historian)

I continue to be deeply concerned that the [Bush] administration underestimates the importance of [drug] treatment and [drug] education. We know that education can inoculate children against drug abuse.

—Edward M. Kennedy

[T]he immune system must *recognize* self in some manner in order to react to something foreign.

—Edward S. Golub (immunologist)

I think AIDS is an interesting disease because it . . . actually causes the boundaries of the human being to be blurred between self and environment. The things that can't [usually] grow in you can grow in you. . . . People become culture mediums. I mean, you become a substance upon which many things can grow, can grow and flourish. If you look at it from the microorganism's point of view, they can now grow and flourish in you. You become this kind of incredible rich ground upon which to multiply. I know that's disturbing from the human being's point of view.

—Allan Chase (medical student)

A good argument for an intensive study of rhetoric is that citizens might thereby be put on their guard against the onslaughts of these vicious forms of persuasion.

—Edward P. J. Corbett[1]

Learning to Produce and Learning to Receive Rhetoric

Why is rhetorical training important and what are the goals of rhetorical training? We might divide those goals into a binary of learning to *produce* rhetoric and learning to *receive* rhetoric; rhetoric as production and rhetoric as reception; changing the beliefs of others and rendering others' beliefs or one's own beliefs resistant to change. As Chaim Perelman and Lucie Olbrechts-Tyteca have written, these interwoven and complementary goals have existed together throughout the tradition of Western rhetoric.

> Epideictic discourse, as well as all education, is less directed toward changing beliefs than to strengthening the adherence to what is already accepted. Propaganda changes beliefs. Nevertheless, to the extent that education increases resistance to adverse propaganda, the two activities may advantageously be regarded as forces working in opposite directions. (54)

In this work I wish to sketch the progression of the idea that rhetorical training might endow the student with a kind of *resistance* or *immunity* against bad rhetoric.

The Immunity Metaphor

"Immunity," as Emily Martin explains in *Flexible Bodies*, her genealogy of the discourse of the immune system, has become one of the "great ideas today." It is, in other words, becoming an idea to think with, a metaphor we take to other topics to understand them. More and more, we are seeing our world through the lens of the idea of the immune system. More and more, we are seeing the "ideal and fit person" (15) as the individual with a sound immune system.

Although I most often criticize the "rhetorical training as inoculation" model of education, the analogy between physiological immunity and rhetorical immunity, perhaps, can help us understand what we have done in the past and what we might try to do in the future. Many health experts and many critics of public discourse (both past and present) have regarded the world as a dangerous place, teeming with dangerous agents, whether microbial or rhetorical in nature. A society's response to any epidemic can take several forms. It might try to clean the place up, wipe out the media (both bacteriologists and cultural critics speak of "cultural media") where these dangerous agents grow and threaten to contaminate the populace. It might try, that is, to make the world a more aseptic place, as was the case in the nineteenth-century hygiene movement or in the various attempts throughout history to deny certain persons and ideas access to the public forum. Or a society might try to separate the diseased from the healthy, stigmatizing the diseased, labeling them as immoral or responsible for their illnesses, as has been the case with leprosy, smallpox, syphilis, and, as shown by writers like Susan Sontag, AIDS. Or, finally, it might try to render the populace more resistant to infectious agents—the prophylaxis/inoculation strategy for controlling disease.

These are not exclusive categories but complementary. In any epidemic, all three strategies are deployed in various combinations. The body that succumbs to disease is portrayed as somehow frail or disordered or out of balance. Individuals are morally responsible for their illness; illness is a curse, a punishment, or at best an embarrassment (Sontag 102). Since the popularization of germ theory in the late nineteenth century, military metaphors have dominated, where campaigns against disease are cast as all-out wars, and where individuals must accept their responsibility for helping to conquer the foe. Illness is portrayed as "an enemy that invades, that lays siege to the body-fortress" (Sontag 96). Or (as in the case of homeopathy and the nineteenth-century "Nature cures") they must restore their *natural immunity*, which has been rendered imbalanced by various aberrant causes (see Fellman and Fellman 25–40). Most commonly, disease is seen as the result of individuals' and societies' deviations from the natural order. Disease could not prevail if we could only restore this natural order.

In terms of rhetoric and rhetorical training, an unhealthful public discourse has often been portrayed in similar terms. As Aristotle portrayed the situation (as I discuss below), bad public discourse results from deviating from the natural order that public rhetoric would take if only the citizenry (or at least its elite leaders) would recognize what constitutes healthful rhetoric and practice it. When unhealthful discourse dominates public discussion, the individual public discursant has two choices: to withdraw from the situation completely into safety, or to acquire a resistance to public discourse so that she might enter that dangerous world with immunity. Individuals must understand how to *receive* this unhealthy discourse properly, so that they might become less susceptible to it. Rhetorical bodies, like bodies in the physiological sense, must become like a fortress that keeps invaders out; or, just as the body must recognize disease-causing agents before it can destroy them, so too must public discursants recognize bad rhetoric so that they can resist being swayed by it.

A Tradition of Rhetoric as Immunity

Within this division of producing vs. receiving rhetoric, the first (producing rhetoric) is perhaps represented most strongly by the Ciceronian ideal, where rhetorical training is conceived as the means for forming active citizens who would enter the public fray and contribute. The classroom was important to rhetorical training only insofar as it could prepare the active citizen. Withdrawing from the realm of public discourse was simply not an option. In Cicero's *Of Oratory*, Antonius objects to the "flower sort of diction," which is "redolent rather of the training-school and its suppling-oil than of our political hurly-burly and of the Bar" (211). Cicero's more idealistic Crassus agrees. While Crassus's perfect orator would be also a philosopher, rhetorical training must never confine itself to the school, which is artificial, unrigorous, and insular. Young students may need such insularity at first, but the rhetoric practiced in the school is not and cannot be true rhetoric. As Crassus insists,

> Then at last must our Oratory be conducted out of the sheltered training-ground at home, right into action, into the dust and uproar, into the camp and the fighting-line of public debate; she [oratory] must face putting everything to the proof and test the strength of her talent, and her secluded preparation must be brought forth into the daylight of reality. (221)

The discussion between the more practical Antonius and the more idealistic Crassus does not question *whether* the goal of rhetorical training is the creation of active citizen-leaders, not even *whether* rhetorical training should include participating in the "hurly-burly" of public life. They argue about *how much* philosophy—how much of the "Greekling" ideals of reflection and "idle speculation"—should be combined with the practical, active, side of rhetorical training.

The other goal of rhetorical training—the ability to receive rhetoric properly—does not stand in simple opposition to its counterpart. For Cicero's Crassus, the perfect orator is a blend of the "real" world of action and the "ideal" world of philosophical speculation. Crassus insists that in order to lead the public toward civic health, the orator must be able to listen to the community (how it conceives itself), listening, that is, with philosophical understanding, so that it can make an informed judgment about what proper course should be advocated.

Aristotle too maintains that a well-practiced rhetoric includes the activity of receiving rhetoric in the proper manner: rhetorical training must endow the rhetor with the capacity to take a distanced (critical and accurate) perspective on public debate. It has been argued for some time that rhetorical training for him was a means of nullifying what Gorgias had called the druglike magic of rhetoric (de Romilly 52), or of neutralizing the rhetorician's "bag of tricks" (George Kennedy 28; Gage, "Why Write?" 10–11). Proper rhetorical training, in fact, represents the *antidote* for corrupt uses of language. As James L. Kastely has argued (though his discussion focuses on Plato), Aristotle's true rhetoric would help us see through "mere" rhetoric as it is improperly and "sophistically" practiced in civic life, so that we might inject into public debate a more accurate vision of the world and the actions that should be taken there. Kastely notes that Aristotle believed that there was a "natural order of truth and justice" that would be adhered to if "true" rhetoric were theorized and practiced. This true rhetoric would help restore this natural order (10–11). The function of rhetoric for Aristotle (at least as stated in the first chapter of Book I of the *Rhetoric*) is "not to persuade but *to see* the available means of persuasion in each case.... [I]t is a function of one and the same art *to see* the persuasive and [*to see*] the apparently persuasive, just as [it is] in dialectic [*to recognize*] a syllogism and [*to recognize*] an apparent syllogism" (35, my italics, brackets in Kennedy's translation). As Kennedy comments on this passage, "Both the orator and the dialectician need to be able to recognize" the true as well as the apparent (or specious) argument, and to tell the difference between them (35, note 30). Rhetorical invention must begin, then, with the proper recognition of right and wrong, justice and injustice; and the function of true rhetoric lies in restoring the proper and true order.

Unlike Cicero's discursants in *Of Oratory*, Aristotle did not worry much over the right blend of the real and the ideal, the right blend of getting things done in a rhetorical world on the one side and of ethical/philosophical speculation on the other. Aristotle's rhetor, immersed as she must be at times in public life, needs to distance herself from the public in order to discover and then advocate the proper actions. So for Aristotle, the way to *receive* public discourse is not to receive it at all, but to see through it, reject it, and correct it. And for this lack of attention, Aristotle's *Rhetoric* and the tradition it has inspired has been radically questioned. Jasper Neel argues we should reject Aristotelian rhetoric as the model for composition studies, since the rhetors he addresses are, at root, antidemocratic aristocrats who desire techniques that will allow them to enter the messy and unclean world of public discourse, and then exit without becoming permanently sullied or altered: "For [Aristotle] and his friends," writes Neel, Athens "was nothing but a cesspool of democratic style and delivery anyway, the sort of cesspool that no self-respecting aristocrat, no enthymeme master would deign to enter. . . . Rhetoric is the prophylactic that demonstration and dialectic wear in order to protect their identities and their processes from the free play of linguistic transfer" (177, 179). True, Aristotle recognized the world of public discussion was fundamentally contingent, but that was merely the unfortunate result of bad rhetorical practice (bad *technē*): "Aristotle saw an agonistic world in which one speaker had to be right, the other wrong. His own maneuvering allows him to extract himself from that situation in order to articulate the general principles whereby rightness or wrongness are recognizable" (203). Rhetoric properly exercised, then, might render its practitioners healthfully distant from the contaminated world of popular public discourse.

In *Rethinking the Rhetorical Tradition*, Kastely too suggests that we question the Aristotelian tradition which assumes that justice will "naturally" dominate if we can only get our rhetorical techniques properly in place. Kastely attends to what he calls "the skeptical thread of classical rhetoric," which might "speak more meaningfully to the present" (4, 2). Today, argues Kastely, we can no longer assume with Aristotle that justice is the natural state of human affairs; Plato's philosophy, by Kastely's reading, teaches us about our rhetorical responsibility in a world where "injustice is the natural state" (9). Kastely's Plato can be seen, then, as challenging the Aristotelian tradition of inoculative rhetoric. Indeed, for Plato, true rhetoric does not safeguard discursants in any sense, but makes them radically vulnerable to ideas that might fundamentally change them. He proposes that Plato (as well as Sophocles and Euripides) are, contrary to most contemporary accounts, "friends of rhetoric." Plato provides a philosophy of discourse that better addresses the problem of persuasion in a world where no single political position and no single argumentative technique can ensure the proper conception of justice or the proper means for pursuing justice. The question of *justice*, rather than *knowledge*, assumes the foreground. Kastely sees Plato's skepticism as the foundation for a "flexible rhetorical practice" (rather than technique for winnowing the true from the false) that entangles "us in a lifelong search for justice in which we can never achieve our goal but which nonetheless engenders not a futile life but rather the fullest life that one can lead" (52). Such rhetorical "flexibility"is fraught with risk since we cannot exculpate our responsibility to justice by nodding comfortably to an order of the true and the good. Such practice places our very *selves* in jeopardy:

> To practice philosophy as Socrates understands it requires the courage to reject conventional understanding. One has to accept isolation as the price of thinking for oneself. . . . One can exploit

dialectic only if one is willing to open oneself to refutation. . . . The terror that always lurks in a dialectical inquiry is caused by the almost certain prospect of finding out that *one is not who one thinks one is.* This openness requires enormous courage because in such an inquiry one risks discovering commitments that were acquired inadvertently and, even more likely, wrongs that were done unintentionally, but for which the inquirer must accept responsibility. (39, my emphasis)

In other words, when we practice "rhetorical skepticism,"[2] we open ourselves—consciously, deliberately, responsibly—to ideas that are not "ours" but foreign. We "risk losing our beloved persons and practices and understandings as we seek to know them and ourselves better through a dialectical refutation" (45). We risk losing who we are.

Like Neel, Kastely, and others, I question a rhetorical training whose goals emphasize the production of qualified, distanced, critical receivers of rhetoric. In particular, I question the idea that good rhetoric might serve as the "antidote" to bad rhetoric—or, as I foreground the term, the idea that sound rhetorical training might serve as an inoculation against bad rhetoric, so that we might become less susceptible to the wiles of the wicked rhetor, so that we might securely remain ourselves, uninvaded by alien and dangerous ideas and discourses. And yet I recognize also how difficult it is for teachers of rhetoric to resist the temptation to merely substitute their authoritative discourses and models of critical reflection for those held by students. As Neel warns, "The call of academic elitism through which we arrogate superior aesthetic and ratiocinative powers is practically impossible to resist" (125). Or, as Kenneth Burke put it, human beings as symbol-using, -making, and -misusing animals are inherently "goaded by the spirit of hierarchy (or moved by the sense of order) and rotten with perfection" (*Language* 16)—the impulse, in fact the necessity, of substituting one hierarchy, one terminology, for another appears to be our lot as symbol users. No matter what terminological or rhetorical system we adopt for taking apart and better understanding the discourses that have laid hold on us and our students, they too gain their own power over us: "There is a kind of 'terministic compulsion' to carry out the implication of one's terminology" (19). Whether or not we recognize the constructedness of our beliefs and our systems of knowing and naming, they are compelling for us and compel us to take certain actions nonetheless.

And of course the pedagogical imperative to help students resist conformity and manipulation is a noble one. The knowing subject who can stand apart from the competing fray of voices in relative autonomy remains at the center of the Western intellectual tradition. As C. Jan Swearingen observes, "The knowing subject who stands apart from nature, apart from self, and apart from previous philosophy, even when problematized, remains the protagonist in Western philosophy and aesthetics" (*Rhetoric* 221). From Isocrates and Plato to Burke to contemporary composition theory, rhetorical training has sought to endow students with the wherewithal to resist the powerful discourses of a culture that seeks everywhere to inhabit them. All this is noble and should remain a part of our pedagogical goals.

But rhetorical training errs when it lapses into mere defense, rather than dialectic, or negotiation, or Burke's identification. To use Burke's terms, when division is emphasized over identification, or when division and identification are not conceived as thoroughly interwoven, then rhetoric devolves into logomachy, the will to persuade the audience at all costs—rhetoric as productive manipulation. Or it devolves into the effort to erect barriers between the self and foreign discourse, an effort to safeguard oneself from any discourse that would threaten the autonomy and assuredness of the self—a rhetoric of reception that *refuses to receive*. Rhetorical training, then, becomes merely a program for safeguarding students from competing discourses that "we" (intellectuals, the academy, teachers of writing, etc.) see as dangerous. Rhetorical training becomes a method, in part, for ensuring that our students receive discourse in a way that enables them to think and feel in ways that correspond to what is really in their own best interests.

Popular Public Discourse as the Disease, and Rhetorical Training as the Immunization

Throughout this work I return again and again to the idea that rhetorical training might safeguard students against pernicious discourse that seeks to inhabit them. There is a long tradition of explicitly portraying bad rhetoric in terms of disease, infection, or other agents that can infiltrate the body and mind and even spread like a contagion. Bad rhetoric is what the citizenry must be on its guard against, and rhetorical training in this sense protects us by showing us *what* bad rhetoric looks like. We learn to recognize bad rhetoric when we see it. According to the viewpoint that sees rhetoric as a "bag of tricks" that diverts us from our pursuit of truth, if we are to respond "properly" to discourse of any sort we must have the cognitive, moral, and ethical wherewithal to distinguish the healthful from the unhealthful, or the tricks of rhetoric from the truth. For instance, a writer who calls himself/herself "R" explains how s/he was able to *resist* the admittedly very powerful rhetoric of Hitler in World War II Germany:

> [Hitler's oratory] was of the kind that speaks neither to the mind nor to the heart of his audience, but plays upon its nerves until

they are strung to such a pitch of intensity that they shriek for release in action. . . . But it can only be practised by one who has a profound and subtle understanding of the secret hopes and fears of his audience . . . ; who can be a conservative with the conservative, a revolutionary with the revolutionary, a man of peace with the pacifist and a war lord with the belligerent, and on occasion all these things at once should it be necessary. Certainly, Hitler was the greatest master of this type of oratory there has ever been, and I have stood among 10,000 people in the *Sportpalast* in Berlin and known that everyone around me was the victim of its spell. Who knows, if I had not been inoculated in childhood against the tricks or oratory, I might have succumbed myself.[3]

Obviously, and as Wayne Booth (who quotes this passage) points out, when we speak of such *inoculation* we are simplifying rhetoric into "mere rhetoric": rhetoric is what we recognize as specious and reject; truth is what we embrace. In this sense, rhetorical training as inoculation is a kind of surveillance system against bad rhetoric.[4]

The "rhetorical training as inoculation" model subscribes fairly closely to what Emily Martin calls the "modernist model of immunity." Here, there is ideally a clean division between self and nonself, and the immune system's mission lies in recognizing and then destroying the exogenous pathogen, which is likened to an invading entity. For at least the last fifty years, modernist interpretations of disease and immunity have been "dominant." In other words, the modernist version of immunity has been the prevailing idea for understanding not only how our bodies work but also the various topics that are informed by the immune-system metaphor. Modernist models of immunity square fairly well with modernist views of argumentation and the arguing self. Here, disease constitutes a "conflict" to be resolved or put down. Pathogenic agents are trouble-making aliens who want to disrupt the natural health of the human body. Here, the immune system is usually portrayed as the body's military or police force or border guard that brutally enforces the frontier between self and nonself, friendly and alien entities (see also Sontag 63–67). With this modernist version of immunity, the outside must not get inside, and when it does, the outside must be exterminated.

The argumentation analog of the "recognize, then destroy" model of immunity would be *eristic* and *agonia*—"fighting for one's life," to use Ong's phrase. To accept this metaphor of rhetorical training as inoculation against bad rhetoric is to accept what many in rhetoric and composition consider an impoverished sense of discussion and disputation. It hardly needs to be said the combat/border-guard model of debate is the contemporary "popular" view of rhetoric, where the line between rhetoric and philosophy ought to be (or would be in a just world or among just persons) conceived as a clean and clear one. Assuming that one could possibly be on guard against rhetoric but still open to knowledge, assumes, as Richard Lanham puts it, that "[r]hetoric is cosmetic, and bad girls wear makeup as well as good ones, probably better" (*Electronic Word* 158).

Wayne Booth, writing in 1982, commented, "We really do seem to be surrounded by masters of 'mere' rhetoric, many of them professional liars using rhetoric to trap us. Every day millions of Americans are taken in by public words that no *educated person* could believe after careful thought and investigation" (*Vocation* 340, my emphasis). Surely, implies Booth, with his tongue firmly in cheek, we might expect the ordinary citizen, the member of the "mob," to fall for such tricks, but not the educated person, who has been taught to distinguish right from wrong, who should have been taught to recognize the difference between good and bad rhetoric. With this bit of irony, Booth suggests one of the main premises of the antirhetorical stance, its antidemocratic, paternalistic bent. Indeed, as Stanley Fish points out, "there is always just beneath the surface of the antirhetorical stance a powerful and corrosive elitism" (*Doing* 473). As Joseph Harris argues, cultural studies pedagogy that portrays the competent observer as somehow invulnerable to the pernicious effects of popular culture (while others, of course, possess no such power) indicates its "deep anti-democratic impulse, a fear of the mob" ("The Other Reader" 228).

Just as the diseased body is conceived as weak or morally aberrant, the rhetorical body that succumbs to "mere" rhetoric is both responsible for its predicament and is labeled as "weak," "cursed," or justifiably "punished." As Sontag notes, disease has always served certain groups well for labeling certain other groups as weak, inferior, or immoral (passim).

The Inoculation and Resistance Theory of Attitude Change

There are other problems with the inoculation/resistance metaphor of persuasion, which can be illustrated through the research of social psychologists and communications scholars, who have been using the "inoculation and resistance" metaphor since the early 1960s. During the late 1950s and the 1960s, with worries over Nazi and Soviet propaganda, with the widespread discussion of such works as *The Authoritarian Personality*, *The Lonely Crowd*, and *The Man in the Gray Flannel Suit*, American society as well as the academy seemed preoccupied with the question of *conformity* (Halberstam 521–36; Larson 63–64). In the field of social psychology, and later in speech communications, academics began exploring why it seemed that people could be so easily manipulated toward obedience. The verdict on attitude change and conformity was straightforward: it was alarming how easily individuals abandoned their beliefs and sense of morality when confronted with even the flimsiest of arguments. People's attitudes were alarmingly open to manipulation. Social psychologists wanted not only to understand why people conformed but also to learn how individuals might be made less "susceptible" to conformity. These social psychologists found, basically, that John Milton was right when he said in his *Aeropagitica* that the best way to fortify an individual's immunity against persuasion was to put it to the test.

The "inoculation" analogy was constructed by social-psychologist William J. McGuire, who first discussed "resistance" and "susceptibility" to attitude change in a 1961 article, "The Effectiveness of Supportive and Refutational Defenses in Immunizing and Restoring Beliefs against Persuasion." Using a medical/biological metaphor, McGuire suggested that just as individuals can be made resistant to a disease or virus by giving them a mild or "attenuated" strain of the germ so that they would develop antibodies, they can be made more resistant to discrepant beliefs by inoculating their initial attitudes. The inoculation "treatment" consisted of exposing experimental subjects to weak counterattitudinal messages prior to exposing them to stronger, truly threatening messages. These researchers found that persons could be made resistant to persuasion by exposing them to such weakened virus-arguments, which stimulate their defenses. They will then be put on guard for *other* potentially damaging counterarguments, that is, on guard against arguments that are contrary to and threaten the individual's beliefs. As a contemporary researcher puts it, "Inoculation does more than simply preempt specific content. The threatening material triggers the motivation to bolster attitudes, thus *conferring a broad blanket of protection* against *all* potential counterarguments" (Burgoon et al. 488, my emphasis). The literature on "attitudinal inoculation" is vast and impressive. Literally thousands of laboratory studies and case studies have shown attitudinal inoculation does occur, in a wide range of situations and across a fairly broad spectrum of attitude types. Young persons, for instance, can be inoculated against peer pressure to smoke (Pfau, Bockern, and Kang); and as I will discuss momentarily, voters can be inoculated against the "attack-ads" of political campaigns.

The inoculation/resistance metaphor subscribes to modernist notions of belief, just as it subscribes to, as Martin calls it, modernist metaphors of physiological immunity, where the body is ideally a fortress that prevents dangerous agents from transgressing the frontier between self and nonself. The attenuated, weak counterarguments (the experimental treatment) are likened to immunogenic microbes, which show the body how to recognize dangerous beliefs when they encounter them and tell the body to put itself "on guard" against subsequent assaults. The arguments that truly threaten the subject are likened to pathogenic microbes, which try to infect the body and compromise its harmony or integrity. Subjects supposedly hold attitudes that are "theirs" (which are created by their true selves), but counterattitudinal beliefs (beliefs that do not rightly belong in the believing body) threaten to invade this integrated and autonomous self. The difficulty, of course, lies in distinguishing the healthy body's beliefs from the invading beliefs. Which are healthy and which are pathogenic depends on which beliefs you hold to be the true ones. Inoculation seeks to render the body or the belief-holding subject immune to attitude change, decidedly not to render it more open to the possibility of entertaining new beliefs and understanding them—or being transformed by them.

Research focusing on inoculation against attitude change has also illustrated how tricky and dangerous such strategies can be. In some cases attempts at inoculation can result in what has been called a "boomerang effect": the effort "backfires" as the attempt to inoculate actually *magnifies* the effect of persuasion you are trying to inoculate against. One very interesting such case occurred when Kathleen Hall Jamieson at the University of Pennsylvania's Annenberg School for Communication and her colleagues devised a program for helping the news media neutralize the power of misleading political "attack ads." During the 1992 presidential campaign they began working on a program called "adwatch." They showed political attack ads to a group of experimental subjects and explained to the subjects how the ads included "errors and misleading claims" (Cappella and Jamieson 342). The adwatch program was seen by the researchers as inoculative in nature: like the experimental subjects, the voting citizenry might be immunized against a broad range of misleading political-ad strategies.

> Inoculation is a way of preempting an attack ad, especially if it can be anticipated. Inoculation forewarns that an attack is imminent, summarizes the lines of argument in the attack, rebuts the attack, and offers a base of evidence and reason to uphold the attacked position. . . . The newscaster [who narrates the adwatch spot] counterargues . . . , thereby reducing the persuasive impact of the ad and inoculating against subsequent exposures to the same or argumentatively similar ads. (Cappella and Jamieson 346–47)

However, the researchers obtained results that were opposite to their expectations. Jamieson and her colleagues were surprised to find that their adwatch segments could—and did—backfire, or "boomerang." Persons "exposed" to the attack ads were *more* likely to favor the candidate who launched the attack ad than were persons with no exposure.

They found that the reason-based critiques of adwatch simply could not compete with the image-based attack ads, which made skillful use of visual information. Visual information, reasoned the researchers, appeals to emotional responses, enhances memorability, and is "processed quickly by receivers, while their minds are virtually at rest." In general, the attack-ad rhetoric often *outtrumped* the effects of the verbal, reason-based critique (Pfau and Louden 326–28). (One might say it is a case of pathos overpowering logos.) Therefore, in this contest between the image-based attack ad and the reason-based attack-ad critique, "the spot is likely to win" (Pfau and Louden 328). Indeed, for some groups of viewers in particular, adwatch critiques not only failed to neutralize the attack ads but also actually *magnified* the effect of subsequent exposures to the original attack ad: "once a television ad plants an image in the mind of the receiver, subsequent airing of the spot, even in the context of an adwatch, may have the effect of reinforcing that image" (Pfau and Louden 328). The adwatch spots had the unfortunate and unintended effect of helping the attack ads bamboozle the subject-viewers further.

In short, the inoculation-and-resistance model does not square with postmodern conceptions of knowledge or of subjectivity and the strategy is fraught with risk. This is not to suggest that *because* this model is not postmodern in character that there is something inherently wrong with it. Rather, this suggests that changes in subjectivity (or even changes in attitudes about specific beliefs) are rarely, if ever, accomplished with ease or assuredness. Human beings are more complex than the inoculation model implies. However, just as modernist theories of inoculation and resistance have informed (and oversimplified and impoverished) modernist theories of attitude change, postmodern theories of resistance might square better with contemporary ideas about what it is we expect to accomplish through rhetorical training. These emerging models might help us better envision the characteristics we wish to have our students embrace. They might help us better envision what characterizes healthy discussion and what characterizes the healthful participant in discussion.

Contemporary Composition and "Flexibility"

Contemporary composition teachers are still—and with good reason—captivated by the problem of cultural conformity, but their conceptions of how students are persuaded not to conform remain, in many cases, unhelpfully informed by modernist ideas of attitude change. As John Trimbur and others have described the goals of cultural studies and composition, it should help students resist "the imposition and reproduction of dominant forms of thought, structures of feeling, and patterns of behavior" (9). In other words, cultural studies helps individuals resist the "subject positions" imposed upon them. To an increasing extent, they recognize further that withdrawing from the world of actual public discourse is not an option. Academic literacy cannot remain in the ivory tower but must engage meaningfully with the world outside the academy. I too find such rationales worthy ones, but I fear that some cultural-studies pedagogies do little more than "expose" our students to cultural theory and critique. Mere exposure cannot fundamentally alter students, or at least such change is all too rare and unpredictable. Believing that teaching cultural studies will lead students to acquiring a lifelong habit of resisting cultural conformity is either naïve or grandiose on our part. While we may think our students have merely conformed to the penetrations of commodity culture, we have to remember that those cultural beliefs, as far as our students are concerned, are *their* beliefs, and that our countercultural intrusions are the alien ones. To put this in terms of the inoculation/resistance metaphor, for our students, the beliefs of commodity culture are those of the healthy body, and the teacher's countercultural beliefs are the immunogenic or pathogenic ones. And it seems likely that rather than really changing our students, we may merely be providing them with immunity to any countercultural arguments they will encounter after our class, leading, in other words, to the boomerang effect.

The question, therefore, should come down to efficacy: *Can* we, that is, in the short time we have with our students, bring about the terribly complex and difficult changes we are seeking (see Alcorn and chapter 7 of this book)? So, with Alan Kennedy I wonder if, "far from being an inoculation against success in late capitalist America, classes founded on resisting the dominant ideology might well be keys to success in it" (25). Richard Ohmann agrees that the issue of achieving real change poses "a hard question that should be asked more often. . . . [S]tudents came to college to gain social advantage, not to defect; to elaborate their individuality, not discard it." Ohmann questions the published accounts of student change in the cultural-studies classroom, and wonders about the longevity of such change: "But what next . . . for those ["transformed"] students—for the ones who say they will never see the world the same way again? All too likely, . . . [they will turn to the pleasure] of 'participation in the construction of a new world, free from class, gender, race exploitation' " (329). Just as Jamieson and her colleagues discovered that reason-based critiques are sometimes no match for the emotional power of visual rhetoric, we might consider that in our cultural-studies classrooms, reason-based arguments against commodity culture may be no match for the lifelong inscription of desires and identities. Do we stand a chance of substantially altering our students by merely "exposing" them to cultural theory?

It is neither practical nor even ethical to have as one's teacherly goals helping students acquire immunity or resistance to their culture or to the ideas of others. We should not and probably cannot help students become like fortresses that exclude all alien agents or ideas, which we teach them to recognize so they can never invade or transform student writers.

Perhaps Martin's description of what she calls the "postmodern model of immunity" can help. As Martin illustrates, our standards for the "ideal and fit person" change, and these changes are informed (to an increasing extent) by our imaginings of what the immune system is. The modernist interpretation of disease portrays illness as a problem of imbalance or as a "conflict" that needs to be resolved or demolished. But a postmodern model of immunity and disease is emergent, partly because science is changing, partly because the AIDS epidemic has necessitated different understandings, and partly because we are thinking about the world and ourselves differently. In the postmodern model, disease is conceived to be something like an "imbalance," but the imbalance does not result from a deviation from the *natural* workings of the body. Rather, imbalances always occur and are, in a healthy body, temporary, part of an exquisite, always-changing give-and-take between self and nonself. In the postmodern model, the immune system is an organizing and systematizing power within us that must be *flexible. Flexibility* suggests that the immune system is capable of adapting to and responding "intelligently" to the changes in what counts as self and nonself. The immune system must alter itself according to the present state of the system and the environment. There is always the interplay between self and nonself. Here it is recognized that outside always gets inside, and in fact that the distinction between outside and inside (self and nonself) is a dynamic one. If our immune systems are to be flexible, they must be clever enough (not just tough enough) to enter risky situations (the world is a risky place of germs and disease), where contagion can never be prevented but only responded to. Whether an antigen (an agent that provokes an immunological response) causes disease depends *not* on the antigen itself, but in many cases on our bodies' reactions to it. Therefore, a healthy immune system does not respond to every agent it regards as foreign (as in the case of hay fever or certain other allergies), but only to those that really pose a threat to the body. If we think about the immune system this way, then the metaphor of "militia" and "fortress" becomes insufficient, and we must move on to metaphors such as a computer interface, or some other metaphor that allows us to think about immunity as a dynamic system that "organizes" and "systematizes" unpredictable and always-changing conditions—something that can constantly renegotiate the relationship of self *with* nonself. Keeping foreign bodies out—keeping the body whole, untainted, and unviolated—is no longer the paramount issue.

Responding intelligently and flexibly, even to the point of self-transformation, becomes the preeminent concern.

Of course, Martin's *flexibility* resembles in some remarkable ways what many compositionists have been theorizing and practicing in recent years. Students are not taught to merely apply an accepted paradigm for reading, interpreting, and deconstructing their culture or the ideas of others. Nor are they taught merely to be "on guard" or "to see through" them. This is not to say writing teachers ought not to teach interpretive strategies, but only that these strategies should not be conceived as methods for safeguarding students from dangerous ideas. The concern becomes not erecting barriers between student writers and their culture, or between students and the ideas of others. Rather, students are taught that outside always gets inside, and that trying to make ultimate distinctions between the two is a difficult, probably impossible, task. Self, culture, and other must be examined together, in terms of one another. The interpretive and rhetorical strategies we teach, in other words, might resemble Kastely's "rhetorical skepticism," where one still strives to reject conventional understandings and one still must take responsibility for their positions, but, rather than erecting safeguards, one opens oneself up to "the almost certain prospect of finding out that one is not who one thinks one is" (39). Student writers strive to understand "who they are" and "who they might become" *through* their investigations of culture and the ideas of others; and they strive to understand their culture and the ideas of others *through* their investigations of themselves.

Part Two

History

2

The Uses of Composition History

A history of the past is worthless except as a documented way of talking about the future.

—Kenneth Burke

Rhetoric has had a long and variegated history. . . . It has been an ambiguous history, because continuing terms assume new meanings in their new applications, and the innovations are seldom guided by knowledge of how renewed terms were used in earlier traditions. Histories of rhetoric, which throw little light on the principles or purposes by which present methods and uses of rhetoric might be evaluated or changed, tend to be pedantic explorations of traditions of rhetoric . . . , which follow through the consequences of pejorative judgments posited as premises.

—Richard McKeon[1]

In his 1967 essay "Where Do English Departments Come From," William Riley Parker makes the analogy between English studies and a child from a broken home. English studies' father is philology (which became linguistics) and its mother rhetoric (which became speech). This "child" has become distanced from both parents, but Parker encourages English teachers and scholars to believe that a reconciliation between the child and one or both parents is possible and desirable. English studies, Parker concludes, "needs still to learn something from its mother . . . and even more from its father" (14). Parker's essay was among the first to sketch out the history of the profession of teaching English and writing in the modern American university, and it therefore has been an important document in the field of composition studies.

But for sizing up composition studies itself, I would suggest a similar analogy but a different genealogy. Here one side of the family tree comes from the rhetorical tradition: the good side, the side whose heritage nurtures us to this day, but with which composition studies has only recently recognized its kinship. The other side of the tree comes from nineteenth-century America, with its limiting views of rhetoric, the institutionalization of the composition course, and what has come to be called "current-traditional rhetoric": the bad side from which we have strived to escape, psychically, pedagogically, and institutionally. To pursue this metaphor, during its adolescence (during the late 1970s and 1980s), composition studies began putting together its past, conceiving itself as a viable and attractive intellectual and academic discipline. In order to do this, it understandably associated its identity with the tradition of rhetoric and distanced itself from what happened in the nineteenth century.

Of course, all analogies break down, and this one breaks down where it suggests that composition's recent reinventing itself is akin to an adolescent temper tantrum. Composition history has done tremendous good for teachers of writing and for the teaching of writing. What it rejected from that part of its heritage—which can be and usually is summed up in the term "current-traditional rhetoric"—was rejected for good reason.

I would argue, however, that in the heat of defining itself through its past (i.e., *against* its past), composition history often surveyed the nineteenth century too hastily and broadly, rejecting most everything, finding very little in the past that had relevance for the moment.[2] As I try to show in chapters 3, 4, and 5, when we look closely at composition through the twin lenses of biography and the social history of American intellectual culture, the relationship between composition's forebears and mainstream society looks different. Because nineteenth-century American intellectuals ("patrician intellectuals") felt very much at odds with mainstream American culture, I think it is misguided to portray nineteenth-century composition as *clearly* in league with capitalism and business, when business (not ideally, but as it was practiced in America) was the *bête noire* of these intellectuals. This enmity between intellectuals and the world of business, entertainment, and profit was particularly felt by academic intellectuals (Townsend; Bercovitch, "Problem"; Hofstadter, *Anti-Intellectualism*). As Myron Tuman writes, concurring with my point:

> Writing instruction, embedded as it was in English studies, saw its principal charge as helping the individual withstand the numbing onslaught of commercial culture, including new empirical academic disciplines, mesmerizing and dehumanizing popular culture, and, just as dangerous, peer pressure. Print literacy in its most rigorous form—the kind of critical reading, writing, and thinking that characterized the best college writing programs—

was viewed as a safeguard against contamination by a world organized around the manufacturing, merchandising, and consump-
tion of goods, organized, in a word for profit. (*Word Perfect* 94)

Therefore, I find many of the generalizations about composition's ideological agendas to be inaccurate and misleading—like this one from John
Schilb: "Historians agree that composition studies was invented *purely* to
train students in the mechanics of language, to help them face the newly
specialized demands of higher education and the emerging circumstances
of corporate life" ("Cultural" 174, my emphasis). To assume that Hill,
Channing, and other patrician intellectuals were in simple allegiance with
business interests is to subscribe to a clumsy and inaccurate model of class
organization. The assumption seems to be that because patrician intellectuals and business leaders were in similar economic classes, they worked
for the same goals.

Certainly, a Gramscian model of civil society and hegemony would be
far more sensitive to complexities of class organization, ideology, and struggle
than are more traditional models for the relationship between economic
class and consciousness (e.g., economic-determinist models of base and
superstructure; see Williams's *Marxism and Literature* 75–82). Although I
do not use Gramsci's models for analyzing the place of patrician intellectuals in American civil society, that could certainly be a valuable extension
of this work. (See Thomas P. Miller's *The Formation of College English*,
which looks at the rise of English studies in the British cultural provinces
and which deftly and helpfully employs Gramsci's models for its analysis of
the cultural and political roles English studies played.)

By looking closely at Channing and Hill (their early writings, their
biographies), I hope I have seen some things not visible to historians who
were surveying the field of composition more broadly. Specifically, both
were worried about the quality of public rhetoric, thinking it dangerous
and a habit of communication that inhabited the citizenry and (potentially,
at least) their students. Therefore, the writing course was conceived as one
avenue for ameliorating the dangerous effects of a dangerous public discourse. I do not suggest that because some of their anxieties are similar to
some of ours, we should therefore admire them. I do not in any sense
advocate that we follow their methods and reasoning for new ways of teaching our students. In fact, they show us (as they seem to have always shown
us) the path to reject. So I have perhaps simply found new reasons for
despising these forebears, but I hope also to show that they were complex
figures, and that understanding that complexity is rewarding. In other words,
returning to the family-lineage metaphor, we may perhaps have more in
common with this nineteenth-century side of our heritage than we have

previously been willing to recognize. Understanding how our problems are both similar and different from theirs may help us determine the future of our scholarship and teaching practices.

Tradition, Community, and the Rise of Composition Historiography

It is difficult to specify why, around 1980, the history of nineteenth-century American rhetoric and composition suddenly captured the interest of the rhetoric and composition community. Before 1980 there was only the occasional article and dissertation. Since then, scores of articles, several anthologies of historical articles, and dozens of book-length studies have appeared. Today, historical research has become an influential and ever-growing discipline within the discipline. In fact, trying to understand our backgrounds as a community of professionals has come to seem almost urgent.

As Susan Miller has pointed out, the practitioners and theorists of composition studies—like any group trying to establish a community identity and trying to attain the power that can accompany such identity—wanted, first, simply to *have* a history that would indicate a "respectable past" (*Textual* 35). They wanted stories about where they came from to help them understand who they were and who they are. The psychological importance of this desire is apparent in the comments of Andrea Lunsford, who describes how in 1971 "my life in the profession began . . . the day I picked up Edward P. J. Corbett's *Classical Rhetoric for the Modern Student*. . . . Though I'd been teaching for several years, it was Corbett's book that actually *invited* me into a community" ("Nature" 4). In the pantheon of influential composition textbooks, Corbett's was at that time distinctive in situating composition within the 2,500-year tradition of "rhetoric," which has been, Corbett informs us, perhaps the greatest and most enduring discipline in Western humanism. Only in the last 150 years has rhetoric experienced its ignominious demotion, from the centerpiece of Western education to the contemned periphery—if you will, from "rhetoric" to "composition." As Lunsford's comments show, Corbett's textbook accomplished more than simply providing another rubric and another method for teaching writing; it provided a much-needed boost in morale for composition faculties, whose work was perceived by the academy to possess only minor—and, it was hoped, passing—importance.

In part, composition suffered from this inferiority complex because, until recently, it had not benefited from anything like a *tradition* of historical inquiry. Unlike, for instance, literary studies, modern rhetoric and composition had no corpus of authoritative historical inquiries that more recent scholars could challenge, support, or augment. Historical investigations revealed that rhetoric and composition had not always seemed an orphan of history. Prior to the nineteenth century, of course, there was a prominent, respected, and relatively coherent historical tradition. One could think not only of Cicero, Quintilian, and Augustine, but also of George Campbell and Hugh Blair, all of whom recognized both their debts to and their departures from a tradition firmly established at the center of Western intellectual thought. Even sixteenth-century Peter Ramus, who insulted the rhetorical tradition at every opportunity, relied on his audience's familiarity with the history of rhetoric, exploiting the tradition as a background with which to distinguish his own theory and practice. In fact, rhetoric and composition history may have become too concerned with establishing its connections with classical rhetoric. As, for instance, Nan Johnson notes, "the classicist bias" has been a prejudice inherent throughout much of composition scholarship: "Pejorative critiques of the nineteenth-century tradition draw their force from the assumption that rhetorical traditions that deviate from classical philosophies of rhetoric . . . are unstable or inherently compromised" (12).

Then, during the nineteenth century, the discipline underwent its rhetoric-to-composition paradigm shift. There would seem to be little wonder that a shift would occur, considering the astonishing and overwhelming cultural changes that affected ideas about what composition was for—changes in communications technologies and ideologies, the change from the small American college to the modern "new" university, and the society-wide changes from oral to written discourse. But despite the apparent abundance of reasons for fundamental transformation, the changes that took place within rhetoric during this period were portrayed by composition historians most often as shrouded in mystery and almost always troubling, painting the period in metaphors of darkness and emptiness. With few exceptions, composition historians, in describing what happened to the once-noble art of rhetoric in nineteenth-century America, have relied on what Robert Connors has called the "decline and fall" historical narrative ("Writing" 64–65). Very often, nineteenth-century composition has been portrayed as an intellectual and social abyss that swallowed up any and all ideas of rhetorical complexity. For whatever reasons, went the argument, the history of rhetoric fell into a period of stagnation and decay. Concomitantly, so declined rhetoric's prestige and sense of mission; so too deteriorated the community's sense of importance and purpose.

The first to call attention to the severity of this lapse was Albert R. Kitzhaber, who in 1953 wrote his ground-breaking doctoral dissertation, which he finally chose to have published in 1990.[3] As he sums up in his characteristic litotic style, "The years from 1850 to 1900 cannot in any sense be called a great period in the history of rhetoric" (226). John E.

Braun describes the lapse with the metaphor of lethargy: "Historians of rhetorical theory seem to be in implicit agreement that little of philosophical significance to rhetoric developed during much of the nineteenth century. Most analyses of modern theories of rhetoric either ignore the period completely, or assign it to slumbering 'repose.' " Other historians describe the period with metaphors of darkness, disaster, and emptiness. Connors calls the years 1830 to 1930 "the Dark Ages of composition"; elsewhere he writes that the "traditional rhetorical histories end abruptly" with Englishman Richard Whately's *Elements of Rhetoric* (1828): "after Whately in 1828, [traditional rhetorical history] falls off the edge of the earth . . . , and the rest of the nineteenth century is an echoing tomb" ("Current-Traditional" 216; "Writing" 50). The late Donald Stewart agreed that composition history had failed to shed much light on these questions, and had instead engendered even greater mystery. Nineteenth-century rhetoric "poses some special problems," explains Stewart, "the greatest of which is that it apparently had no intellectual, philosophical, or theoretical center" ("Nineteenth" 51). Stewart did not mean that historians had failed to *perceive* a center or even that there were many scattered centers of intellectual brightness; he meant that sophisticated rhetorical thought *did not exist* in nineteenth-century America, and any movements that were sophisticated were swallowed up by the violence of history.

Nonetheless, composition historians have continued to make their inquiries and their interpretations, all as part of composition's larger effort to understand and define itself as an integrated and distinct discipline. This conception of history has been crucial to the historical arguments of many academic communities that, like composition, perceive themselves as having been systematically excluded from traditional histories. As Stewart has noted elsewhere, the most significant insight or attitude gained from composition history lies in

> remind[ing] ourselves that ours *is* a discipline with a history and
> *that* history is inextricably linked, on the one hand to the history
> of the modern profession of English, and on the other hand to one
> of the oldest intellectual traditions in the Western world, the tra-
> dition of rhetoric. ("Some History Lessons" 22)

By and large, I would agree with Lunsford, Susan Miller, and others that composition history has succeeded in drawing the rhetoric/composition community together. By labeling its recent past as an "outworn history," composition history has played an important role in "both unif[ying] and motivat[ing] composition professionals, giving them a readily perceptible sense of . . . themselves as group" (Miller, *Textual* 189). Likewise for

Theresa Enos, in the past "We have worked too often not as a community of teacher scholars drawn together by a sense of history but as discoverers of a 'brand new world every morning' " ("Brand New" 11–12). This created past, then, provided a space for identity and solidarity for the discipline of composition teachers.

"Current-Traditional Rhetoric" as Villain: The Problem with Historical Agency

Composition history has always been rhetorical in the sense that it has strived consistently to bring about changes in the world. It is remarkable, in fact, how self-consciously it has strived to be useful, to help *reform the way we teach our students*. These histories, in other words, were more than intellectual delights for those interested in history; they acted as a *social force* that shattered (for many) the pat, tired notions about how compositionists thought about their discipline, how they conceived of themselves as members of the English-department community, and how they taught their students. In historiographic terms, it has been a *critical* history, or, to use Nietzsche's term, it has been a "strong" history, "break[ing] up and dissolv[ing] a part of the past . . . by bringing it before the tribunal" (75–76).

The counterpart to community and acceptance is rejection or "breaking up" the past. In general, composition history has rejected the composition portion of its past and has embraced the classical portion. Because of this, many histories have concentrated on the victimizations and on failures of composition and compositionists—victimization at the hands of literary studies and failure to carry on the noble art of civic-minded rhetoric. While historians have argued for the hero status of a few forebears (e.g., Fred Newton Scott, Gertrude Buck), most historical studies have focused on composition's villainous forebears and the pernicious pedagogical traditions they established. Understandably, composition studies (in its history and theory) has been striving to distance itself from much of its not very distant past.[4] As I have suggested, it has strived to redefine itself and its image, aiming its arguments at two different audiences, its own community and the academic community at large. And while this project has been most successful in persuading those already in composition (and not our colleagues in English departments and throughout the university),[5] composition has certainly made important strides in reforming classroom practice.

Composition history has concentrated on practice—in particular the practice that was labeled "current-traditional rhetoric." This term of opprobrium was seized upon by James Berlin, first in his series of early-1980s articles and later in his book-length studies. More than anyone else, he was responsible for bringing this term to the profession's attention.[6] Although "current-traditional rhetoric" has become something of a catchall term for almost *any* theory of composition one finds objectionable, it is analyzed in Berlin's work and the work of others along four dimensions. First, current-traditional rhetoric ignores invention, assuming that good writing just happens once the writer has decided what she ought to say and has lined up the proper methods and modes. Second, it subscribes to positivist theories of language: thought occurs before language, which is the mere "clothing" for ideas and which exists as a kind of memory bank for thought; ideal language has little to do with the meaning but should merely be perspicuous and correct. Third, current-traditional rhetoric subscribes to a positivist theory of knowledge: knowledge and nature are orderly and discrete; truths, always external to the social and personal, may be arrived at via rational investigation, and conflict, therefore, is a sign of something having gone wrong. A fourth dimension to current-traditional rhetoric concerns its intellectual and ideological origins: with roots in (the aristocratic and idealist) Scottish Common Sense Realism, current-traditional rhetoric participated in a larger system of cultural, economic, and institutional hegemony.[7]

To generalize, 1980s composition history argued, perhaps above all else, that contemporary compositionists must learn what current-traditional rhetoric is, how it still exists in composition textbooks and teaching, and why it is ineffective and dangerous. It urged that contemporary teachers extirpate it from their teaching practices. This practical bent is seen in the first lines of Sharon Crowley's *The Methodical Memory*: "I undertook this study because the status of current-traditional rhetoric as a historical artifact is not evident to the many people who think of it as a natural, self-evident, and universal system for the invention of discourse written in school" (ix). There has, in fact, been a kind of "working class" pride in the teaching mission, as in Robert J. Connors's comments (which are imbued, obviously, with some irony):

> Because we're writing teachers. We're where the rubber meets the road. . . . We can't be neutral because we have to meet those kids tomorrow and look 'em in the eyes and tell them what we think the true names of things are. ("Foreword" xi)

Donald Stewart foregrounds the importance of reforming practice in his "Foreword" to Berlin's *Rhetoric and Reality*: "ignorance of the history of writing instruction . . . is the single greatest deficiency in the majority of this nation's English teachers. . . . Berlin has drawn a map of the territory we call English. . . . He has told us who we are and why we think the way we do about the field of English. Parochialism in our field will undoubtedly persist, but because of this book, it can no longer be excused" (ix, xi). Indeed, historians, as Stephen North points out, have been unabashedly— and I would say healthfully—"propagandistic" in their aims (87–90). One can find similarly laudatory expressions about the relationship between history and reforming practice in Enos ("Learning from our histories of rhetoric has enriched composition teaching" ["Brand New" 5]), Lloyd-Jones ("have [histories] made me a more useful teacher?" [22]), and others.

While this practice-minded focus has been one of composition history's great virtues, current-traditional rhetoric—which is of course the historian's abstraction for a congeries of complicated and often contradictory rhetorics—became almost reified. As some historians have portrayed things, current-traditional rhetoric *itself* has come to resemble one of the villains. That is, current-traditional rhetoric has assumed so central a place in much of the history that *it* often seems a central figure in American rhetoric's great lapse—a historical agent itself. Or if not current-traditional rhetoric per se, it is the *period* of the late nineteenth century that gets tagged with villainous agency. Such historiography is described aptly by Nan Johnson (though whether her syntactic agency was deliberate, I cannot say): "what is distinctive about recent [historical] scholarship . . . is its overall assessment of this era as that *period most responsible* for the theoretical impoverishment of the rhetoric of composition and the academic marginalization of rhetoric studies in modern English departments" (11, my emphasis). It is the period, then—not individuals, not cultural exigencies—that gets blamed.

Certainly, one can read Johnson's words more generously and see that she is trying to bundle up a congeries of historical forces into "period." Nonetheless, I argue that composition history might benefit by moving beyond academic/intellectual traditions and beyond generalities about current-traditional rhetoric and the "period." I argue there is much to be discovered by examining the relationships between American ideology and composition ideology. Scholars can start by looking at culture more broadly (looking not just at universities but also at specific social forces they were reacting to) and at individuals more closely (looking more deeply into their biographies).

Many histories, somewhat hermetically, focus on the intellectual evolution of current-traditional rhetoric; such histories (e.g., Crowley, *Methodical*; Johnson) specify quite successfully a chain of causes and effects that occurred within the *intellectual* traditions and close circles within which composition's forebears thought and taught. Because such histories select and focus upon strategically limited segments of culture, they succeed in positing plausible causational links between culture (however one defines and limits that concept) and rhetoric and composition. But more can be done. As Sharon Crowley indicates in her preface to *The Methodical Memory*, examining the intellectual tradition of current-traditional rhetoric is only part of the historical project and is, left by itself, almost dangerously incomplete. Crowley writes of her

> uneasiness about the fact that I have pulled the texts under study here out of history, so to speak. . . . I ignore the historical detail that surrounded their composition—the biographies of their authors, the social and political circumstances surrounding the teaching of writing . . . and the like. I am acutely aware of the fact that my account is susceptible to the same charge I level against the textbook authors I study—that in eliding difference, I have reiterated the hegemony of the same. (xv)

Connecting composition theory and practice to "the biographies of [composition textbook] authors [and] the social and political circumstances surrounding the teaching of writing" is fraught with risk. But I would argue that the histories that have attempted to do what Crowley acknowledges must be done—link *larger* cultural issues to specific phenomena in composition—have been content to demonstrate merely that such relationships *exist*. They do not specify *how* larger cultural issues have actually influenced the transformation of composition theory and practice.

James Berlin's Histories and the Problems of Causation and Scope

Those familiar with the course of composition historiography may at this point be wondering about the accuracy of my criticisms in light of the highly influential histories of James Berlin, who, in his book-length studies especially, strived to demonstrate the relationship between late-nineteenth-century ideology and the emerging composition course. As he wrote in 1987, rhetorical histories must understand and explain how "rhetorical systems [are] scenes of conflict." But it is often difficult to discern what precisely *is* the conflict and more important *who* is acting in this conflict.

My first point about Berlin's historiography concerns the scope of his analysis: his critical horizons are enormous. One of the first composition historians to concentrate on these important relationships, Berlin tried to manage an unmanageable and undefinable swath of culture—all of culture, a culturewide ideology. Berlin assumed a macrophysics of power, but did not focus on the microphysics of how ideology gets translated into composition theory and practice. Rhetoric seems simply to have changed in concert with something that might roughly be called "culture." Or sometimes a nameable but unfathomable source is identified, such as "managerial capitalism" (Ohmann, "Reading and Writing"), or a "noetic field" at one point in Berlin (*Writing* 2). Things just change, at times, it seems, without agency, energized by a cumbersome and vaguely defined thing labeled ideology. This problem is exemplified by the syntax of the following sentence in which Berlin describes the provenance of positivist epistemology in late-nineteenth-century composition: "Encouraged by the business community, with the tacit approval of science departments, composition courses became positivist in spirit and method" (*Writing Instruction* 9). My guess is that the dangling modifier ("Encouraged by the business community") is more than a blunder; the syntactic agency is indicative of Berlin's failure to uncover a tangible (or demonstrable) source for this change in epistemology. If we ask "*who* is encouraged by the business community?" we find it is a thing: not human beings but composition courses. One gets the feeling here (as in much of Berlin's work) that composition theories and courses are not generated by human beings but operate as elements in a commanding, overarching oppressive structure—a totalizing narrative with no one living within it, or at least no one striving, however slyly or futilely, to resist it.

Certainly, exploring such a theory yields helpful insights, but Berlin often seems to take theories of cultural domination for granted. To make sense of his historical causation, we must infer that there exists a rather direct line from the ruling class's interests to the university and then to the composition course. For instance, Berlin states that in learning any rhetorical system "the student is being indoctrinated in a basic epistemology," a statement most compositionists would agree with. But he goes on to assert that this "epistemology [is] usually the one held by society's dominant class" (*Writing* 3). The question is, *how* does the society-wide epistemology get transported into university culture and into composition instruction? We are left asking, is the composition course dictated by the current "noetic field," which is in turn dictated by society? How does society-wide culture get into the university—wholesale, without interpretation, without significant alteration? Berlin assumes an isomorphic relationship between society and what counts as sound rhetorical theory.[8] *How* do these different levels—society, the university, the composition course—*communicate*? These very sticky but important historiographic problems are not explored, and we are expected, it seems, to take these power relations on faith.

While there of course *exist* relationships between ideology and composition (who today would disagree?), it is yet to be explained *how* ideology might have been translated into composition practice. The causal links between ideology and practice have mostly been too clean and too pervasive. In trying to examine the place of composition within the *whole* of society, Berlin is forced to make generalizations about culture, ideology, and composition that he simply cannot validate. Perhaps I am asking for too much—a "smoking gun"—but if I (as a late-twentieth-century composition teacher) am to be helped by a history (if it is to be "useful"), I need to know, as precisely as possible, what it is I am resisting. Urging me to resist an overarching and largely invisible thing called "ideology" helps me only a little. Because the horizons of such history are enormous, focus and clarity are sacrificed. And as far as the reader's response, also sacrificed are pedagogic and social *action*.

My second criticism of Berlin's work concerns its limiting conception of ideology as an always and everywhere malevolent force. This conception of ideology, reinforced by the massive scope of his investigation, leads to an unhelpful and, perhaps, paranoid representation of the relationship between society at large, the composition course, and the students and teachers who labored there. The nature of his argument forces him to assume tremendous and awful powers of social control that reach into every nook of social life, from the corporate office to the assembly line to the freshman composition course. In Berlin's work it is assumed that "society" (or "ideology" or "culture") possesses the power to control composition. Because the connections remain so mysterious, "society" takes on an eerily omnipotent character. In reading Berlin's work, one rarely gets the feeling that one has sufficiently got a grip on culture—or, as I will be proposing here, even some "slice of culture"—enough to understand or resist it. One certainly feels enraged, but not empowered. It might be said that Berlin does not provide a model of resistance or even an outline of something to resist against; rather, his histories can lead ultimately to a feeling of despair, which can in turn eventuate in a form of intellectual quietism.

My criticism of Berlin's historiography restates criticisms of similar historiography written during this period. Frank Lentricchia, for example, criticizes "New historicism in its strong Foucauldian vein," for positing a "metaphysics of power," which is impossible to know, let alone to resist. Its result is not social action, but a form of radical quietism:

> [S]uch knowledge, if that is what it is (I prefer calling it a paranoid fantasy, one especially characteristic of the recent literary mind), is necessary to the sustaining of a totalitarian culture (or, as I prefer to say, to the sustaining, in ostensibly democratic contexts, of the illusion of totalitarianism). . . . New historicism in its strong Foucauldian vein is an important because representative story of the American academic intellectual in the contemporary moment of literary history, a moment which we had presumed to be a definitive break with the business as usual of literary study. (95, 97)

Because there is no specifiable source of oppression or of always-already instantiated ideology, historians and practitioners alike may as well take "a long weekend that defuses the radical implications of our unhappiness" (96).

Similar to the way that society has been portrayed as omnipotently diabolic, much composition historiography has portrayed composition's forebears—especially the most influential of them—as either willing participants in hegemonic maneuvering or unwitting stooges. It has too simply assumed that the architects of composition were in cahoots with the dominant structures of power and under the unmitigated influence of the dominant ideologies. As Berlin put it recently:

> Ruling classes after all have always made certain that their members are adept at the signifying practices that ensure the continuance of their power. Rhetorics . . . have been forwarded in the name of a "true" discourse, a discourse, however, that actually best served the interests of a particular ruling group. ("Composition Studies and Cultural Studies" 116)

The problem is that Berlin had assumed that the interests of the "ruling classes" and the interests of composition's architects were identical.

This kind of narrative misleads in its simplicity. More local, more focused narratives of these individuals yield different conclusions. Like the laws of physics, these culturewide tendencies can be said to apply to everyone, but they apply to no one in particular. In physics, aberrations can be attributed to friction, mechanical anomalies, and the like; in cultural studies, these anomalies *are* the story. I am arguing that, in the case of composition and ideology, when we look at individuals *closely* and in a sustained fashion, we find that such culturewide depictions look less and less accurate.

Here is an example of the kind of problem that arises when biography and localized accounts are ignored in favor of broad, transcultural ideologies. James Berlin identifies Charles Francis Adams Jr., E. L. Godkin, and Josiah Quincy—the principal authors of the Harvard literacy reports—as "representatives of the world of affairs" (*Writing* 60), an opprobrious label for Berlin, roughly equivalent to "businessmen." Of course, this is true, but as John Brereton ("Business Writing") and I ("Who Wrote?") have shown, there is far more to the story. Adams and Godkin were also public intellectuals who certainly did not simply represent the interest of the business class. In fact, though they were conservatives in many respects (e.g., both were leaders in the movement to curtail suffrage rights [see McGerr]), both were highly critical of American business, and both were fierce reformers. In short, it is a more complicated and interesting story.

As John Gage has argued, we have barely begun to cataloge the problems and questions related to nineteenth-century American rhetoric. In what sense, then, are we positioned to create universalizing theories about this vast phenomenon ("Doing")? This is not to suggest that every lesson we have learned from nineteenth-century composition history must be radically questioned, only that we slow down and make room for new ideas. It seems important to closely examine the myriad intersections of culture, individuals, and composition. This may help us discover "representative anecdotes," which may help us understand this historical background—as well as our current problems—differently. Jean Ferguson Carr writes that

> [h]istories of instruction need to negotiate cultural complexity and attend to multiple intersections of traditions and terms, rather than erecting artificial barriers between school and the world. Such a historical model would . . . acknowledge the multiple hierarchies of power and influence that monitor the crossing of their boundaries. . . . We need to rethink the notion that influence and tradition are produced in straight lines, that theories are uttered and then get "implemented" somehow and the influence spreads down and out until it is diffused in the hinterlands. (96–97)

Susan Miller expresses a similar impatience with composition history that fails to explicate the multifarious links between ideology and practice:

> Without jettisoning the intellectual history we have retrieved from traditional and new historiographies for rhetoric, we must explicitly understand and elaborate on this *cultural* context and its ideological workings if we are to explain why so few root metaphors for composition studies have changed in the light of recent theories and research. ("Composition as Cultural Artifact" 31)

Such cultural histories, she suggests, would be far more helpful to contemporary compositionists in their efforts to change practice.

Composition history needs narratives that are more complex and that more accurately illustrate the relationships between culture and composition. To put this another way, composition historiography needs *more* narratives—narratives that shave off smaller, more manageable and analyzable, cross-sections of composition and of culture, but that are thus able to examine those relationships more thoroughly. Rather than categorizing all nineteenth-century compositionists in terms of the hero/villain dichotomy (as if all figures really fit within a standard category or two called the "nineteenth-century compositionist"),[9] we need detailed accounts of individuals in which the motivations and actions of individuals can be seen in a richer and more illuminating light.

To examine the rise of composition—or any historical phenomenon—solely in terms of a predefined ideology makes for a clear story of cause and effect: the ideology caused such and such persons to do what they did. But the foregrounding of ideology without biography and the details of cultural history also negates the role of human agency by rendering humans powerless in the face of culture. And this makes for a paranoid representation of power. As Frank Lentricchia describes those who use the terministic screen of ideology, Marxists, new historicists, and other Foucault-inspired historians, "will have virtually nothing to do with biography—impatient with the secret plot, they get there too quickly. I think we most believe in secret plots when they are hard to see" (23). Composition history (like the composition classroom, as I suggest in chapters 6 and 7) must make room for the stories of individuals, not just mass ideologies.

Before ending this discussion of Berlin's work, I must point out that this "problem" (i.e., his tendency to take on huge swathes of culture and to read the actions of individuals through culturewide, standardized ideology) is precisely what made his histories so important and so beneficial during the 1980s. His work has demonstrated that any composition theory and practice is fraught with ideological assumptions and therefore inevitably has political, social, and cultural import. He insisted on the grave importance of composition teachers "getting their politics straight" in their own minds and then carrying out practices that would further their political goals as effectively as they can. For this almost magisterial accomplishment, and for his insistence that composition and composition history never lose sight of its political foundations and political roles, composition studies will always owe a great debt to Berlin.

Some Different Models of Ideology, Culture, and History

Composition forebears are seen primarily as flat characters (villains or heroes) because the concept of "culture" in composition historiography has remained somewhat flat. As I have suggested, even with more revisionist histories, the boundaries of composition historiography could stand some jostling. Specifically, by examining more localized narratives (even biographical narratives) in greater detail, *and* in terms of what we know of broader cultural practices, conventions, and anxieties, we might further reconceive the ideological origins of nineteenth-century composition and further complicate the portrait of early composition architects as somehow "in league" with much larger malevolent cultural forces.

More important, such examinations, I think, would make composition more useful. As Richard Lloyd-Jones writes, "We prefer to use history to tell us that we are the same as our ancestors when we should also note that in crucial ways we are different" (22). I would alter this idea slightly to: We seem to prefer to use history to tell us that we are *either* very much like or very different from our forebears, when we should also note that our relationship with the past is highly complex. Furthermore, this complexity is useful to us since "we must," as Lloyd-Jones writes, "always seek another way" (23). As he concludes, such a history would "not [be] so tidy, but it may be more useful" (25). Specifically, it would be more useful because composition studies is inherently highly sensitive to the always changing attitudes, abilities, and needs of its students. Therefore, compositionists, by the very nature of their work, must continuously rethink their practices as the institutions and culture around them change—as their *students* change *with* these institutional and cultural changes. Perhaps histories that are more sensitive to the cultural and other forces that change students will help composition teachers become more sensitive to and thoughtful about student change.

Therefore, we need to remember that—and we need to recover *how*—the relationships between composition teachers and composition students are always changing. In composition studies especially, where there has been so much attention paid recently to students and their writing, it seems we might pay closer attention to the individuals—their lives, their work, their ideas about what they were creating—who helped create the institution of composition. When, for instance, we examine nineteenth-century (or any era's) teaching practices, we must remember: (1) students actually *were* different from our students; (2) teachers' *perceptions* of their students differed from our perceptions; (3) teachers' beliefs about who their students *should be* differed from our ideas about who are students *should be*. So, we need to recover more than just the composition methods and theories; we also need to recover our forebears' sense of the underlying assumptions about the relationships among students, the students' culture, and teaching composition. We should investigate what assumptions—what guiding philosophies about their students—were at the root of nineteenth-century composition pedagogy. What was it like, we should ask, to *think with these ideas*?

I have no grand schemes for "redeeming the historical subject" in composition history, though I do believe we need to at least move in this direction. In any case, a dose of biography can, perhaps, make composition history more "useful." In a sense, this call for historical and biographical detail touches on an old debate in composition historiography. As early as 1984, Sharon Crowley mildly criticized a historical article for portraying nineteenth-century composition theory as *obviously* wrongheaded ("Response" 89). To extend her argument (and North extends it in just this way [85]), to paint nineteenth-century compositionists as adhering to *obviously* foolish beliefs and practices is to belittle them to the point that we have little or nothing to learn from this history. Such a clear-cut history portrays these forebears as mere pawns or idiots, and if they are idiots what does that say about us who are engaging them in a trans-century dialogue? Such a portrait certainly defines them as "other," thereby enhancing the sense of community to which "we" belong. However, it seems to me more important to understand why these nineteenth-century theories seemed to make sense for them. Again, what was it like to think with these ideas? Perhaps the metaphor of "transference of learning" is appropriate here. When we witness how our forebears struggled to bring into teaching practice the results of their cognitive and ideological beliefs, we are better prepared to examine our own practices. When we examine how their beliefs made sense, we are better positioned to critique our beliefs, which of course make sense to us.

In a sense, this historiographic model is merely the extension of the model which Crowley and some others have followed. Crowley "makes sense" of what may seem to us the irrational faith in current-traditional rhetoric. She explains, for instance, why it made sense to nineteenth-century-textbook writers to divorce invention from the writing process:

> If one accepts a faculty model of the mind and if one subscribes to the notion that method represents mental movements in discourse, it is an easy leap to the supposition that a writer who wishes to appeal to one of the faculties, say, the passions, can first devise a formal strategy that is peculiarly suited to stimulating emotional responses and, further, that this strategy can be embodied in a finished text. (*Methodical* 97)

Crowley's *Methodical Memory* is very self-consciously an account of the development of current-traditional rhetoric in academic/intellectual terms, and not a historical or cultural account. Nan Johnson's "cultural history" (as she calls it), *Nineteenth-Century Rhetoric in North America*, does something similar. Both authors limit the horizons of their analyses in a way that allows them to reconfigure composition studies' nineteenth-century heritage. As Johnson argues, nineteenth-century rhetoric has not been measured in terms of that period's cultural and intellectual imperatives.

The historico-rhetorical objective in these histories (and in this work) resembles the kind of reassessment that has been occurring for some time in literary history.[10] Sacvan Bercovitch's distinction between "extrinsic" and "intrinsic" criticism is helpful here. He argues that to criticize an ideology (or myth) *extrinsically* is to "see through" or "expose" its historical functions, usually from an antagonistic perspective. Such critique sees ideology as "a system of ideas in the service of evil rather than (like any ideology) a system of ideas wedded for good and evil to a certain social order" ("Problem" 638). To criticize an ideology *intrinsically* is to "appreciate" it from within, explicating it in order to understand how such an ideology made sense to those subscribing to it.

This is not to suggest, of course, that historians should be absolved from making "strong," "activist," or even rancorous readings of history.[11] I'm suggesting only that "extrinsic" and "intrinsic" reading might constitute two elements in a dialectical historiography. To use the term I will explore in chapter 6, I think historians must assume the *responsibility* to listen and to understand these past figures on their own terms, not merely in terms of the supposedly standardized nineteenth-century compositionist. In addition to criticizing them, we should also strive to learn from their knowledge.

Such historiography might bring us toward a history of rhetoric that has a human face. This admirable quality can be seen, for instance, in Donald Stewart's work on Fred Newton Scott and in JoAnn Campbell's "Controlling Voices: The Legacy of English at Radcliffe College 1883–1917." By examining the diaries of three turn-of-the-century Radcliffe students and exploring the emotional impact of agonistic, male-centered rhetorical teaching, Campbell helps us understand what *it feels like* to never be affirmed, but only corrected. "In a pedagogical context of struggle," she writes, "the writer's voice may be the prize" (474). Rather than ceasing at the moment she discovers the origins of contemporary models of agonistic pedagogy; rather than concluding that these women's experiences were wholly alien to ours, Campbell discovers similarities between past and present, giving vitality and historical perspective to some of our current pedagogical concerns.

Johnson's, Crowley's, and Connor's recent histories challenge the long-held assumption that rhetoric in nineteenth-century America was *merely* dormant, reductive, pernicious, or just generally inferior. In this way they succeed in examining this rhetoric according to the terms, biases, and values of the culture that produced it. With this "intrinsic" approach, Johnson uncovers complexities and syntheses that have previously gone unnoticed. As Johnson puts this:

A commentary that seeks to profile nineteenth-century rhetoric against the backdrop of its indigenous circumstances must resist assumptions of such partisan critiques in favor of an analytical reading of nineteenth-century scholarship as a body of work from which general conclusions regarding the nature and function of rhetorical theory can be elicited, conclusions that clarify how the nineteenth-century tradition responded to the intellectual and social will of its age. When existing scholarship is reviewed from this perspective, significant presumptions regarding the character of nineteenth-century theory, the range of the nineteenth-century rhetorical arts, and the cultural function of rhetorical education can be derived. (13–14)

She recognizes that in the nineteenth century the role of rhetoric changed dramatically and fundamentally. New institutions (Johnson focuses almost entirely on the institutions of "high" and university culture) required new ideas about the purposes and modes of rhetorical exchange. Many of the characteristics and purposes of former rhetorics were abandoned or fundamentally altered. But the most dramatic and laudatory characteristic of nineteenth-century American rhetoric was its capacity for *synthesizing* old ideas and old requirements with the novel ideas and requirements of the emerging culture. In this sense, argues Johnson, the nineteenth-century rhetorical tradition "exceeded the accomplishments" of its predecessor traditions "by synthesizing the epistemological, belles lettres, and classical rationales to justify a broader range of rhetorical practice" (227).

I find Johnson's and Crowley's work exemplary for other reasons. Unlike Berlin, each takes up a fairly modest "slice" of culture to examine: what today we might call "intellectual" or "academic" culture. Each demonstrates how, within the confines of this culture, the changes in rhetoric were not only internally consistent but prudent and powerful. Therefore they need not posit (as did Berlin) an overarching ideology that invaded and corrupted rhetoric and composition. Both offer their readers "tangible-enough" agents (or causes) of historical change. For Crowley, the intellectual, psychological, and social assumptions of the academic class who wrote textbooks led, almost naturally, to their conclusions. For Johnson, the requirements of an altered "high" culture necessitated an altered rhetoric, and nineteenth-century rhetoric fulfilled these requirements.

Johnson's "corrective" history perhaps marks the beginning of a rhythmic reshifting in rhetorical historiography, which is similar to what has been occurring within other genres of history. Before historians in composition studies began their late-1970s historical investigation in earnest, rhetorical history in America was dominated by historians who worked in speech departments. Both Connors and Johnson have called speech-department histories the "first wave" of American rhetorical history, and composition studies histories the "second wave" (see Johnson 7–11; and Connors, "Writing the History" 50–53). By comparing Albert Kitzhaber's dissertation (1953) to Warren Guthrie's series of *Speech Monographs* articles (1946–51), one can readily grasp what have become the traditional differences between composition studies history and speech-department history: not only has speech-department history focused almost solely on oral discourse, but also it has been primarily celebratory—that is, it looked to its forebears for inspiration and definition. Composition studies historiography, to say the least, tends to be more suspicious of the motivations of early composition theorists and practitioners.

The change marked by Johnson's more complex account of the origins of American composition is analogous to the changes that have been occurring in the historiography of literacy and education. As several education historians have noted, the early literacy and schooling historiography is epitomized by Ellwood P. Cubberly, who optimistically, unproblematically glorified the American common-school movement, praising its advocates and damning its opponents. Literacy for historians like Cubberly was unquestionably beneficial, leading to progress, freedom, and enlightenment. (This seems analogous to the "first wave" of rhetorical historiography carried out in speech departments.) Then, in the late sixties, "radical revisionism" (as it was later called) was ushered in, most notably by Michael Katz's *The Irony of Early School Reform* (1968). As David Tyack explains, with Katz's book historians of education began examining "the links between ideology, school formation, and social structure"; they became suspicious of literacy, seeing education as covert indoctrination, "class imposition," and social control (302; see also Carl F. Kaestle's "Literacy and Diversity"). This revisionist history seems analogous to the censorious and distrustful historiography that has typified much of composition studies historiography and has been epitomized in Berlin's work.

But more recent literacy historiography has rejected the nice, clean cause-and-effect relationship between ideology and practice, and has been richly complicated, most notably (but certainly not solely) in the work of Carl F. Kaestle, who concurs with revisionist history that "public schooling had been an imposition in various ways, that it was both culturally conformist and economically unfair, and that it had been resisted" ("Literacy and Diversity" 524). But he also recognizes that the efficacy of such dominant-class hegemonic efforts cannot be assumed. In other words, he questions the complete-domination model assumed by Katz (and, as I argue, Berlin). To summarize, historians of literacy have gone from viewing literacy unproblematically, to viewing it as dominant-class hegemonic imposition, to viewing literacy as a complex factor in a vast web of social relations that cut across class lines, institutions, and time periods.

More recent questions in the history of literacy focus on the formation and function of "readerships": what does a particular readership *do* for society and for the individuals within a readership? What this new trend in literacy historiography teaches is that the cause-and-effect relationship between ideology and reading practices was not (nor can be) a one-way street. All segments of any literate society are affected by the definition and function of literacy within virtually every other segment. Literacy is neither wholly hegemonic nor wholly subversive; rather, diversity and consolidation are always in tension (see Kaestle et al., *Literacy in the United States*, especially 272–93).

This effort to discern the complex interaction between individuals and more broadly cultural conditions and ideologies is nothing radically new, as scholars have exploited such understanding for some time. One notable example is Cathy N. Davidson's *Revolution and the Word*, which is both a literary history and a literacy history. While treating ideology as an always complex and dynamic force and while scrutinizing the role of the individual in society, Davidson examines not only the sociology of book publishing but also the marginalia of book *readers*, thus constructing "an ethnology of the early American novel reader" (10). She makes her point that the early American novel (thought subversive by early-nineteenth-century American authority figures and thought hegemonically oppressive by revisionists) played a complicated role for both readers and society at large and that by examining the interrelationships among both texts and historical contexts we can arrive at a historical understanding far richer than would be possible by examining each by itself. As her work makes abundantly clear, literacy is a tremendous social force that is neither wholly good and liberating nor wholly evil and controlling.

Similarly, Kaestle says he has come to understand that in order to better answer these questions about literacy in America (which he began with his studies of the common school), he has moved beyond historical records of the schoolroom, of schoolteachers, and of the planners of the common school, the university, or other curricula makers. He has found it necessary to investigate all segments of culture, "high" as well as "low," "intellectual" as well as "mass" or "popular" culture. And in order to do this, he has also investigated such diverse matters as the economics of publishing and of distribution, and the effect of changing communication technologies (such as the telegraph, the rotary press, cheap paper, etc.). These forces also cut across all social lines, affecting with equal power the newspaper editor in the pressroom, the mechanic reading a tract or newspaper, and the professor of English contemplating how students ought to be taught. Just as the consumers of popular culture are influenced in complex ways by what they read, also influenced were the defenders of "high

culture," who reacted strongly against popular culture and felt it their
solemn duty to help society resist its onslaught.

So, what would count as a "cultural" history of nineteenth-century
composition? I am, for instance, uncertain about Johnson's characteriza-
tion of her work as a *"cultural* history." (Crowley explicitly defines how her
work is *not* a cultural history [xv].) The borders of what seems to count as
"culture" for Johnson seem narrow, limited to academic, intellectual culture, which seems to be untouched by wider, larger, and perhaps more
influential and important historical forces. Nonetheless, Johnson succeeds
because she examines the place rhetoric and composition intersect with a
relatively small area of "culture." The culture she examines is primarily
what we would today call "intellectual" culture. When she speaks, for instance, of "cultural imperatives," she means the imperatives that the (white,
wealthy, male, fairly traditional) intellectual stratum of culture perceived as
imperatives. To use the terms of the traditional ("high, low, middle-brow")
model of "culture," Johnson looks at the intersection of two aspects of
"high" culture: the intellectual tradition intersecting with the origins of
American composition. Johnson, in other words, elects not to examine the
relationship of these cultural imperatives to other cultural strata.[12]

However, while Johnson shows how nineteenth-century rhetoric strived
to become culturally important and how nineteenth-century rhetorical theory
was well adapted to *intellectual* ideas about what culture was (or ought to
be), her work does not distinguish between the various competing versions
of what "culture" was or of whose discourse should dominate the public
scene. For instance, when she speaks of the "cultural imperatives" of rhetoric, she is speaking of culture in rather hermetic terms: not "American"
culture but the culture of the patrician, educated classes, that is, the intellectuals who wrote rhetorics and rhetorical philosophy. These imperatives
have yet to be analyzed in terms of the individuals who were the architects
of modern composition. In other words, these figures have been examined
in terms of our *contemporary* cultural and intellectual values, without
much consideration for the cultural complexities that shaped their beliefs
about what writing instruction should be and what it should do for students. It is precisely these modest horizons that give Johnson's book its
strength, since they allow Johnson to provide a convincing and precise
rendering of the role of rhetoric in society as its theoreticians perceived it.
However—and perhaps I'm quibbling that she fails to state a truism—she
might have acknowledged the limited scope of her "cultural inquiry."

As intellectual history of the past twenty or so years has revealed, we
cannot depend solely upon what the lives, actions, and words of prominent
intellectuals and educators can tell us about American culture, "except as
mere windows into a small sector of highly elite culture, of whose nature

we seem already to be well aware" (Cayton 597). Historians have recognized the importance of going beyond merely interpreting the utterances of intellectuals within intellectuals' own cultural circles; history can profit from interpreting such utterances as reactions within the larger, heterogenous web of culture. We can profit from noting the larger contexts of intellectual discourse, which is always part of the contest between conflicting groups over symbolic meaning.

My work is in its objectives similar to Thomas P. Miller's recent history, *The Formation of College English*, which expands "the historical frame of reference beyond histories of *ideas about* rhetoric" (28, my emphasis). He shows how the work of intellectuals is helpfully conceived as a response to these broader historical forces, specifically those forces—mass literacy, the rise of the middle class, and their need for its assimilation into the conventions of high culture—that led to the institution of English studies in Scotland, Ireland, and (to a limited extent) the United States. If we are to understand how we got to the present, Miller argues, we must examine not "*the* rhetorical tradition" but the various competing rhetorical traditions, as Miller puts it, "the rhetoric of traditions—the ways that political parties, ethnic groups, social movements, and other discourse communities constitute and maintain the shared values and assumptions that authorize discourse" ("Reinventing" 26). In order to do this, Miller argues, we need to "look beyond the rhetorical tradition"; "we need localized accounts of the shared experiences of the community as well as more broadly focused research on discursive practices, social conventions, material conditions, and political ideologies" (31). In writing a history that examines how rhetorical instruction reacted to real social exigencies, Miller maintains he has tried to "establish a more rhetorical perspective on the formation of college English—a perspective defined by rhetoric's traditional concern for assessing how discourse is used in specific contexts to accomplish specific purposes" (*Formation* 6).

I hope to extend composition historiography by focusing on Harvard Boylston Professors of Rhetoric Edward T. Channing and Adams Sherman Hill, two central figures in American rhetoric and composition, both of whom have been almost exclusively regarded as villains in composition history. They seem to me worthy test cases, since their composition theories are considered so influential, so pervasive, and so unworthy of emulation. The case of each provides a "representative anecdote," to use Kenneth Burke's term, that might help explain the cultural forces that nineteenth-century composition instructors felt as they were constructing their theories and writing curricula. I do not argue (as for instance Johnson does) for the accomplishments of synthetic complexity of the figures I study, but I do argue for the virtue of some of their motivations. While I do not always (or even often) agree with their conclusions, I try to show that they faced and tried to respond to cultural imperatives that are very similar to those we are facing today.

3

To "Fortify the Immunities of a Free People"

Edward T. Channing's Response to Emerging Forms of Popular Public Discourse

[The modern students'] minds are surfeited with what other men have said, and toiled hard and all alone to come at. No wonder that they grow sickly, acquiescing, and unproductive.

—Edward T. Channing, 1816

Television, film, and photography, far from making culture democratic, have fostered the wide dissemination of industrialized entertainment so that the capacity of persons to produce their own culture . . . has become restricted.

—Stanley Aronowitz and Henry Giroux, 1985

This country is filling up with thousands and millions of voters, and you must educate them to keep them from our throats.

—Ralph Waldo Emerson[1]

Prologue: Conformity versus Resistance and the Real versus the Ideal

Edward T. Channing's theory of communication and composition resembles in some interesting ways our current ideas about "critical pedagogy" and "culture and composition studies" pedagogy. Specifically, both Channing's theories and our contemporary theories of critical pedagogy attempt to rescue the active, discerning subject from an uncritical immersion in her/his surroundings—her/his "culture." As modern education theorists insist, "critical learners" strive not to imbibe and describe reality, but to gain "critical perspective" on it; they strive not to "reproduce" their culture, but to step outside of it, to "resist" it. But these goals may be achieved, I would argue, at the expense of silencing students' actual, lived experience.

The problems of conformity, coercion, and domination have been much discussed in the research on composition and pedagogy, as have their counterpart solutions—resistance, dialogue, and empowerment. It was Freire, of course, whose models of liberatory pedagogy got us to question the practice of "banking pedagogy" and conceiving of our students as docile receptacles to be filled with our knowledge. In more recent years, the debate has turned to the purposeful injection of politics in the classroom (the curriculum debates at the University of Texas at Austin perhaps being the most memorable incarnation of this discussion). The conversation has turned to the problem of defining literacy; we recognize that "our" literacies—"academic" literacy, "critical" literacy, and so on—exist among many forms of literacy, each doing different kinds of work and encouraging different ways to view the world for those who practice it. Indeed, then, imposing our desired form of literacy can reasonably be seen as an act of "violence" (e.g., Stuckey, Godzich). Therefore, we must take responsibility for imposing upon students our ways of seeing the word and the world.

But can such an approach really work—this approach that foregrounds ideological critique and intellectual distance at the expense of students' lived experience and their habitual ways of seeing the world? Can it change students? In a rancorous exchange at the back of a recent *College Composition and Communication*, respondents Alan France ("Theory Cop"), Donald Lazere ("Spellmeyer's Naive Populism"), and Kurt Spellmeyer ("Culture and Agency") confronted the politics and problems of students' subjectivity, how it might best be changed, and the ethical and political implications of such change. Lazere suggested that Spellmeyer lapses into a "comfortably clichéd idealization of students," which leads to a lazy model of expressivism or of pluralism in which teachers fail to confront their responsibility to lead students toward better and more critical stances toward their world and its politics (292). In his rejoinder to Lazere, Spellmeyer contends that when teachers remain so assured and enamored of their politics and of their forms of literacy, they themselves may lapse too comfortably into elitist indoctrination to leftist beliefs and methods. Spellmeyer argues that it becomes all too easy and dangerous to conceive our students as simply "incompetent readers," who are sorely in need of political and cultural remediation—where *our* methods of reading culture dominate (or should dominate) classroom discussion. Lazere accuses Spellmeyer of idealizing students, and Spellmeyer accuses Lazere and others of idealizing their own methods and beliefs.

Edward T. Channing's rhetorical training resembles the kind of elitist indoctrination that Spellmeyer (and I) objects to. Both Channing and many modern-day cultural studies teachers want their students to reject the clichés of their culture; both see culture as inhabiting student subjectivity. Both want students to adopt *their* ways of seeing the world and their ways of demystifying society's discourse. Social and political conformity is the very problem that teachers must help their students overcome. Both, in short, define rhetorical training as a process that pushes *against* a society that instills a standardized consciousness into the citizenry and into college students. Or perhaps Channing and these modern-day teachers represent mirror images, since Channing (by the standards held by most of us) was decidedly conservative in his beliefs. But even so, both want to keep popular communicative "habits" *out* of their students.

In this way, my argument differs fundamentally from the way most critics have viewed Channing: I do not criticize him for striving to help his students "fit into" society but for the way he attempted to help them "resist" an increasingly coercive and dangerous society—his way of helping his students distance themselves from their culture at all costs. According to Channing and much cultural studies teaching, students with a sound training in rhetoric—for Channing, training in both reading and writing—might turn their backs on society and pursue what is *really* in the best interest of themselves and their society. So Channing's elitism resembles our own. Channing, like all of us, perhaps, abided by what Richard E. Miller has called "pedagogy's master narrative," where "the violence of the educational process is always already understood to ultimately have been for the good of the student, the master narrative in teaching," where the student overcomes her resistance to our ideas and in the end becomes "just like us" ("Making").

Channing too navigates between two worlds, the real one and the ideal one. The real world was where actual public discourse was enacted. It was a dangerous place that was becoming increasingly perilous and powerful as forms of public discourse were changing in step with changing technological and political practices. It was also a place where men of his elite and refined stature were becoming less and less influential. The ideal world was where Channing felt more "at home," as he put it, at Harvard, in the pages of the *North American Review*, and, so he thought, among his coterie of colleagues and students. Like all of us, perhaps, Channing believed the real world should be more like his ideal world and that the best way to judge the real world was to use the critical methods of his ideal one. His rhetorical training sought to teach students to "resist" that real world—where citizens were coerced into certain habits of communication—and to bring their newly invigorated versions of proper and ideal discourse, bit by bit, moment by moment, into that fallen world. The problem with such an approach, as I argue throughout this work, is that it encourages students to regard their society as insidious, as something that infects them and their ways of regarding reality, something to be resisted, something that rhetorical education can inoculate them against. It does not teach students that their culture, and that their beliefs about culture, provides rich material to work with. The part of students that culture has created, says Channing's model, must be ignored. Such pedagogy cleanly separates the real from the ideal, rather than blending the two.

Channing's Discourse Immunity

Channing's theories of rhetorical education and healthful political discourse resonate with the "inoculation, resistance, and immunity" metaphor of education. This claim is admittedly an act of anachronism since the very idea of physiological resistance, as we know it, was not available to Channing. It was not an idea he could think with, consciously or otherwise. But Channing's models do share, I maintain, the idea that "the ideal and fit person" (as Emily Martin expresses it, 15) has an inner strength (like the immune system) that helps defend against alien violators (like infections and crafty viruses) of the self. For centuries it has been common, even for Channing, to speak of questionable ideas as "infecting" (as in "corrupting" or "invading") certain persons, and for dangerous ideas to spread like a "contagion," especially among the masses.

For Channing, the key to a "fortified immunity" (to use his phrase) is not just a steady diet of information; indeed, the Enlightenment and early-American idea that knowledge would make falsehood powerless became less tenable for Channing as increasing numbers of less-educated voters elected the nation's leaders and as print technology democratized communications media, so that a less-select class of persons was now bringing new habits of writing to an increasingly large newspaper-reading public. What was crucial to the citizenry's moral and political health was the ability to consistently and independently discern truth from falsehood. Channing, in agreement with the Scottish Enlightenment philosophers who so powerfully influenced him, believed that humankind's "common sense" (endowed to every person by the "Author of Human Nature," as Francis Hutcheson put it) allowed individuals to perceive the world in "proper" ways. In other words, this capacity to perceive the difference between truth and falsity was part of who each of us is, so long as alien phenomena did not warp the natural character and thus the ability to perceive the world and ideas properly. But such alien ideas, for Channing, abounded in nineteenth-century America as republicanism was veering into liberal democracy. Therefore, the citizenry needed some kind of protection against alien and dangerous ideas, and that protection had to come from within, since democracy cannot make the world a safe environment.

Channing believed that emerging forms of public discourse were in very large part responsible for compromising Americans' critical capacities. Emphasis on factionalism and disembodied facts was causing Americans to see the world, ideas, and truth itself as fundamentally contentious rather than cooperative. The remedy for Channing was a steady diet of healthy public discourse that would instill into the populace calmer and better "habits of thinking." Such a steady dose of healthful public discourse would have salutary effects. It might "fortify the immunities" of Americans.

The era in which Channing lived was undergoing an exceedingly complex transformation from an ideal (somewhat nostalgic) view of republican civic virtue to an ideal of liberal self-virtue. While the clichés of American history (those old-fashioned grand narratives about abrupt, clean changes in cultural attitudes) portray these ideals as nicely separated, that is hardly the case. And it was even less the case for persons who lived during that era and were trying to make sense of a rapidly changing nation and (as it seemed to many) its rapidly changing citizenry (for a revealing account of this progressive but imperceptible transformation of ideology, see Watts). And for a Whig-Federalist like Channing, whose Federalist, government-interventionist, paternalist ideals had been popularly trounced during the first years of the century but were resurfacing in various ways during the decades after the War of 1812, the story becomes even more troublesome and subtle.

To be clear, "Ned" (or "Potty") Channing was no radical pedagogue—at least not in the contemporary sense of the word. He was aristocratic in temperament and conservative in politics. From a Boston Brahmin family, an editor and contributor to the *North American Review*, a Unitarian, a Whig, Channing's most ardent desire in education was to reinforce the status quo and ensure that "the multitude" learn to respect America's established institutions of law and order. As for his Harvard students, his pedagogy was aimed at helping them gain some distance from (as we would call it today) popular culture, so that they could see the reality of human nature (and thus *themselves*, who they were and should be) properly; then they might go out into the world and lead the citizenry toward respecting America's institutions.[2]

I hope that Channing will remind us of ourselves, those of us (from the right as well as the left, those of us recommending public writing as well as those of us who advocate expressive writing) who ardently want to alter the way our culture influences the consciousness of the citizenry and of our students. For Channing, culture was becoming horrifyingly proficient and subtle in its capacity for colonizing consciousness. Cultural forms of communication threatened to create a citizenry of docile subjects, who might accept, believe, and die for ideas not in their own best interests. Like many of us, he thought that education and the understanding of discourse might help provide Americans with the means for resisting the overwhelming power of their culture. Channing hoped to stir his readers and students from their passive immersion in culture and provide them with the means for becoming critically aware, active citizens.

Today, of course, the debate is conceived differently. Today, cultural spokespersons from both the right and the left portray their movements as "rebellions"; it seems that every faction in America today portrays itself as the outsider, the underdog, struggling to gain a position to be heard in the public forum. In fact, the very notion of "resistance," which has long been a slogan in critical and "radical" pedagogy, depends upon this underdog position: culture is not only pernicious but also very powerful; it inhabits our students; they need to learn to "demystify" culture, so they can resist its awesome power.

For Channing, a subscriber to the paternalist social theory of the Federalists and the Whigs, the relationship between culture and power was different: he wanted to ensure that his class would *maintain* its cultural influence; he wanted to ensure that the citizenry—or at least the upper echelons—maintained its critical distance from *emerging* pernicious forms of popular culture.

The Historical Reception of Channing in English Studies

Edward Tyrrel Channing (1790–1856) is an important historical figure for both composition studies and American Literature. Harvard's third Boylston Professor of Rhetoric and Oratory, Channing achieved literary historical status, in part, by way of his involvement in *The North American Review*, a politically conservative, scholarly magazine whose contributors were primarily the "cream of New England intellectuals" (Tebbel and Zuckerman 4) and whose editorial policies included "the encouragement of American Literature."[3] Channing helped found the magazine in 1815, acted as its third editor, and contributed articles throughout his life. He resigned the editorship in 1819, when he accepted the Boylston Professorship, a position he held until his health began to fail in 1851 (Felton 35–36, 40). At Harvard, he made his most prominent mark on the American literary scene by teaching rhetoric and literary philosophy to such future literary celebrities as Emerson, Edward Everett Hale, Holmes, Lowell, Parkman, George Ripley, Thoreau, and Thomas Wentworth Higginson, among other notables. "In fact," remarked Van Wyck Brooks, "the whole New England 'Renaissance' was to spring so largely from Channing's pupils ... that the question might have been asked, 'Did Channing cause it?' "[4] Literary historians usually cite Channing as a salutary influence on American letters, as he challenged American writers to move away from the literary models of the ancients and the British. Clearly influencing Emerson's "American Scholar,"[5] he challenged intellectuals to turn away from books, fame, and society, advising them instead to find intellectual independence by looking to Nature and their own sense of genius.[6]

However, Channing has fared much less favorably with historians of American rhetoric. These critics generally fault him, in various ways and to various degrees, for moving the ancient, proud discipline of rhetoric toward that tedious subdiscipline of English studies, composition. Historians have provided ample evidence that much of current-traditional rhetoric can be traced to the influence of Channing.[7] Indeed, on every matter for which rhetoric historians denigrate current-traditional rhetoric, they have criticized Channing for participating in its formation. Thus, for instance, he is portrayed as an aristocratic Whig who tried to initiate an aristocratic stylistics of exclusion through elitist education;[8] as a proto-professional who initiated the styles and ethos of the expert (Clark and Halloran 16–17); as a literature-department oppressor who privileged literature and the literature teacher over composition and the composition teacher;[9] and, in general, as one of the central figures who turned American rhetoric away from classical rhetoric's tenets of public oratory, pragmatism, and democratic discourse, and toward a rhetoric of the written word, belletrism, and private discourse. All these interpretations possess validity, some a great deal of validity. I agree, in general, that Channing's work had some decidedly pernicious effects upon American rhetoric and that his rhetoric almost certainly helped lay the foundations for current-traditional rhetoric.

But such criticism glosses too easily over Channing's deep concern for the eclipsing of the individual in American society. This criticism has not examined how Channing's culture was arguing over the definitions about what *society* was and should be, about what an *individual* was and should be, and about what the *relationship between the two* was and should be. In terms of composition, there has been little attention paid to Channing's concern for the status of the writing *subject* and his concern for how composition might help students resist (what today some call) cultural coercion. There is more to the story than merely charging that Channing divorced rhetoric and language from politics and culture deliberately (see especially Douglas). To the contrary, Channing recognized there had been radical changes in American culture and that the philosophy and practice of rhetoric must accommodate those changes. He recognized, to some degree, what has become in the last decade a commonplace in historical investigations of rhetoric, to use James Berlin's apt and much-quoted words, "A Rhetoric is a social invention":

> It arises out of a time and place, a peculiar social context, establishing for a period the conditions that make a peculiar kind of communication possible, and then it is altered or replaced by another scheme. (*Writing* 1)

Like many of his contemporaries, Channing in fact criticized American rhetoric for failing to *keep up* with the monumental social changes that had occurred since the ancient Greeks invented and developed rhetorical argument. And most important to my argument here, Channing recognized that in this changed world, the individual—the citizen, the auditor of discourse, the *knowing and acting subject*—had been fundamentally altered and lived in a fundamentally different world. Profoundly influenced as he was by Scottish Common Sense rationalism, Channing believed that humankind and its institutions had undergone tremendous and beneficial *progress*. His rhetoric and his theory of literacy—however conservative, aristocratic, and misguided they may ultimately have been—attempted to preserve for the writer and reader a critical space, a space where individuals could distance themselves from society and analyze the merit and impact of certain cultural assumptions.

Channing's Critique of Communications Media

Channing seemed aware that his rhetoric was new, or at least responded to new ideas about rhetoric and engaged America's new political and cultural scene. He quite consciously proposed this rhetoric, furthermore, to meet the demands of a radically new nation—a radically different "rhetorical situation" that presented scholars and students of rhetoric with new demands, new possibilities, and new dangers. On the one hand, America (as its debaters on democracy had been discussing since the Revolution) was immense in geographical size and cultural diversity. While new technologies and new forms of communication had made it possible to unite the country, these technologies and the forms of discourse they spawned also threatened America's citizens, Channing believed, with what might be called uncritical habits of belief. In contrast to face-to-face oratory, the written word healthfully separated auditor/readers from the vagaries and confusions of a increasingly complex world of competing ideas and ideologies; while reading, auditors could distance themselves from the writer to reflect quietly, in solitude. Reading offered refuge, a place for reflecting on competing truths and the leisure to discern the one and only truth.

What Channing confronted most notably were America's changing forms of discourse. American culture had once been dominated by modes of communication that were predominately oratorical in nature, but these modes were fast becoming more print-oriented.[10] On the one hand, Channing championed written forms of public debate, because he believed they fostered superior forms of thinking and reflection. To put this in more modern terms, for developing the kind of "critical consciousness" needed in a democracy, print culture was superior to oral culture. At the same time, however, Channing challenged emerging forms of print-culture for the same reasons he challenged oratory: they inhibited the capacity for critical reflection.

The Rhetoric of the American Experiment

Channing, like most educated Americans, knew that the American experiment required a system of communication that was fundamentally different from the democratic models of society inherited from the ancients. It demanded also a fundamentally different system of rhetoric. Like many of his contemporaries, Channing would compare the American scene to the rhetorical scene of ancient Athens. Because Athens possessed no technologies for disseminating information (such as large-scale writing technologies or a transportation system), the medium of political debate and political "news" was the human voice and its mode of transportation the human foot. Even without communication technologies like writing (at first), printing, or highways, the Greek city-state could become and remain a cultural unity because of its relatively small size. It had to be small enough for any citizen to travel readily to the assembly area, yet large enough to remain (with some trading beyond its borders) self-sufficient.[11] The inspiration for the Greek model was the *agora*, where all free men could (at least in theory)[12] *converse* within the public assembly.

But the American nation was far different from the Greek city-state, and the architects of American government knew it. As both Jefferson and the authors of the *Federalist Papers* realized, the new nation had to meet the challenge of bringing together a vast, diverse, and growing population scattered throughout a vast, remote, and growing continent. The answer lay in providing a government-subsidized postal system[13] and employing the power of the printed word in order to promote the dissemination of information throughout the republic. Whereas the Greek city-state was small and could depend upon face-to-face communication, America, enormous in geography and in population, had to depend upon the technologies of transportation and printing. In short, American thinkers, and especially Channing, were acutely conscious of the important roles played by communication and its technologies for a smoothly running democracy.

The transition from oratorical to written discourse occurred gradually and steadily throughout the nineteenth century. As Gregory Clark and Michael Halloran have argued, this transition was accompanied by larger shifts in "political and economic realities, and resulted in a cultural change from a communitarian ethos to a professional" ethos. And while my work here does not attempt to provide the kind of grand-scale analyses made by Clark and Halloran, I do want to point out how Channing's position on discourse media reflected the confusion over which modes of communication were best suited to America's needs.

Even in the second decade of the nineteenth century, America remained, it seemed to many, always on the verge of splitting apart at the seams. As the United States underwent its gradual but unmistakable transition from the ideal of republicanism's civic virtue to the ideal of liberal self-interest and of the magical power of the market, many feared the unity of America was becoming increasingly splintered: among states and regions; among commerce, industry, and agrarian interests; among the "eminent," the "middling," and the "humble"; and among atomized individuals pursuing their own interests over the general welfare of the republic. In short, the anxieties concerning factionalism voiced by the authors of *The Federalist Papers* (and numerous others) had only become more acute and difficult to make sense of during the early decades of the nineteenth century. All too commonly, public commentators—from politicians to authors of "self-cultivation" guides—put the issues of factionalism, cohesion, and character at the forefront of their discussions (see Watts, chapters 1–3).

In the years just prior to and continuing through Channing's early years as Boylston Professor, the debate over communication and transportation[14] had become central to political discussions about the future of democracy and the nature of republicanism. As Charles Sellers explains in his history of the "market economy" in early nineteenth-century America, the federal government's role in democratic communication and economics was at the heart of a debate between "old Republicanism" (Jeffersonian style) and "New" or "National Republicanism," which looked a great deal like the old (now unpopular) Federalism, but which rationalized its federal government interventionist ("developmentalism" it was called) positions with standard Republican rhetoric (appeals to equality, opportunity, etc.). The debate was galvanized by New York Governor De Witt Clinton's decision to financially back the Erie Canal,[15] and the specific issue concerned whether the federal government would financially support canals and turnpikes, which were needed, according to the arguments of National Republicans like John Calhoun, for the "general welfare" of America. Employing traditional Republican rhetoric, Calhoun argued that such a system was necessary if America were to remain a single nation: America's rapid growth in size and population threatened the greatest of all calamities, next to the loss of liberty, and even to that in its consequences—*disunion*. . . . Let us then bind the Republic together with a perfect system of roads and canals. . . . Let us conquer space.[16]

What was more deeply at stake, as the "old" Republicans feared, was the character of the nation itself: Would Jefferson's yeoman farmer continue to define America, or would this ideal be supplanted by the market-economy-induced wage earner? Jefferson was appalled when his protégé, Monroe, in 1822, construed the Constitution to mean that the federal government ought to aid capitalist ventures and a market economy.[17] In all, there existed throughout the early years of the republic powerful ideological, technological, and government-sponsored measures for helping disseminate communications, all in an effort to prevent disunion and discord.

Channing employed a similar justification of cohesion and anti-factionalism to forward his theories of rhetoric and to argue for his versions of healthy democratic discussion. Within such a culturewide discussion of communication and democracy, then, Channing's preference for written, reasonable, noncontentious discourse echoes (or at least resonates with) the political anxieties of his day. Specifically, as I will show in detail below, Channing would argue for the superiority of print-based public discussion. There were several advantages to print. First, in the second decade of the nineteenth century, it was still primarily a medium controlled by elites (though that was quickly changing, and this worried Channing). Second, print was a technology with deep roots in pre- and post-Revolutionary republicanism (see Warner). And third, print was *inherently* a "quiet" medium that fostered reason.

The Written Word and the American Character

It is worth noting that Channing's preference for written over spoken discourse provided his detractors with their greatest ammunition against his appointment as Boylston Professor. Channing was skilled in writing but not in declamation. Furthermore, he had already published *North American Review* articles that championed writing and denounced the effects of oratory. He therefore seemed to many a poor choice for a professor who would teach oratory. This was the case especially in New England, which represented the center of America's "Greek revival" and the ensuing "cult of oratory." Oratory seemed part of the American historical fabric; among the most beloved heroes from the Revolution was the martyred orator James Otis. (Thomas Paine, of course, was no orator, but by this time he also had lost his popular reputation as hero.) And at the time of Channing's appointment, America's most prominent cultural heroes, according to Lawrence Buell, were men "who won local and sometimes national literary reputations primarily on the ground of their speaking ability" (138). The most influential of the Greek-style public orators was Edward Everett, the German-trained scholar of ancient Greek studies and of philology, who took his position at Harvard (in 1817) two years before Channing.

Channing's detractors believed the Boylston Professor should instruct future leaders who would influence society through oratory. One detractor, writing in a Republican-inspired newspaper, demanded that Harvard select "an *able, practical orator. . .* who had moreover some knowledge of mankind, and of the nature & operations of our government, derived from actual observation and experience."[18] Furthermore, they pointed out that the Harvard overseers, who established the endowed Professorship of Rhetoric and Oratory in 1804, specified instruction in classical models of eloquence and persuasion, which were, of course, geared toward oral discourse. Although the overseers directed the professor to "instruct [the students] in speaking *and* composition" (my emphasis), they meant by composition "written translations of elegant passages of Latin and Greek," with some instruction in "their own compositions as their progress in letters may permit" in "the latter part of the year."[19]

This debate was, in part, about reforming the means of educating future generations of college students. That Channing was in fact appointed indicates significant sentiment that the system needed to be moved in the direction of the written word. Channing's call for an increased presence of the written word anticipates the reformations suggested in 1842 by Francis Wayland, who bemoaned the way colleges encouraged superficial learning and proposed (in addition to increased competition and practical value) the institution of written examinations (see especially 90–112). More influential was Charles W. Eliot, who called for (and later implemented) many of Wayland's suggestions in his inaugural address of 1869. Seen in this light, Channing's inaugural lecture represents a strong break with the past.

Those who wanted to ensure that Harvard rhetoric remain focused on public oratory had legitimate cause for distress. Under Channing, the Harvard rhetoric curriculum would be fundamentally altered. Channing's rhetorical instruction was dominated by the written word. The number and importance of declamations was reduced, and the number of compositions increased (Anderson 69–81; Anderson and Braden xxxviii–xl). Channing's reasons for altering the rhetoric curriculum were most likely connected with his awareness of the relationships I have been discussing—among rhetorical training, the nature of a particular government, and communications technologies. In his 1819 address "The Orator and His Times" (which was delivered on the occasion of Channing's controversial induction as Boylston Professor and reprinted as the first chapter of his *Lectures*), Channing provides his rationale for fundamentally refocusing rhetorical theory and practice on the written word. First, he addresses the issues of geographical size and diversity among the population—a concern, as I have shown, of particular prominence in the public forum. The Greeks, he explains,

> were not, as is the case in powerful states now, spread over a wide territory, and agitated, and influenced in their public conduct, by a great variety of interests. A diversity of pursuits and local interests did not split the commonwealth into parties. . . . The ancient republics were, for the most part, of small extent. The efficient and governing population was crowded within the walls of a city [and the] . . . whole state could assemble at public deliberations. (5)

To his learned audience of 1819, the message would have been unmistakable: "in an age like this" and in a nation like America, oratory had become impracticable and undesirable.

But for Channing, the printing press and superior transportation systems provided far more than the means for meeting America's practical needs of disseminating information across the continent. Channing argues further that, as compared to oratorical argument, published argument was culturally and epistemologically superior. In fact, like the Scottish Common Sense rationalists he admired, Channing believed that whatever rhetorical system emerged from a society would be just and practical, so long as its principles were grounded in the fundamentals of human nature and the nature of society.[20] The nature of society, Channing firmly believed, had progressed dramatically from ancient Greece: its "moral character" and its institutions had become vastly superior. There was still room for oratory and argument in America, but it would have to be of a different order; since the institutions and character of America were more "settled" than the Greeks', oratory would have to be more calm and reflective.

> Raise the moral character of a state as high as you please; give all classes a proper regard for the institutions, habits, and opinions that alone can establish their happiness; let the public conduct of men be invariably the result of settled principles, and not of vague, transient impulse, and you will find, indeed, that society is tempered and softened, but not tame and lethargic. The earthquake and whirlwind are stilled, but an active and abundant growth is going on everywhere. (19)

Political debate in America, then, would be of a higher moral character. Because the institutions in America had progressed far beyond those of ancient Greece, American institutions could be depended upon to work for the public's best interest; they would ensure stability and reason in the nation. Therefore, political debate would be less moved by the winds of passion and the tumult of constant political upheavals.

In addition to institutions that encouraged order and lawfulness, the *character* of the ideal American, argued Channing, was far superior to the character of the average Greek, who used and was dominated by oral, passionate, self-serving debate. Americans were less inclined to exploit or be exploited by oratorical passion and possessed a greater capacity to play an *active* role in understanding, criticizing, and supporting its governing bodies and figures.

Written Discourse, Ideally, Is Reasonable

Channing's most noteworthy criticism of discourse—especially of oratory—is leveled at its tendency to fall into passion and contention. When this happens, argues Channing, the role of reason in creating and evaluating arguments is inevitably diminished. Of course, we should not be surprised that Channing would be alarmed at discourse that threatened to swell beyond the boundaries of harmony and order. Indeed, considering how powerfully Channing was influenced by the Scottish Common Sense rationalists, and considering (as Broaddus more fully develops the argument) how Channing was fundamentally affiliated with the Federalists, then the Whigs, the Harvardians, and finally the Unitarians, it should come as little surprise that Channing valued these qualities in life and especially in discourse: serenity, calmness, "the public good," and above all reason and reasonableness.

But even beyond Channing's select society of Harvardian Unitarian Whig/Federalist Brahmins, the issue of reasonable, polite, and calm discourse resonated throughout the political and cultural discussions of Channing's contemporaries. Specifically, there was intense nostalgia for the kind of public sphere that was imagined to have existed during late-colonial and republican-era America. As Michael Warner has demonstrated, republican ideologies about reading, literacy, publicity, and reason had developed through the eighteenth century and peaked in the 1790s. Within the ideology of republicanism, the literate citizen could participate in the national public sphere. In that sphere, the citizen regards herself and is regarded as "normally impersonal," not as a specific individual speaking to a public but as a *depersonalized* and highly rational representative of the people who participates in a disinterested act of public discussion. In public participation of this sort, the individual—as writer *or* reader—advanced the public good. It mattered little what specific position the citizen took; merely participating and advancing this public conversation was beneficial to the body politic. As Warner sums up, the very "act of reading was linked closely to the performative values of civic virtue" (xiv). And print itself was regarded as an *inherently* desirable medium for invoking and furthering "disinterested participation in the public sphere" as well as general civic virtue (65).

However, this idealized public sphere—especially from the elite point of view—would not endure. From this early-1790s conception in which print, diffusion, and public discussion were imagined as inherently good, disinterested, and reasonable, America was to move through a series of jolts. In the late 1790s, marked by the Alien and Sedition Acts, political discourse sank into bitter invective and into literally *physically* partisan politics. Public print discourse (newspapers, broadsides, pamphlets, etc.) would become vicious and thoroughly partisan. Frank Luther Mott called the years 1796 through 1814 "the dark ages of [American] partisan journalism" (*American* 167–80). For men like Channing, the ideal, disinterested, and rational discourse of republicanism was distant (and in part fictional) nostalgia, but *parts* of that ideal may have been worth recapturing.

Just as republican ideology would conceive of print as an inherently "reasonable" discourse medium, Channing too would argue that written discourse was inherently superior to spoken discourse. But Channing's era was not the republican era. During the republican era, the public sphere was imagined to be "ideal" when *all* (propertied white male literate) citizens might participate. But things had changed for Channing. For one, journalism (magazines, pamphlets, and especially newspapers) had become a bit *too* democratic and a bit *too* factional—and factionalism, as Madison (in *The Federalist* 10), Fisher Ames (in 1803), and many others had argued, was an immense threat to America, its politics, and its citizens.

And indeed, during the years 1816 through 1824 (1824 marking the period when Andrew Jackson's populist campaigns and his campaigns' supporting newspapers would once again dash such hopes for ideal public discourse), America's elite saw what many perceived as a new era of discussion. Although the latter half of 1819 witnessed a sobering financial depression (the "crisis of 1819"), the years just prior had witnessed an ebullient postwar boom. Furthermore, with the weakening of the Federalists, political discussion had been moving away from a very uncivil norm. The "Federalist collapse," writes Charles Sellers, "allowed Monroe to revive the ideal of united elite leadership after a generation of bitter party warfare." Federalists and Republicans alike hailed the waning of factional strife as Monroe's "era of good feelings." Now the president and Congress might do their job—governing rather than bickering. As Sellers points out further, class hegemony made the waning of factionalism possible: "Gentlemen knew best the public good," and there was little standing in their way in bringing about the best for America (Sellers 82–87). Clearly it was time for rhetorical training that would nourish such an atmosphere and that would flourish there.

With this widespread cultural hope for rational, good-natured debate, Channing's criticism of Greek passion would have been particularly resonant. Members of the Greek "rabble," argued Channing in his inaugural address, not only *allowed* but *desired* their orator to sway them whatever way he pleased; decisions, though often made with enviable efficiency, were often made rashly. To use the term popularized by Walter J. Ong, Channing emphasized the *agonia* of Greek public discourse. As Ong describes the "litigious Greek world,"

> an assembly, a getting together to discourse, was rather essentially a mobilization for a contest. The assembly came together to debate, to match pros and cons, to struggle, not fatally, but seriously and in dead earnest, man against man.[21]

In further agreement with Ong's twentieth-century criticism, Channing believed this *agonia* was due in great part to the Greeks' dependency on oral debate. The ancient model of rhetoric, thought Channing, pits personalities against personalities, rather than ideas against ideas. To use Aristotle's nomenclature, ancient rhetoric emphasized pathos and ethos over logos, and eristic over dialectic. As Ong and many other "consciousness and media" theorists have argued, in oral societies, it is less possible to "separate the knower from the known" and therefore less possible to perceive ideas as standing by themselves, Platonically, transhistorically, without human agents to envision or argue for them. Therefore, in oral societies, debate is much less a contest of abstract ideas and much more about the debaters themselves.[22] In other words, Channing's 1819 address concurs in remarkable ways with some of the recent historiography of ancient Greece that addresses the issues of media, epistemology, and public discourse.

Such subjective and ephemeral tendencies of truth, argued Channing, were reflected in the Greek polis, which was dominated by a very few, very powerful, and very selfish public men. They strove not to enlighten the public, but to dominate their wills:

> But what were liberty and patriotism then? Did they show themselves in a love of social order and temperate government . . . ? Did they lead the citizen to value the . . . substantial improvements and ornaments of life, the solid institutions of a deliberate and virtuous commonwealth . . . ? No— . . . we can easily discern that the spirit of their governments was thoroughly *warlike*, that their love of freedom was another name for *ferocious lawlessness*, and that their

love of country cloaked a boundless ambition of power. He was the favorite who could swell the empire, . . . and make the world itself the *prison-house of one master*. (6–7, my emphases)

Rather than working toward a common good, the "influential [Greek] orator," with his "tremendous power," strived "to produce always the strongest possible *excitement*, and to carry his point by appealing to any principle of human nature which would aid him, without feeling any responsibility," all in an effort to "tempt the rabble" and satisfy his own "selfish" goals (8–10, my emphasis). As he concludes, "The style of speaking which was irresistible in an ancient assembly . . . might now be despised" (12).

Such a rhetoric was ideally suited to Greek government, which Channing labels an "unchecked democracy" in which all free men (who were for the most part "unschooled") voted equally.[23] While it is true that action was taken much more swiftly, it was also taken with much more passion and with a greater threat of demagoguery (74). The Greeks were victims of their own passions: "They had not sufficient confidence in themselves to expect that the judgments they should form under the influence of powerful eloquence, would be approved by them in their cooler moments" (75).[24]

Channing believed that the classical, entirely oral model of rhetoric was no longer suitable for, as he put it, "an age like this" (*Lectures* 25). Responding perhaps to the adherents of the Greek revival, Channing tried to show that American government is very different from—and far superior to—ancient democracies. American citizens (those of the elite order at least) were better able to think independently of social pressures. Able to distance themselves from the fray of a debate, today's "men [are] the most deliberate, and most incapable of rashness of delusion," whereas the citizens of ancient Greece "had nothing more to do than add the storm of eloquence to that of the state" (18). Unlike the Greeks, whose government was efficient but often rash in its decisions, America's political debates would proceed less efficiently and less passionately, but with more prudence. Something like modern consciousness and media theorists, then, Channing realized that there arise epistemological and practical repercussions to alterations in communication media.

The character of society—its citizens, government, and institutions—had *progressed*, and so too must the character of debate. With a tremendous (and, as I will show, unrealistic) confidence in the ability of American institutions to ensure a lawful and just society, Channing confidently asserts that America's governing officials had nothing but the best interests of the population in view. With its representative democracy established, America's government was much more responsive to the needs of its citizens, with public leaders less likely to employ persuasive powers selfishly.

Therefore, fundamental to modern debate was the dominance of reason. Although there are moments when passion is appropriate, citizens today, whether from "temperament, or from circumstances, live less in a habit of passion" (79). Men today, he argues, are less likely to abandon careful reflection for passions and to tolerate an orator's selfish irresponsibility. Such prudence results from improved social circumstances and from the improved character of American citizens,

> who are in the habit of demanding a warrant or justification for passion. And it is in unconscious obedience to the demands of [the citizens'] known character that he becomes the eloquent expounder of deep, wide-branching, far-stretching political truth. (80–81)

Governed by reason and according to higher, sometimes abstract, needs of the public, American rhetoric, in its ideal form, is thoroughly disinterested.

> The deliberative orator is at least supposed to have adopted no opinion which he will not abandon for a better. He is not to think so much of bringing a majority to his side, as of ascertaining which side is *the true one for all*, by offering his own views and listening to those of others. In short, all the parties have but one and the same client. (83)

Channing's is a Platonic rhetorical system: when carried out properly, rhetoric helps human beings, as a community, discover the truth. In sum, Greek debates were oratorical, American debates written; Greeks were swayed primarily by passion, Americans primarily by reason; Greek citizens were governed by a selfish few, American citizens by the communally discovered truth.

Written Discourse and the Philosophy of Rhetoric

As professor, however, Channing needed to address not only the immediate political exigencies of discourse of his times, but the philosophy of rhetoric. Since he wanted to elevate the status of both written discourse and reason, Channing works throughout the *Lectures* to undercut the traditional elevation of speech over writing in a way closely tied to his effort to undercut the elevation of passionate discourse over reasoned discourse. He does so by implicitly challenging George Campbell's distinction between "persuasion" and "argument" (*Philosophy of Rhetoric*, published 1776). Both Campbell and Channing were disciples of Scottish Common Sense "faculty psychology," which held that the human mind possessed distinct faculties (or organs) that could be addressed by the orator. Not only could psychology inform the study of rhetoric, but rhetoric could inform psychology, with rhetoric providing, Campbell suggests, "a sketch of the human mind."[25] For Campbell "argument" was one of four rhetorical "characteristics" or "forms"; it was used to appeal to the faculty of "understanding" (or "judgment") and its "purpose" (or "end") was "conviction." "Persuasion" was Campbell's most powerful and complex "purpose." In order to persuade, the orator must not only appeal to the understanding, but also to the "imagination" and "passion," using the form of "vehemence," which was not a form in itself but a combination or culmination of "instruction" and "conviction" and "pleasure" *and* "passion."[26] Persuasion is Campbell's highest and most difficult end of rhetoric.

> Finally, as that kind, the most complex of all, which is calculated to influence the will, and persuade to a certain conduct, is in reality an artful mixture of that which proposes to convince the judgment, and that which interests the passions, its distinguished excellency results from these two, the argument and the pathetic, incorporated together. These acting with united force, and . . . in concert, constitute that passionate eviction, the *vehemence* of contention, which is admirably fitted for persuasion, and that has always been regarded as the supreme qualification in an orator. (4)

Furthermore, contrary to Channing's preference for written discourse, Campbell reserves his greatest praise for spoken rhetoric. When Campbell does address writing, he considers it a special case, and even suggests vehemence resides naturally with spoken delivery. He notes, for instance, that the orator need not be much concerned with accuracy or correctness when she or he is speaking with vehemence, but that accuracy *is* essential to effective written discourse, as writing implies "more leisure and greater coolness than is implied in speaking" (81). Furthermore, Campbell most often conceives of language primarily as an audible, not visible, medium: for instance, "Without perspicuity, words are not signs, they are empty *sounds*; speaking is *beating the air*, and the most fluent declaimer is but as a *sounding brass* and a *tinkling cymbal*."[27] Finally, in defining vehemence, passion, and persuasion, Campbell clearly finds a speaker almost indispensable:

> [A] *person present with us, whom we see and hear*, and who, by words, and looks, and gestures, gives the liveliest signs of his feelings, has the surest and most immediate claim upon our sympathy. We become *infected* with his passions. We are hurried along by them, and not allowed leisure to distinguish between his relation and our relation, his interest and our interest. (90, my emphases)

Passion, according to Campbell, is difficult to arouse when the auditor has the "leisure" to acquire a distanced perspective on the rhetorical situation. Such distance is more difficult in the presence of a human speaker. Since passion requires the presence of a human speaker, and since passion is a necessary condition for vehemence (the "supreme" form of rhetoric), "persuasion" requires a human speaker.

Channing, as we have seen, did not trust passion. Those aspects of passion that Campbell celebrated (lack of leisure, lack of distance) are precisely what Channing most feared about the spoken word. He strives, therefore, to dismantle Campbell's hierarchy, which places persuasion on a level above argument. Instead, Channing demonstrates the two need not be distinct:

> What, then, is meant by the alleged distinction? We hear frequently that argument addresses the understanding and persuasion the passions; and that reason or the judgment is proverbally prudent and safe, while the passions are as proverbally headlong and dangerous. (37)

Furthermore, he advocates an address to passion *through* reason. In fact, responsibly excited passion is "a brief and informal kind of reasoning": "Topic follows topic, proof is heaped upon proof, till . . . we seem to be in the midst of fiery shafts and grand peals, with the reason as clear as the brave eye in storms and peril, and with conviction as seated as the rock" (38). For Campbell, appeals to the "understanding," to the "imagination," and to the "passions" were discrete appeals; for "persuasion" to occur, all kinds of appeals had to be made. For Channing, the distinction is a supple one; passion is (or should be) subsumed under reason; passion is a "kind of reasoning."

Separating the Real from the Ideal: The Dangers Posed to Americans and Their Institutions by Changing Forms of Discourse

Channing was very un-Platonic in the sense that he believed written discourse was superior to oral in discovering the truth.[28] Writing, for Channing, was superior to speech because writing fostered superior "habits of thinking." For Channing, the act of speaking was primarily a matter of delivery, the act of hearing primarily a matter of being passively influenced. The act of writing was primarily an act of thinking, creation, and accuracy; the act of reading was a critical, active process. Furthermore, the act of listening too easily lapsed into uncritical immersion in the speaker's discourse, whereas reading afforded the auditing subject the critical distance to evaluate that discourse more thoroughly.

Channing equated proficient writing habits with proficient thinking habits. Learning to write allows a person to "acquire such self-command that he can give his whole attention to a subject, so that he shall be in a way to comprehend it perfectly" (*Lectures* 208). The "habit of writing," in fact, can "do more than make us skillful in composition":

> It will prepare us in a degree for active life, by giving us habits of self-denial, industry and close study, a general and ready command of our faculties, a clear, direct way of thinking on all subjects and occasions, a promptness and decision in our opinions, and a natural and precise method of expressing them. A man who writes much and with consideration is doing himself an incalculable good in respect to every other study. (209)

Channing also wanted Americans to become (as we might say today) *critically aware readers*—that is, readers who do not accept whatever their culture offers them at face value, but who take care to examine it in detail. Unlike Greek oral eloquence, which sought to immediately but completely dominate the opinions of its passive listeners, the new American eloquence "is suited to have a growing and *permanent influence* over the character and opinions . . . on the decisions and conduct of men." Modern eloquence was more suited, thought Channing, to the "habit" of active, critical thinking: "It aims at making men think patiently and earnestly, and *take an active part themselves* in giving efficacy to another's arguments or persuasions" (19, my emphasis). Critical, active auditors are not merely supplied with the truth, but offered arguments that they themselves actively consider and evaluate: eloquence "has only to secure a lodgement for truth in the mind, and by and by the truth will quietly prevail" (19).

The Changing State of Public Discourse

So much for Channing's *ideal* audience, the audience approximated most closely, perhaps, by the readership of the *North American Review* and by the one addressed during his "Inaugural Address"; so much for the ideal audience Channing was trying to invoke in his *Lectures*. In fact, this ideal audience, like all such audiences, never did exist, not even during the socially imagined *"Res Publica* of letters," a public sphere that was imagined to have existed just prior to Channing's birth. As Warner describes this idealized, largely fictional public sphere, it was a place made intelligible by the dissemination of print: "print discourse made it possible to imagine a people that could act as a people and in distinction from the state" (xiii), a place where the "paradox of disinterest coupled with common interest" could be dissolved (28). This ideal public sphere was imagined to have allowed any citizen (if he was male, white, literate, and landowning) to assume a "normally impersonal" role as disinterested participant, bracketing his self-interest for the common good. In the very act of reading, argues Warner, citizens could imagine themselves as idealized citizens participating in an idealized public sphere.

But as Raymond Williams has noted, English-writing elites have perennially waxed nostalgic about such ideal lost ages of organic community that existed just before their own times (*The Country and the City* 8–12). (And of course we do the same today.) And while the imagined pre-1890 "Republic of Letters" (according to Warner) may have in reality helped to create an approximately ideal public sphere, Channing, with his contemporaries, believed (with good reason) that popular American discourse and Americans themselves were changing for the worse. This posed an immense threat, thought Channing, to the character of the nation and its citizens. At stake, of course, was the political and social influence of persons of Channing's class, their authority to define healthy public discourse.

The power of the printed word cut (as it always cuts) both ways. If the printed word isolated the reader and gave the reader the psychic distance, calm detachment, and the leisure to reason carefully, it also offered the opportunity for "unauthorized" interpretations and therefore demanded a measure of responsibility on the reader's part. As Cathy N. Davidson has shown in her analysis of early-republic novels, new reading materials challenged elite authority because these new forms of popular literature (the newspaper, the novel, etc.), unlike traditional poetry, could be read by *anybody* who was even modestly literate. There were no established rules for interpretation (13–14). Likewise, the traditional limitations concerning who was at liberty to publish were changing. So, while the printing press might, per Enlightenment optimism, offer a salutary means for spreading knowledge throughout the republic, it might also spread forbidden ideas and in this way threaten civilization.

Related to this change in the nature of public discourse was the growing enfranchisement of the "voting multitude" in America, so that the very conception of democracy was fundamentally changing.[29] Cultural and political influence was being relinquished to an entirely new and alien breed of spokespersons. As Hofstadter describes the change:

> As poor farmers and workers gained the ballot, there developed a type of politician that had existed only in embryo in the Jeffersonian period—the technician of mass leadership, the caterer to mass sentiment; it was a coterie of such men in all parts of the country that converged upon the prominent figure of Jackson between 1815 and 1824. (*American Political Tradition* 63)

Educators and other cultural spokespersons were surprised by and apprehensive about these changes, especially the changes they were creating in the character of public discourse. The current "decay of argument" argument, the current "decline" in public discourse, and the current concern over a horribly powerful and pernicious popular culture—these are not in any sense unique to our times. Neither is it unique that rhetorical educators have attempted to engage and strive to reform such problems.[30]

Furthermore, historians have often noted that the years between 1790 and the Civil War (roughly the years of Channing's life, 1790–1856) saw a profound and (according to many) permanent transition from Republican ideals to Lockean liberal ideals.[31] It would be a simple—and simplistic—move to argue that Channing's rhetoric nicely reflects the change from republicanism (with its emphases on public discussion) to liberalism (with its ideal citizen as a person who engages in self-cultivation). For instance, Channing's emphasis on reading as a private but ennobling and self-improving activity depends upon the ideal citizen-self as proposed by liberalism (and, indeed, it is this aspect of Channing that his late-twentieth-century detractors have noted).[32] But in other ways, his rhetoric harked back to a bygone era of republicanism: his belief that a healthy society depends upon a public that considers the common good over the good of atomistic, Hobbesian individuals, that engages in productive, reasonable, communal conversation that never stoops to mere factionalism and discord, and that has the power to resist the allurements of tyrant public leaders and of discord. In other words, with his admixture of both republican and liberal ideology, Channing was very much like the majority of his contemporaries, and much like America itself (see Watts).

In emphasizing the political and cultural debates of early nineteenth-century America, I may be ignoring what may be a more direct and plausible influence upon Channing: the intellectual heritage of the Scottish Common Sense philosophers. Crowley (*Methodical*), Johnson (*Nineteenth*), and Thomas P. Miller (*Formation*) have all demonstrated, in various ways, the immense impact of the Scottish moralists on nineteenth-century rhetorical theory in the United States. Miller, in a remarkably thorough and compelling argument, reveals how this tension between civic humanism and liberal (or bourgeois or laissez-faire) ideology was a result of the Scottish moralists (and others who taught English in the "provinces" of Great Britain) attempting to teach English to students who were not from the elite classes but from a more heterogenous reading and college-attending public. The epistemological theories of Thomas Reid, the economic and social theories of Adam Smith, and the rhetorical theories of George Campbell and Hugh Blair, argues Miller, encouraged a conception of rhetors as disinterested "impartial spectators" within civil society, rather than the rhetor of the Ciceronian ideal, where practical action was deployed in the public sphere in order to constantly renegotiate popular public sentiment with ever-changing political exigencies. Indeed, Miller's history provides numerous instances in which the Scottish moralists criticize the public sphere (the kinds of discourse that occurs there, and the kinds of persons who use rhetoric there) in sentiments that almost certainly influenced Channing. For instance, these eighteenth-century socio- logical scientists of the mind and society also lamented the pernicious influence of public orators on the unwashed public (similar to the way that some composition scholars complain that popular argument adversely influences our students' conceptions of argument). Most important, Miller establishes that the eighteenth-century political exigencies and the social changes con- fronting the Scottish moralists moved them, like their follower Channing in the nineteenth century, to depoliticize rhetoric at all costs, and to value peace and tranquility over the messiness of the public sphere.

It is indeed striking how closely the Scottish moralists' conflicts be- tween civic humanism and liberal humanism (as described by Miller espe- cially) parallel the transition that was taking place between republican ideology and liberal ideology. These overlapping ideals—sometimes in ob- vious conflict, sometimes resonating with each other—can account for an important part of Channing's rhetorical theory. These overlapping ideals resonate with composition's current controversies about what student writ- ing is for: whether its purpose is best seen as some version of civic virtue (as in the republican ideals of civic humanism, citizenship, and public- mindedness) or best seen as some version of expressivism (as in the liberal ideals of moral and ethical responsibility, self-fashioning, and discerning the self, one's "voice," behind the public facade).

Popular Oratory and the Unschooled Public

An 1817 *North American Review* essay provides Channing's most direct commentary on the political, social, and epistemological differences be- tween oratorical and written discourse, and between his ideal audience and the audience of typical Americans (becoming less ideal and more "rabble"- like daily). "Ogilvie's Philosophical Essays" ostensibly reviews a new book by James Ogilvie, an American orator of considerable fame who was striving to acquire, in Ogilvie's words, "permanent and extended celebrity as a philo- sophical writer" (quoted by Channing 386). More importantly (for Channing and for my present argument), the review is an attack on oratory and a celebration of written communication. Most notably the essay celebrates the effects of writing and reading on the American citizen, as they foster superior "habits of thinking."

As always, Channing's diction provides an immediate clue to his attitudes about spoken and written discourse. When describing oratory and the effects of spoken discourse on hearers, Channing's diction turns to phrases that would strike most modern readers as shamelessly antidemocratic— terms such as "the wild rabble" (381), "men given up to passion," "publick sympathy," "criticism of [i.e., by] the mob" (382), "drowning judgment" (383), "bluster," "clamour," "strength becoming zeal," "unmeaning vehemence" (384), and "inflated emptiness" (385). In describing written discourse, Channing's diction changes to far more positive terms, such as "emotions more inward and lasting," "restraint," "secret contemplation" (382), "independent opinion," and "knowledge" (383).[33]

As in the *Lectures*, Channing discusses the changed nature of humankind. In the Ogilvie essay, however, he cites the source of that change specifically, the printing press: "It should not be forgotten, that men are readers now. The art of printing has probably done more for independence of mind than all legislation or revolution" (383). Literacy and printing had changed humans, making them more thoughtful, active, and discriminating about the information they received. Indeed, reading for Channing was a more active and critical activity because it put "the thoughts of men into the hands of others, where they may be ransacked and proved. We can bring them down to skeletons, and then see if they have strength, connexion and object." With the habit of intelligent watchfulness throughout the reading populace, the public speaker or writer as well becomes a more incisive thinker. He aims less

> at forcing publick sentiment and *drowning judgment in declamation*. . . . He is under the rebuke of controversy, and feels the influence of keen observers about him, deliberating with him upon common interests, which they value more than his exhibitions. He remembers that they are fond of looking into their work before they begin; of approaching it with the confidence of knowledge, not of ignorance. . . . He must work *through the judgment to the heart*, and when he has reached and moved it, he will leave there a deep and inextinguishable energy. (383)

Channing rebukes Ogilvie for continuing to think and argue in nonrational, *oratorical* ways. In fact, for Channing, Ogilvie epitomized the problems with oratorical "habits of thinking." "Mr. Ogilvie," Channing begins,

> has long been known in this country, for fine recitations and rather indifferent discourses, delivered from what he calls the Rostrum;

and we are among those, who think that he has some essential qualifications for an orator. (378)

Channing goes on to say that oratory is not in itself an unworthy art, but that in America its influence is mostly pernicious. This is the case because the character of audiences had changed for the worse: Channing's contemporary audiences, he argued, expected from the orator little intellectual or political *substance*. Audiences make judgments solely on orators' abilities to ornament their speeches:

> [H]earers have fallen into the habit of inspecting the manner of an orator, and guessing that he has nothing else to offer, if he is only bold enough to venture out of the old walk of tranquil utterance. (380)

American oratory has become, for various reasons, little more than entertainment.[34] Nevertheless, Channing will not side with those who would propose that all discourse ought to be stripped of ornament: unlike unnamed "others," Channing will not "rail against the evils and abuses of eloquence, and shew how much better it is to leave truth to its own power"; eloquence remains, for the time being at least, a necessary evil, because "the world has yet got to . . . [achieve an] etherial purity and susceptibility. Men must be quickened."[35]

While Channing concedes Ogilvie's competence—or at least effectiveness—as an orator, he pronounces him thoroughly incompetent in the area of written discourse. Although he finds mild fault with Ogilvie's overwrought ornamentation on the rostrum, Channing is "more disgusted" at such discourse in Ogilvie's written work, "at seeing sober philosophy arrayed in such sorry and unbecoming finery" (406). Ogilvie cannot separate his "facts and conclusions" from "light graces" and "flaunting ornaments that lay near" the truth of his statements. These habits that arise from the medium of the rostrum,[36] Channing implies, lead to pernicious and unforgivable habits in written composition, most notably "mistaking words for substance": "We believe that his defects of [written] composition are nearly connected with important defects in his mind and ways of thinking" (407). Channing, like Campbell, maintains that defects go unnoticed in oratory and have no immediate effect, but they undermine the validity of written products because readers have the leisure to examine arguments carefully and are much more likely to discern defects.

Furthermore, Ogilvie cannot separate *himself* from his arguments. Part of this noxious aspect, Channing suggests (with a large dose of New England bigotry), comes from his Southern environment: "we fear that he has lived very much out of those wholesome regions, where a man learns to rein in his enthusiasm" (387). But by and large Ogilvie's inflated sense of self-importance results from years on the rostrum, which have infected him with an unhealthy sensitivity to public reception of his orations: "There seems to be a perpetual disease, a malignant *sensitiveness* hanging over him" (388). Channing quotes many lengthy passages (several pages from his life narrative) in order to ridicule Ogilvie's overreaction to both adverse criticism and "heart-felt plaudit[s]" (392).

Channing, in short, criticizes oratory through the example of Ogilvie. Oratory, according to Channing, fails in two basic matters: (1) it fosters uncritical, undisciplined habits of thinking, and (2) it leads too often to a confused mingling among the personality of the speaker, his/her argument, and criticism of the argument. So again, in oratory *ethos* too easily over-shadows *logos*.

Oratory is a fine pursuit for small minds with little to say. Written composition, however, requires another kind of expertise that resides on a much higher level. After ridiculing almost every aspect of Ogilvie—from his style, to his philosophical readings, to his "constitution"—Channing con-cludes his review by making a joke at the expense of both Ogilvie and oratory: "and in parting, we beg him, whatever he may do for the improve-ment of our boys in speaking, by all means to let their composition alone" (408). A ridiculous thinker like Ogilvie may indeed be qualified to teach oratory, but is certainly not qualified to teach composition, which demands different and more refined "habits of thinking."

Channing believed that rhetorical education should do more than teach citizens to make good—that is, effective—arguments. Both communication and "habits of thinking" went hand in hand: a person without sound com-munication skills probably could not possess sound thinking skills, and vice versa. Just as sloppy-thinking oratory like Ogilvie's depended for its effec-tiveness on the superficial and sloppy thinking of its audience, such oratory also encouraged pernicious habits of thinking. If Americans were to have any chance of maintaining the distance between themselves and overwhelm-ing cultural rhetorical forces, they would need to possess the means for resisting mass culture, represented for Channing by oratory and other emerging communications conventions (such as the new species of news-paper discussed below). Channing wants to help Americans prevent cultural discourse from "drowning [their] judgment in declamation" (381). As Channing says of Ogilvie's written and oratorical arguments: they "would hardly raise the character, or fortify the immunities of a free people" (381).

Here we come to one of Channing's fundamental conceptions about the purpose of education. Like his Scottish Common Sense predecessors, like his culture-preaching successors Matthew Arnold and F. R. Leavis, and like many contemporary cultural-studies theorists, Channing maintains rhetorical (or belletristic) education should seek to *distance* the student from mainstream culture and thoroughly indoctrinate the student into university culture. In the terms Joseph Harris has used for criticizing some cultural-studies teaching approaches, students are led to "feel required to adopt an adversarial stance toward their own culture, to side somehow with the university and against the media" ("Other Reader" 233). *Proper education gives students a kind of immunity or durable resistance against the pernicious cultural forces that work against or otherwise weaken, undermine, and atrophy the thinking capacities of the citizenry and that thus threaten democracy.* If citizens were unable to gain critical distance from an argument, their examinations of argument can be little more than superficial commentary. Oratory, with its immediacy and emotional domination, debilitated hearers' efforts to distance themselves from the speaker and the argument, and they are thus capable of only the most superficial examinations of argument.

Channing's indictment against popular oratory resembles some of our contemporary indictments against American mass culture. Stanley Aronowitz and Henry Giroux argue that the fundamental

> problem engendered by mass culture . . . consist[s] in its assault on the capacity to engage in critical thought as a meaningful form of social discourse. . . . [T]he capacity of humans to distance themselves . . . in order to gain critical perspective upon their social world can no longer be taken for granted. (*Education under Siege* 49)

Channing's arguments harmonize also with Aronowitz and Giroux's contention that "critical thinking is the fundamental precondition for an autonomous and self-motivated public or citizenry, [and] its decline would threaten the future of democratic, social, cultural, and political forms" (49–50). Or, to use the language of Ira Shor and Paulo Freire, Channing wanted rhetorical training to help students become capable citizens, helping them get beyond their "uncritical immersion" in the discourse of their culture (*A Pedagogy for Liberation* 14). Finally, Channing's assertion that "habits of thinking" should provide "immunity" against cultural discourse resembles (both semantically and conceptually) the modern idea of "resistance through education." While Channing's "immunity" differs significantly from the modern concept of "resistance," the crucial component for both modern pedagogical theorists and Channing is critical distance: improved "habits of thinking"—"critical thinking"—enable students and citizens alike to lessen the impact of the dominant culture upon their consciousness; they learn to achieve, as Channing called it, "active independence and self-reliance." They learn, that is, to be more themselves, not vessels passively containing their culture.

Emerging Conventions in American Culture: The News

For Channing, the price of democracy was eternal vigilance of communications culture, because a culture's habitual forms of communication dictated how a citizenry thinks and how it thinks of itself—what it conceives itself to be. Because "habits" of communication are inextricably bound together with "habits of thinking," any alteration in communication conventions inevitably alters the character of a culture. Channing challenged oratorical discourse because it fostered passionate, rather than reasoned, response. Further, it fostered an unhealthy obsession with the individual; the cult of oratory directed the auditor's attention to the individual rather than the larger community. Oratory made people believe that the "real" resided in the speaker and in passion, but for Channing, the "real" was constituted by ideas.

Channing's attitude about communications resembles what James Carey has called "communications as culture." Carey offers two conceptions of communication, "a transmission view of communication" and a "ritual view of communication" (*Communication as Culture* 15). The transmission view, which dominates popular and academic discourse, sees communication as the "transportation" of information from sender to receiver. Analogous to scientific models of cause and effect, and to the geographical, transportation model,[37] it sees communication

> as a process of transmitting messages at a distance for the purpose of control. The archetypal case of [transmission] communication is persuasion; attitude change; behavior modification; socialization through the transmission of information, influence, or conditioning or, alternatively, as a case of individual choice over what to read or view. (42)

The ritual view of communication, inspired by ethnographic models of causation, focuses on the ways that communication constitutes a community. In this way, the "forms" or "conventions" of communication fall under scrutiny.

> [It] is directed not toward the extension of messages in space but toward the maintenance of society in time; not the act of imparting information but the representation of shared beliefs. . . . [It is a] projection of community ideals and their embodiment in material form . . . [which] creates an artificial though nonetheless real symbolic order that operates to provide not information but confirmation, not to alter attitudes or change minds but to represent an underlying order of things, not to perform functions but to manifest an ongoing and fragile social process. (18–19)

Communication as transmission provides us with information that we can consider, believe, or reject as false; communication as ritual tells us what is real and who we are.

Channing was at least close to realizing that whoever controlled the nature of communication controlled the popular conception of what is real and "who we are." If, for instance, the cultural elite (readers of *The North American Review* and his Harvard students) could control the conventions of communication, the ideological substance of communication would fall in line. But Channing did not limit his concerns to the communication aimed at aristocrats and neither did he limit his criticism to oratory. The printed word—more and more the dominant mode of communication in America[38]—could also be the site of communication rituals that provided Americans with unhealthy definitions of themselves. In this vein, like many of his contemporaries, he harshly criticized an emerging organ of public communication, one which, in 1817, was just beginning to reach out to a less wealthy and less educated audience—the newspaper.[39]

Like Channing, most American intellectuals were acutely aware of, and often appalled at, the increasingly powerful role of the printed word. The newspaper had already established itself as an important component of American culture and politics, playing a crucial role in the Revolutionary War, and serving as the battleground for the Constitutional crisis and the Federalist-Republican debates over the nature of the republic.[40] After Hamilton's party had lost the bitter "war of the newspapers" to Jefferson's party, newspaper reading in America continued to rise and the diversity of the newspaper audience widened. Between 1810 and 1825 the number of newspapers doubled; by the time of Channing's adulthood, the newspaper as a strictly aristocratic medium had vanished (see Schudson, *Discovering* 12–60).

The News versus Rational Discussion

In "The Abuses of Political Discussions" (1817) Channing focuses on the relationship between the real world of actual public discourse and his ideal world's methods for critiquing public discourse. Here he lays out how men of his class (addressing his readers as "teacher" and "political teacher") might reform public discourse and thereby reform the citizenry. Harshly criticizing what he thought were pernicious trends in American newspapers, Channing is less interested in the effect of communication habits upon an elite readership (such as the readers of the *North American Review* or Harvard students) but very concerned about the effects of such communication upon the "hurried, raw, and unprepared," that is, the "unlearned" "publick," who "cannot be schoolmen" because they are "men of action. . . . [t]heir school . . . out-of-doors, under the hot sun, in the very stir of the world. They cannot retire to sheltered porticos to argue about the rights of man; the blessed level of society" (196). Channing recognizes that his audience will be somewhat learned. But Channing focuses on the newspaper's impact on the "publick," "the people," or "fellow-citizens," who become, when they read "irresponsible" journalism, "the multitude," "the crowd," and "people in an uproar."

On the surface at least, the essay is nonpartisan and mentions no specific political issues. Channing was not particularly concerned with certain factions "monopolizing truth" but with how they were "shaming her [truth's] spirit" (193). It is not political issues that Channing challenges, but the "habits" of published political discussion—to use James Carey's terminology, the *rituals* of political discussion. Since, as Channing believed, the manner of communication tremendously influenced the character of those involved in communication, highly contentious journalism fostered a highly contentious populace and thus a restive populace. In this sense, when Channing implores political journalists "to understand publick sentiment and direct it wisely" (195), he means that journalists must eschew the "corrupt eloquence" of belligerence because it destroys "habits of calm thinking," which are crucial to social control.

Throughout his life, Channing consistently insisted the good man speaking well must abjure short-term goods for the sake of the more durable character of the citizenry. While it was true, writes Channing, that a political writer *could*, for the sake of political expediency, employ passion "to bring about some definite good," the "responsible" writer *must* not, since exposure to excitement instills in readers an habitual craving for excitement, which may then be used by any writer, good or bad.

> And if you want bad men to succeed, the best thing you can do for them is to form and cherish in the people a *habit of excitement*, of approaching their interests with heated mind, of looking upon truth as cold and spiritless, unless it is fairly on fire. . . . Once get up this taste, . . . and by and by you will find other teachers in your places . . . lighting the torch of hell at your pure vestal flame of truth. (197, my emphasis)

He encouraged America's "teachers" to influence the character of public discussion. Channing did not propose that diverse opinions be buried; to his credit, Channing insists throughout his writing that all voices be heard. What Channing proposed was calm and honest discussion, which would form in the citizenry the "taste" for reason over passion and "calm habits of thinking." Such a citizenry, "less subject to sudden changes of sentiment or condition," could constitute a "nation [in which] you will see every thing brisk, healthy and conscious" (201).

What may seem most puzzling to the modern reader is Channing's failure to distinguish vehement, passionate journalism from what today we call "the news." But we need to remember that "the news" for Channing was a relatively recent invention, so recent in fact that Channing does not have our contemporary sense of "the news," but feels the need to *describe* this journalistic practice for his readers, often employing some fascinating metaphors such as fire and crashing waves. This is not to say that the word *news* was a recent invention (it had been in use for centuries), but the nature of the news was changing into something Channing could classify only by metaphor. Specifically, the idea of reporting on everyday events was for Channing and his contemporaries an alien one—and a dangerous one. In fact, the pernicious effects of such journalism were, for Channing, indistinguishable from contentious journalism:

> [The reader's] mind, his calm judgment may be swept away by the tempest about him; or [the judgment] may become so buried in the present, as never to stretch to other times; never to regard evils and dangers as if they had causes, bearings, or connexions. (199)

Note the metaphors Channing deploys to describe events-oriented news: The reader sees only

> events crowding upon each other in a sweeping and wasteful tide. The crimes and wonders of yesterday are lost in the vaster ones of to-day. The wave that now rolls on the shore, is washing away even the desolations of the retreating one. (199)

This emergent model of the news, Channing feared, was more subtle and dangerous than the journalism that had preceded it. During the "dark ages of journalism" and "the war of the newspapers" (1796 through 1814), bitter and wild political arguments had created a wild and intractable politics. Now that America seemed on the verge of an "era of good feelings," reporting daily events would misplace readers' priorities about the importance of various aspects of their world. As contemporary critics of the news (especially television news) have put it, event-oriented, context-deprived news confronts viewers with merely the accumulation of events, one upon the other, without providing a guiding context that would tell us the meaning of those events. And in doing so the news changes our understanding of the world and who we are within that world. In such an arena of public discussion, the "teacher" has much to do.

Channing's contention that "the news" would create a taste for more news is not just the conservative claptrap we might expect from a Whig journalist. Contemporary journalism historian Michael Schudson agrees, pointing out that it was not until "the early nineteenth century . . . [that] news became an intimate part of citizenship." Furthermore, there was no public "thirst for news" until the habitual presence of news in newspapers created that thirst ("Preparing" 434–37). In general, Schudson agrees (implicitly, that is, as his work does not deal with Channing per se) with Channing on the newspaper's potential for influencing the way its readership perceived reality. According to Schudson, the version of reality presented by a newspaper is not the only possible rendering of reality: "The newspaper, as the carrier of news stories," writes Schudson, "participates in the construction of the mental worlds in which we live rather than in the reproduction of the 'real world' we live in relation to" (423). Neil Postman more directly confronts the "epistemological" impact by the electronic transmission of information (beginning, for Postman, with the telegraph [c. 1849]):

> [T]his ensemble of electronic techniques called into being a new world—a peek-a-boo world, where now this event, now that, pops into view for a moment, then vanishes again. It is a world without much coherence or sense . . . ; a world that is, like a child's game of peek-a-boo, entirely self-contained. But like peek-a-boo, it is also endlessly entertaining. (77)

Significantly, both Channing and critics such as Postman stress the infantalizing force of such news, and both (Postman implicitly) stress the need for paternalistic intervention.

Channing objected to the news version of reality that was becoming increasingly common in the nation's newspapers because "reality," for Channing, was constituted not by "events crowding upon each other," but by enduring ideas. Just as "the mob" and "the crowd" (as Channing variously puts it) pose threats to America and to healthy public discussion, events themselves that *crowd* "upon each other" become like the mob itself and can be just as dangerous. The prominence of "news" events crowd out what needed to be promoted in the citizenry's consciousness—higher moral and intellectual principles. The elite "guides of society" should concentrate on promoting reflection: the public

> should be *constrained to think*, when there is time for it, for they have much to learn. . . . The safety of a free people is in the principles, taste, and calm habits of thinking, which they acquire when the mind is sober, and looks widely and fairly. (200–201)

The public, in short, has no time for the entertainment of America's emergent mass culture. It actually harms their critical habits, as it promotes a misleading view of the world as a tumultuous place, where events take precedent over ideas and principles.

Habits of Reading and the "Original Mind"

Channing emphasized *forms* of discourse, rather than specific *messages* or forms of argumentation (lapses of logic, etc.). Channing was concerned with what might be called "habits of auditing" (with "habits" in general being one of his most important concepts). He was concerned with *how* auditors (whether hearers or readers, citizens or students) receive communication; how they position themselves in relation to what they read/hear.

Sound "habits of thinking," for Channing (as for many of today's cultural studies teachers), was a process of distancing oneself—erecting enduring barriers—from the chaos of culture, that body of increasingly competitive and diverse discourses, so that one might have the "leisure" and "solitude" to examine ideas closely—as we say, to examine them "critically." As he put it in his critique of Ogilvie, Channing thought "calm habits of thinking" best suited a free citizenry. For Channing, gaining "critical" distance often involved literally physically removing oneself from the world. *Solitude*, as Elizabeth Larsen has shown, was one of the key terms both in his rhetorical theory and in many of the themes he assigned his students.

Distance from the immediate cultural surroundings allows the student/citizen to discern her "original mind," that is, to separate her own self from the biases of others' ideas and from immediate events as they confront her, "crowding upon each other": "The word *original*, is commonly used to denote the character of a mind which, from its constitution and natural action,—not from weak and random eccentricity,—takes its own view of things and makes its own use of them" (*Lectures* 194). In fact, for Channing, the paramount issue in evaluating the healthfulness of any communication was, "does it make us more ourselves?" When looking at books, for instance, he says the answer to this question should be the single criterion in their evaluation: "The only question is, do books make us less independent, less ourselves, than any other source of knowledge or exhilaration?" (193)

His answer, it seems, is "it depends." It depends on *how* one receives books. (He devotes an entire chapter to "Habits of Reading," in which he points out the danger of reading superficially, trying to read a great deal, instead of reading deeply.) The reader who allows books to overwhelm her—to swamp the self—has lost touch with her original mind. This is a potential danger in any literature, popular as well as great: "a student is *exposed to perils* from his constant association with great writers" as well as popular ones (198, my emphasis). Whether the student/citizen is reading great books or attending public lectures, she must maintain boundaries between the self and what she hears/reads. Although the auditor certainly benefits from the thoughts and ideas of others, they must undergo a mysterious, "hidden transmutation" so "that a man makes what he reads his own" (197–98). Reading—or auditing of any kind—should make one *more* oneself. One can ensure the maintenance of the self by being aware of—fortifying oneself against—the "perils" of influence (194). Something must stand in the way between our ideal selves and the real world. The student—the citizen—must know how to erect and maintain barriers between these two realms, so that our "exposure" to this dangerous world imperils us to a lesser degree.

Channing did not criticize journalism for failing to be objective. Indeed, journalism's emphasis on secluded facts and on objectivity would not emerge strongly until the economics of telegraphic journalism forced newspapers to grind down stories into atomized morsels that would be palatable to an variegated audience spanning an ever-growing continent, and even then other larger cultural changes would be required before objectivity would become the standard of journalistic public discourse (see Schudson's *Discovering* and chapter 4 of this work; see also Schiller *passim*). Rather, Channing criticized journalism for infantalizing its readership. Such journalism, which focuses on disembodied facts and events and on contention over calm and peaceful deliberation, warps the character of its audience, away from what is true, lasting, and universal among humankind. He feared such journalism might inject into the citizenry alien and dangerous ways of understanding their world; it made them not themselves.

Channing's theory of rhetoric falls in line with much of nineteenth-century rhetorical thought, which, in turn, has much in common with classical and Scottish Common Sense rhetorical thought. Specifically, rhetorical education is conceived as intimately connected to the moral and intellectual health of the individual as well of society. As Nan Johnson sums up the age-old belief of the function of rhetorical training, it is "crucial to individual development and cultural harmony" (50). For nineteenth-century theorists of rhetoric (as for classical theorists), sound moral character and the ability to persuade were inseparable: "it is the good person speaking well who is best able to persuade" (Johnson 166). Furthermore, they posited an almost unquestioned "cause-and-effect relationship between the *cultivation of taste* (through the study and practice of rhetoric) and the acquisition of intellectual, moral, and civic virtue" (45). In order to possess virtue, one must possess good taste.

According to Scottish Common Sense philosophy—and according even to the skeptic David Hume and to later critics like Matthew Arnold—standards of taste were universal. All persons are endowed with nearly identical faculties of taste, and, furthermore, this faculty was improvable through education. Therefore, all persons—unless they lacked the proper education or had been corrupted by improper experience—possess the capacity for apprehending beauty, and thus they possess the capacity for understanding moral and civic virtue and acting upon that understanding. Furthermore, it was considered incumbent upon the person of letters to engage in critical writing (writing that assessed the literary or intellectual merit of some work) for the purpose of promoting "standards of taste among the reading public" (Johnson 216).

This theory of taste may seem democratic, but it was used, as William Charvat argues, for cultural and political leverage, since it was maintained also that one's faculty of taste was all too easily "corrupted" by accidents of society:

> The fact is that [the Scottish moralists were] not speaking for mankind, but for [their] own economic and social class. [Lord Kames tells us] that "those who depend for food on bodily labor are totally devoid of taste," and that the standard is to be found among people of education, reflection, and experience.... The rationalists found arbitrary rules distasteful, but they had no intention of granting intellectual and aesthetic freedom to the mob.[41]

According to the Common Sense school, "human nature" is universal among humankind; this element of Scotch philosophy has been termed by Gladys Bryson "uniformitarianism." Any diversity among persons' taste or reason is the result of accident. Therefore, the goal of society's teachers— its public intellectuals—involves discovering natural standards and inculcating them into society's members: "The object of the effort of the religious, moral or social reformer, as of the literary critic, is, therefore, to standardize men and their beliefs, their likings, their activities and their institutions; 'nature' means ... uniformity" (13). Again, this *seems* democratic, but also common to all of Scottish moralism was the idea of, as Dugald Stewart called it, a "natural aristocracy":

> it has pleased the author of Nature to mingle, from time to time, among the societies of men, a few, and but a few, of those on whom He has been graciously pleased to confer a larger portion of the ethereal spirits than in the ordinary course of His providence He bestows on the sons of men. These are they who engross almost the whole reason of the species, who are born to direct, to guide, and to preserve. ("Government, Unintended Developments, Expediency, Innovation," in Schneider 113)

Although Johnson elides any commentary on the snobbery and undemocratic nature of such a conception, she does suggest how this belief was important for the establishment of canons of taste in American English departments: that is, the model of taste, reason, and virtue exemplified in the world's finest works display what is (or ought to be) universal in all persons.

By coming into contact with the works of genius—the most beautiful productions of that "natural aristocracy"—persons not only strengthened and refined their faculties of taste, but also discovered their "true" nature— "human nature," their "true self." One becomes *more* oneself by coming into contact with the genius of eras past.

Elite Rhetorical Leadership, "at Home" and among the "Popular"

To summarize, I have tried to show how Channing's theory of rhetoric and of rhetorical education can be seen as a response to his class's perception that public discourse was deteriorating, threatening both the civic sphere and its citizens' "habits of thinking." It is not surprising that Channing's prescription for reform was a paternalistic one: raise the character of the public and public discourse by adhering to our standards of public conversation, our standards of taste and propriety, and our standards of what a properly functioning human being should be. While it is a patently predictable observation, it is still important to note that it seemed never to have occurred to Channing (or others like him) to reform public discussion by eliciting a dialogue between the community (growing as it was with legions of "unschooled" citizens) and the persons who were actively creating this new forum for public discussion, what was emerging to become the "news." Instead, Channing imagines the healthy citizen as one who is always distancing herself from a dangerous world.

The early decades of nineteenth-century America saw a gradual, mostly imperceptible, change from republicanism to liberalism. As Watts portrays it, there was a gradual but relatively permanent shift from the "public virtue," "independence," "organic society," and "civic humanism" of republicanism to the "self-interest," "possessive individualism," "market society of competing interests," and "self-culture" of liberalism. This alteration of the individual and society posed for those living through the period a troubling cultural dichotomy. How might factionalism, unbridled avarice, and self-interested political ambition be tempered? For many upper- and middle-class writers, the key lay in "self-culture": because individuals were no longer so tightly bound to the republican-imagined social sphere of mutual obligation and respect, because social control and cohesion seemed far less secure than they had before, it was incumbent upon all individuals to cultivate within themselves the capacity for confronting a world of competing ideas and fractious discourse. It was important, therefore, to separate the self from society. The auditor of public discourse—whether its form was oratory, responsible or irresponsible journalism, or high literature—needed to be "on guard" against a dangerous society, because *where* one uses and hears rhetoric in large part determines *who* the orator and *who* the auditor is.

In all of his writing and throughout his *Lectures* Channing maintains a clean distinction between "popular" and elite venues, between the real world of crowds and politics and the (closer-to-) ideal worlds of judges and literary tribunals. Predictably, Channing assumes his students will be more "at home" when arguing among their equals or superiors. For instance, in distinguishing the character of the political orator from the legal orator, Channing maintains that "In a court of justice [arguing to a judge rather than to a jury or to a political gathering], he is perfectly at home, in his natural atmosphere, and surrounded by objects that long custom has made important to the free and prosperous exercise of his powers" (*Lectures* 118). In fact, the two venues seem to Channing to have little to do with one another, since "popular influence" demands that the orator does "what he can to determine [the auditor's] choice" (117). The popular venue offers no "protecting genius" to save him from the ugly customs of the public sphere, from the "browbeating, from the assaults of clamorous prejudice, from the charge of public apostasy, and from awkward revelations of his private history" (118). Channing wonders, in fact, whether one venue for rhetoric and the forms used there have anything at all to do with each other. He doubts whether a principled orator can really have public influence, or whether the "popular" orator can have influence over learned persons: "A rude street orator would manage a mob far better than Burke could do. A popular preacher or advocate might thin the seats of the senate house" (117). He ends his lectures on the relationship between politics and advocacy this way, unwilling or unable to say whether popular rhetoric has anything to do with ideal rhetoric:

> As you will certainly find that some of the greatest statesmen have also been the greatest of lawyers, you are to consider whether they became politically eminent in spite of their profession, or by virtue of it, or (to be perfectly safe) whether is was not, in their case, a wholly indifferent matter. (119)

The responsible rhetor, then, like the writer of great lasting literature, must shun the "selfish" urge to become popular in the eyes of the masses. In fact, such a rhetor most likely *cannot* have popular influence. But by attending to higher ideals, rhetors might have (what might be called) a "trickle-down" salutary effect on the public, "however humble" that public might be. Such humble readers (if they could really understand their best interests) do not really want rhetors to "write down" to them: "so much more agreeable is it to feel one's self growing stronger by exposure to difficulties, and to the influence of grand thoughts intrepidly uttered, than to be nursed into a life-long imbecility" (165). Auditors "among all classes" grow stronger, more themselves, when exposed to rhetoric and literature in their ideal forms. Good rhetoric and good literature might act as the linchpins in the growing need for self-culture among Americans.

4

A. S. Hill (i)

Nineteenth-Century Journalism and the Making of a Patrician Intellectual

I sat up during the evening, reading by the light of the fire the scraps of newspapers in which some party had wrapped their luncheon. . . . Almost all the opinions and sentiments expressed were so little considered, so shallow and flimsy, that I thought the very texture of the paper must be weaker in that part and tear more easily. . . . [T]he reading matter . . . struck me as strangely whimsical, and crude, and one-idea'd like a school-boy's theme, such as youths write and after burn.

—H. D. Thoreau

Going to college, you will make life friendships, but you will come out filled with much that will have to be unlearned. Going to newspaper work, you will come in touch with the practical world, will be getting a profession and learning to make yourself useful.

—Henry George

[W]hen taken up young, I consider [newspaper work] destructive both to mind and character. I would nearly as soon see a son of mine opening a faro bank or an assignation house. All the influences of a newspaper office on a young man are extremely demoralizing.

—E. L. Godkin

I wish you had a widow's purse of money to draw from; for I believe that, in the long run, newspaper wheels require the grease of filthy lucre, as do most things in this worldly world.

—A. S. Hill[1]

From Channing to Hill

Edward T. Channing, after serving thirty-two years as the third Boylston Professor of Rhetoric and Oratory at Harvard University, retired in 1851, prepared his *Lectures* for press in 1852 (published in 1856), and died in 1855. The fourth Boylston Professor was Francis J. Child, perhaps the first and most definitive instance of the English professor who loved literature and hated composition. Child, forced to teach students how to write, taught it contemptuously, abandoning almost entirely the mundane subject of composition and student writers for the more high-minded subject of literature and great minds. Trained in Germany, he preferred the philological approach to literature and criticism, which was little concerned with nonliterary composition (Ronald Reid 249–52). And like so many English professors who followed him, Child resented his composition duties largely because they took him away from his genuine scholarly interests; as Albert Bushnell Hart reported, "Francis James Child used to say with a disarming twinkle that the University would never be perfect until we got rid of all the students. This was a hint at one of the strongest and most beneficent duties of the modern university, namely, to contribute to the world's stock of knowledge" (64).

Child's national influence was immense. As much as any other figure, Child set the standard for elevating the study of belles lettres and devaluing the teaching of writing. This standard, which segregated literature and composition, was adopted throughout American English departments in a process Donald Stewart called "Harvardization" ("Two Model Teachers"; see also Berlin, "Rhetoric and Poetics"). In 1875, when Johns Hopkins University, which had just opened its doors, offered Child a professorship in English, Harvard released him from the composition grind and conferred upon him the title Professor of English (the first at Harvard). Child is one of the villains in composition historiography, but his animosity toward writing instruction was something Child always acknowledged and even joked about. He cared little about composition or composition students; he was not a compositionist; he was not "one of us."

But Adams Sherman Hill, Harvard class of 1853, Channing's student, and the fifth Boylston Professor (1876–1904), was an enemy within the ranks, and for this traitorship he has become "composition's *bête noire*." In other words, as one of the leading architects of composition, one of Kitzhaber's "big four" composition-textbook authors, Hill represents a more tangible and appropriate target of criticism. He was a member of the "community" of composition. Composition historians, almost universally, consider Hill's influence on composition immense. Similarly immense and pernicious is the damage historians feel he did to the profession. Hill has become the emblem for almost everything *wrong* in writing instruction.[2]

I concur that Hill, his textbooks, and his followers indeed left an impoverishing legacy to the teaching of writing and to teachers of writing. However, I find that deeper and more thorough consideration of his biography and the assumptions of his culture renders a somewhat different, and perhaps more sympathetic, representation of his motivations. Indeed, perhaps to our discomfort, but I hope to our enlightenment, Hill's rationale for teaching writing has much in common with our own.

While it is difficult to square Hill's methods for teaching writing with his cultural-improvement motivations, I situate Hill in a similar position to Channing's. Specifically, both thought composition could help reform a dangerous and powerful cultural discourse that threatened every citizen and every student. Because of his experience in journalism and because of his social position as a Harvardian "patrician intellectual,"[3] Hill, like Channing, found himself "at odds" with mainstream late-nineteenth-century American culture. And whereas Channing's commentary on public discourse and the culture it bred sought merely to have the students turn their backs on society, Hill, in step with turn-of-the-century Harvard's messianic impulse to reform society, wanted his teaching and his students to take an active part in changing the world. (This conclusion is diametrically opposed to those historians who argue that Hill wanted his students above all to *fit in* with modern managerial capitalism.) The most influential forum for pubic discourse, and according to patrician intellectuals the most dangerous one, was the American newspaper, whose style and approach threatened the health of Americans' political and moral selves. Sound composition skills, thought Hill (himself a "newspaper man"), would endow students with a vigorous, healthful, and *manly* style, which would render them less susceptible to the infectious reach of newspapers.

Deepening Crises and Further Transformations

The social crises that confronted Channing's America had not lessened. If anything, they seemed to those who lived through postbellum America to have become even more acute. Concurrent with the transformation of American education, postbellum America agonized through numerous other monumental and permanent transformations: in class structure and the nature of the professions, in intellectual/academic epistemology, in demography, and generally, in the way Americans thought about the relationship between themselves and their society.[4] In general, cultural historians have portrayed this period as one dominated by cultural uncertainty and fear; questions of class hierarchy, authority, and democracy were punctuated by fears of class and racial violence and by the prevalent anxieties over the toppling or disintegration of American civilization.[5] The transformation I focus on here occurred so rapidly and forcefully that it is usually termed a "revolution"—the "communications revolution."[6]

Channing's generation experienced the first (and lesser) wave of communications changes, and Channing's rhetorical theory addressed and responded to these changes. Channing realized that our habits of communication determine in large part who we are. For Channing rhetorical training was largely a matter of learning how, in what manner, and in what medium one could best communicate. He was mostly optimistic about the new emphasis on written communication over oratory because writing seemed (1) the most reliable form of communication for holding together a vast, culturally diverse citizenry, (2) the medium that best fostered thoughtful, reasonable discourse, (3) the medium most easily controlled by an elite, ruling class, and (4) the best medium for the reader to distance herself from an alien and dangerous culture. Such a writing theory seems quite suitable for Harvard, one of the principal gatekeepers in American society and, in Channing's time, a reliable certifier of class values (see Bledstein 202–206, 223–27).

But the changes in communications witnessed by Channing were minor in comparison to the sweeping changes that occurred during and after the Civil War, when printed matter became even less the province of an elite class of merchants and thinkers. From the late 1840s to the 1870s and beyond, communications technologies—the railroad (1827–40), the telegraph (1849),[7] inexpensive (non-rag) paper (1844),[8] the rotary press (1847), the steam-powered press and mechanical compositors (1880s)—acted synergistically with one another, with the rise of public schooling and literacy, and with the rise of a market economy and a market ideology to revolutionize the nature of communications. During this period, the number of American publications expanded almost exponentially and the real cost of publications plummeted.[9] More and more, for America's patrican intellectuals it seemed that *anyone* could afford printed materials. Even more dangerous, almost anyone could produce and distribute printed materials. For the intellectuals at Harvard and at the editors' desks of the elite publications, one of the most troubling new sources of written communication was the ever-distending world of journalism.

Furthermore, this era was characterized not only by sweeping changes in American institutions, but also by frantic confusion and fear of disorder and by multifarious efforts to restore a lost order and to impose organization and control.[10] American intellectuals, especially, were fearful of the rise of "mass culture." Adams Sherman Hill, like most of his contemporaries who were concerned with educating the elite (and like many educators today), believed that mass culture was, for most Americans and for most college students, pernicious, overwhelming, and almost irresistible. According to Hill and other intellectuals, mass culture dulled one's critical capacities; it took over one's thoughts as well one's communication habits (one's manner of expression, one's style); it divided the citizen-student from what was "truly" in his or her own best interests. Patrician intellectuals consistently charged that amoral business interests—the "plutocracy," anathema to the nineteenth-century intellectual—were using America's growing literacy to control Americans' thoughts, expressions, and sense of self. Hill believed he was witnessing the cultural disintegration of the natural self and the cementing of the massified self; no longer did the masses or his students possess definitive boundaries between self and an abhorrent new imposter culture. Consciousness was being colonized. Hill's social theory and his pedagogy, then, were "countercultural": what counted as "culture" for most Americans had become for Hill something to "resist." These forces might be better resisted if students were provided with an "English . . . hardy enough to withstand the chilling influences that surround it" (*Our English* 139).

Hill the human being has been caricatured in composition historiography, as has his rhetorical theory. (Hill's historical reputation has been especially vulnerable to the kinds of distant, sweeping readings of nineteenth-century composition I discussed in chapter 2.) But, his rhetorical theory has been criticized for the wrong reasons. I find his ultimate motivations rather generous. His *theories* of teaching writing, anyway, have some things in common with contemporary "critical pedagogy." His greatest fault (and the fault not only of current-traditional writing instruction but also of some cultural-studies instruction) has been an unrealistic sense of the writing self—that a unified, pre-thought, integrated self exists before writing has begun, and can thus be transferred onto the page. A unified individual, says this theory, makes a unified composition. It is this obsession with unity, both in Hill's day and in our own, that kills vibrancy in student writing.

A Biographical Sketch of Hill

Kitzhaber remarked in his 1953 dissertation that "It is difficult to find out much about Hill," and forty-six years later it remains difficult. There is simply very little material available. Considering Hill's status as a Harvard graduate, a named professor, and a department chair, Hill's Harvard Archives "general folder" is remarkably thin (the letter to E. M. Bacon cited in the epigraph is the only Hill-written material in it). If he saved either his book manuscripts or his lecture notes, they have not come to light. It would seem also that he was not much of a letter writer—or at least he wrote very few letters to persons whose lives would be deemed important enough for an archive center to catalog.

Harvard University Archives does possess two of Hill's diaries, one an unrevealing one-month account of teaching composition at Harvard during 1900. The other diary dates from his final year in preparatory school and his first year at Harvard (1849–50), revealing the candid thoughts of what was probably a typical middle- to upper-class sixteen-year-old who had literary aspirations and was prone to purple passages on almost any subject.[11] The diary includes fanciful (I presume) stories of romance with his prep-school French teacher, Miss Henshaw ("thrice she kissed me. Twice did her lips touch mine, once press my cheek"); his humiliation at having his composition "murdered . . . most barbarously"; his intense guilt and fear about masturbation, about his "passion for female society," and, possibly, about some homosexual activities with a boy named Jim Hammond ("more have been rendered insane by this habit than by all other intemperances");[12] and, lastly, the intolerable food served at his freshman boarding house.[13]

Perhaps because of this dearth of material, Hill has been portrayed by composition historians as something of a mysterious misanthrope neurotically fastidious about details—a fussbudget about grammar and other aspects of mechanical correctness. As I will suggest in this cultural and biographical analysis, that caricature has a great deal of truth to it, but there are some interesting and significant angles to the story. If nothing else, then, I hope to fill in some of those mysterious gaps, bringing forth a human being where before there has been just a caricature. I hope also to offer a more thorough and accurate depiction of his rhetorical theory, which, rather than representing merely what contemporary compositionists ought to shun, might be criticized for more substantial and relevant reasons, and which might yield some insights into our own teaching and our own attitudes toward our classroom.

Temperament and Characteristics

Hill was born in Boston in 1833, christened Abijah Adams Hill, his named changed by "Act of the Legislature" shortly after his father's 1838 death. Both parents suffered from poor health, his father succumbing to yellow fever in 1838 while on a family voyage to Cuba, his mother, "who had long been an invalid," dying in Worcester in 1846 (Rantoul 135). He was raised by his uncle, Alonzo Hill, the junior minister in Worcester's First Unitarian Church and charter member of the Temperance Club (Lincoln 170, 256, 397–98; Abijah Marvin 98, 105), who later was called by Hill in his diary "my Savior from the continuance of [the solitary] vice." That is, "Uncle Alonzo" recognized, somehow, that Hill's physical infirmities resulted from masturbating, and it was he who set him on the straight and narrow path to moral and physical salvation.

Hill was a small man with a high-pitched voice. He wore humorously thick eyeglasses that made him look "like a wide-eyed child" (Starr 123). He possessed a noticeably infirm constitution, which was consistently remarked upon by his contemporaries. For instance, Barrett Wendell, Hill's "lieutenant" in Harvard composition and later an esteemed literary scholar, described Hill in 1897 as having always seemed worn down by age: "Professor Hill is in aspect an elderly man, and has been so since he was really a young one" (*Letters* 117). The available biographical sketches of Hill and the surviving letters to and from him suggest a man prone to frequent "breakdowns," principally involving his eyes.[14] The first major breakdown occurred during the spring of 1859 after working three years for the New York *Tribune*, first as a law-courts reporter, then as its New York desk editor. After Hill spent a year in Worcester recuperating, several colleagues—including notables Samuel S. Wilkeson and Charles A. Dana—advised him not to "work in news until your eyes get better."[15] After continuing to work in newspapers, Hill suffered another breakdown in 1865 and again in 1868, and was prone to them for the remainder of his life. It was Hill's frantic work habits (his letters reveal he was constantly moonlighting) and the nature of newspaper work that are most often blamed for Hill's ill health, but whatever the cause, Hill's weak constitution was among his signature characteristics. Even his Harvard-publication biographers stress his lifelong infirmity. J. H. Gardiner, writing a eulogy for Hill, *begins* his biographical sketch of Hill with a statement of his chronic ill health and "frequent breakdowns," and he also *concludes* with a comment on his health:

> We all knew how frail he was, and what staggering illnesses he had to contend against, but he seemed to take the minimum of interest in such matters himself. One can only wonder at the amount of work achieved with such minimal equipment. (377)

> One cannot look back with pity on one who, in spite of bodily distress and sorrow, played a man's part in active life and left a broad mark on his generation. (380)

It seems odd that a man so racked by ill health and poor eyesight would choose a profession grading student themes. Physically speaking, Hill in no way epitomized "manly good health," which is something worth considering in the context of Harvardian manliness, a stolid self, and resistance to social conformity.

Another signature characteristic was, in the words of his friend Barrett Wendell, Hill's "dry . . . manner and comments" ("Recollections"). Others interpreted his manner less sympathetically, as merely acerbic and rude. In

1862, a fellow *Tribune* correspondent berates Hill for possessing "an amount of crass I have rarely seen equaled" and for his "peremptory style of speech." He offers Hill this advice:

> Perhaps you do not know,—perhaps your friends, from delicacy, have never told you,—that the airs of arrogance mingled with frivolity which you affect sit upon you with little grace—and that your dictatorial manner is most disagreeable to all gentlemen who are, at least, your equals, and who expect to receive the common courtesies of life.[16]

Hill also seems to have left similar impressions upon persons to whom he had reason to be especially courteous. For example, Francis H. Underwood, prime mover behind and editor of *The Atlantic* writes to Hill about his "querolous" (*sic*) correspondence (Hill had apparently attempted to get something published in the magazine): "The somewhat irritable tone you choose to adopt is not agreeable in a correspondent. You write like a man under a sense of injury."[17] In fact, one gets the impression from the correspondence to Hill that this "sense of injury" bordered on paranoia. Hill indignantly resigned from his work with the Chicago *Tribune* because editor Whitelaw Reid discredited one of Hill's dispatches (December 3, 1863), and Reid responded, "Since when did you imagine that I was [not (?)] bound to 'throw discredit' on dispatches you happened to make which I happened to believe untrue" (December 9, 1863). And later in life, among his composition contemporaries and among composition historians, Hill left unfavorable impressions. The late Donald Stewart, whose impressions of Hill come from his readings of Hill's younger contemporary, Fred Newton Scott, has stated:

> When we speak of Harvard's influence on composition instruction, we are really talking about A. S. Hill, his texts, and his program. And no one has succeeded yet in convincing me that this man was not mean-spirited, arrogant, dogmatic, and, on the subject of rhetoric, intellectually shallow. ("Harvard's Influence" 470)

On the other hand, Barrett Wendell in his private journal calls Hill "not only my chief but a tenderly and considerately affectionate friend" and attributes Hill's seeming aloofness to "his infirmity of health . . . , his extreme near-sightedness . . . , his dry and biting manner . . . , the thin rigidity of his hard-headed countenance, and most of all a temperamental shyness" ("Recollections"). The writer of his biographical sketch in *Harvard Graduates Magazine* also suggests that behind the veneer of aloof manners was a generous teacher:

The ultimate basis of friendship is frankness, and no man was franker than he. To casual acquaintances the untempered directness and the keen wit with which he would speak out the truth was sometimes disconcerting, and in rare cases repellent; but such feelings vanished with closer acquaintance. His kindliness was unfailing; and he had a peculiar faculty for free intercourse with younger men. . . . [T]o no man, young or old, was respect for Mr. Hill ever blurred by familiarity. (Gardiner 380)

It is not hard to detect the fancy footwork and careful phraseology that was most likely motivated by the famous filiopiety shared among Harvard graduates, but this theory of a kind underlying nature was shared by others.

In terms of his manner, I would make one suggestion further: Hill may have been largely unconscious of the impressions he left on his students, colleagues, superiors, and his composition followers. This was the belief of Wendell, who wrote that

his tendency as a teacher was grimly to eradicate fault rather than sympathetically to stimulate promise. So far as I could ever see, though, *he never suspected himself this propensity, meaning rather to be a helpful friend.* ("Recollections," my emphasis)

A similar representation of Hill as having a hard exterior covering a caring personality is given by LeBaron R. Briggs (for years, Hill's composition colleague, and later dean at Harvard and Radcliffe, supporter of women's education at Harvard):

The essence of Hill's method was common sense ruthlessly applied, surgery; wounds which left scars, and at first, it may be, bitterness toward the operator, a bitterness which time transformed into gratitude and affection. A smart undergraduate characterized him as "pungently Philistine." No man could take the conceit out of a pupil more rapidly, or with more memorable phrasing. Of method, in a formal sense, he had none; he was scarcely coherent; but at his best he had a sparkling spontaneity peculiarly his own. Moreover, the discerning pupil soon discovered in him a mind as quick in responding to the significant and genuine as in exposing and damning the empty and insincere; a judgment whose praise was worth working for and treasuring long. (*To College* 2–3).

The caring interior beneath the gruff exterior is an aspect of Hill that composition historians seem to have chosen to ignore. For instance,

Kitzhaber quotes the first disparaging part of the above Briggs quotation but not the remainder, which clarifies Briggs's belief that Hill was actually a caring teacher (61).

For Hill, as with any teacher, there was a gap between theory and practice, between the pedagogical impression Hill believed he was leaving and the impression he actually made, between what Hill thought a composition course ideally should be and the composition courses he actually taught. Hill was probably *not* a very good teacher of writing, but his motivations, I find, were decent ones.[18] As I want to point out in this chapter, there was a large gap between his theory of composition instruction as manifested in his popular but theoretical writings and the theory of composition instruction tacitly prescribed by his textbooks. That is, by examining Hill's textbooks *only*, composition historians have concluded Hill's theory of teaching writing involved nothing but instruction in grammar, concision, and the four modes of discourse; however, within the covers of a freshman rhetoric it has always been, and remains, quite difficult to communicate one's full theory of teaching writing.[19] It is unfair to expect Hill to have done so.

The Impact of Journalism on Hill

Like Channing, Hill was a journalist before he was a teacher of rhetoric, though the social meaning and character of journalism had changed dramatically in the five decades that separated their entries into the profession. But even more than Channing, Hill was profoundly influenced (mostly unfavorably) by his work in and his knowledge of journalism. Indeed, as early as 1856, on the eve of Hill's anxious plunge into a profession in journalism, Hill expressed his perception that the newspaper in America and newspaper readership were changing steadily for the worse. Just after passing the bar exam in New York City, at the age of twenty-three, Hill wrote to his Harvard mentor James Walker (Harvard president, 1853–60) to solicit his opinion about whether he should enter the dubious and possibly dangerous profession of journalism: "Will you inform me whether an inclination to become an editor, which I am beginning to feel is in effect an inclination to throw myself over a precipice—whether, if yielded to, this would be inevitable, moral or mental? [*sic*]." The letter, full of youthful anguish, goes on to discuss his dissatisfaction with law, his doubts about a literary career, and, most important to my argument, his belief that journalism, *because* it was powerful and in disrepute, *needs* persons like Hill, who possess high moral character and "a fine and vigorous style." While Hill worries whether his moral constitution can withstand the challenge of newspaper work, he portrays such a career choice as morally righteous: "As

I perceive the influence which the newspaper is exerting . . . , I debate with myself whether any mission be more noble in this country . . . and whether any [profession] call more earnestly for the right man, with right aims?" This perception about the demoralizing influence of newspaper work upon journalists and of newspapers themselves on the public was widespread among persons of Hill's class, and one has to suspect that Channing's tutelage had some bearing on Hill's personal beliefs.

The Civil War, Hill, and the Transformation in Journalism

But Hill did pursue a journalism career, and he did so when journalism was undergoing rapid and irrevocable transformation. At the outbreak of the Civil War, newspapers were still a collection of unrelated, locally owned periodicals that concentrated on local news and that limned global events in local color—when they covered them at all. After the Civil War, the values underlying journalism had changed from those of the particular communities each paper served to the more nationally defined values of objectivity, fidelity to the facts, and speed. The advent of the telegraph made possible the concentration of news gathering, and high-speed presses made possible timely and widely distributed news coverage. The so-called "public's hunger for news" (a phenomenon that was new to mid-nineteenth-century America) was either a product of the Civil War or was greatly intensified by the Civil War. This hunger, made possible by communications technologies, had begun with the penny papers and was cemented into the American psyche during the Civil War. With the Civil War came broad solidarity among Northerners for the cause of the Union, and Northern journalism was practically unvarying in its support. Before the Civil War, competition among the dailies was based in ideological and political debate. With a more unified North, competition was transformed into matters of "scooping" a rival newspaper, which responded to and increased the citizenry's burning desire to know the outcome of the latest war campaign.

The nationwide hunger for early intelligence coupled with the new economics of news-gathering culminated in the New York Associated Press (NYAP), a wire-services monopoly ruled by the iron and unforgiving hand of Daniel Craig, who (as I detail below) "wield[ed] a power in the realm of news service akin to that of absolute monarch" (Rosewater 74; see also Reilly 236–38; and Schwarzlose 1:186–254). Nevertheless, the Civil War created huge profits for the Northern newspapers, even though they were gouged financially by the wire-services. Furthermore, because of the citizenry's, as one of Hill's contemporaries put it, newly "acquired habit of reading daily papers,"[20] profits and popularity for newspapers were sustained after the war was over. Hill had reason to be particularly bitter not only about Craig's monopolization of the news, but about the nature of the newspaper business and its pernicious (as he saw it) effect on its readers.

News-gathering had not only become big business (with Craig as its robber baron) but also enormously competitive. No longer was a fine style the hallmark of journalism. With the nation's new-found hunger for news, the public's willingness to pay for the hottest items, and intense competition among newspapers, different qualities became paramount for the newspaper correspondent: the ability to "scoop," to follow leads, and to make "connections."

And Hill was among the best of this new breed of reporters (though the favorite story about Hill concerns his alleged cowardice on the battlefield).[21] According to press historian Louis M. Starr: "Perhaps better than any other correspondent, Adams Hill personified the new journalism in which speed, efficiency, and a nose for the news supplanted the old emphasis on rhetoric, bombast and belles-lettres" (124). Hill was described by Henry Villard ("immigrant boy" who had become a celebrated Civil War reporter, Northern Pacific Railroad financier, benefactor of the *Nation* and *The New-York Evening Post*) as "a sharpwitted and indefatigable collector of the news" (*Memoirs* 1:339). Starr describes Hill, his work habits, and his importance to the *Tribune*:

> Sydney Gay [managing editor of the *Tribune*] had occasion to thank his stars for the nervous, bespectacled little man who held the fort for him in Washington. Adams Sherman Hill, introverted, pathetically nearsighted, frail, awkward, . . . took command of [the Washington office], and proceeded to run it with dispatch. Hill's high-pitched, excited voice might be heard at almost any time of the day or night. . . . Hill not only filed a nightly news budget sufficient to keep the *Tribune* abreast of the *Herald*, often a jump ahead of it; he also directed the assignment of war correspondents with the various armies, . . . kept track of them, sped their copy on its way, recruited new men, bought horses for them, and the while served as the *Tribune*'s insider and Gay's confidential adviser. . . . Hill cultivated his [inside government] sources assiduously, and they were legion. (123–24)

Unknown to Gay (and probably to Starr), Hill was also earning extra cash by writing dispatches to various western papers, which only makes his successes at the *Tribune* even more impressive.

But Hill thought of himself as more than a mere "gatherer" of news, and this belief was justified. Hill's government sources—his close ties with the Lincoln administration, its cabinet, and various persons in Congress— allowed him to play a key role in the most important political event of the

Civil War, the Emancipation Proclamation. With his inside sources and his keen ability for synthesizing disparate masses of facts into a unified whole, Hill understood the political difficulties behind the emancipation issue, and he passed on his knowledge to Gay. Hill theorized that Lincoln was "out of touch" with public sentiment on the issue. Gay, in turn, as editor of the second-most influential newspaper in the country,[22] possessed enough political/popular clout to gain a serious hearing from Lincoln, informing him of the "deep-seated anxiety [about emancipation] on the part of the people"; Lincoln urged Gay to "Please come see me at once.[23]" The support of Horace Greeley and his powerful paper was important to Lincoln ("as helpful to me as an army of one hundred thousand men" [quoted in Starr 127]), and therefore Hill—through his influence with Gay and thus with Greeley—became an important player in perhaps the most important political move of the Civil War. In fact, according to Starr's account, Hill was a vital, though invisible, mover behind the whole affair.[24]

Nonetheless, rubbing elbows with senators and congressmen, staying up till late hours, engaging in intense competition with rival newspapers, Hill's work was exceedingly demanding. At times he "hated" his work, and at others he seemed to relish it. In a letter written to Gay (n.d. [ca. November 1862]), Hill tells Gay about a new "source" he has secured for the *Tribune* ("I think we shall get along with [him] & suffer not even the smell of a grindstone upon our garments," that is, he would be a source that does not require a great deal of goading for the latest information), but then, inexplicably, launches into a discussion of his fatigue, his infirmities, his boredom, and his request for an assistant. (Hill would often complain about being overworked, but apparently his request for an assistant was never granted by Gay.)

> The worst of it is that through nearsightedness and other natural disqualifications I am unable to effect much in the hotels work, and should be if I had plenty of time for it, in a word floor "reporter," using the word in its strictest sense. Then, too, to draw from the more aristocratic fountain of news, Secretaries, Under Secretaries, Generals, I have to spend much of my time waiting and in some cases being bored after admission. Others too let down their news very slowly & water it with talk. To be bored is to pay the price for some news. Indeed, I am bored from after-breakfast till bedtime pretty steadily: and at times I hate this life with my whole faculty of hating.

But there were also many times when Hill celebrated with Gay his part in scooping the rivals—for example, "we beat the *Herald* out of sight and today we have beaten them *all*" (September 19, 1862). At other times, he resorts to bragging, for instance, about his wheedling information out of a drunken senator (n.d. [ca. June 1862]) or about his beguiling a capitol-building "custodian" into allowing him and his "aid de camp" to sneak out a draft of a controversial tax-bill: "Cerberus ate a poisoned cake of words and gave me the sheets of the Conference Committee. . . . [and returning hours later] So Cerberus ate some more cake & the golden apples were carried down to the Tribune rooms" (June 28, 1862).

My point is not only that Hill was very good at newspaper work, but also that he experienced it in its most intense and influential aspects. He was an important person who was never seen, never acknowledged publicly. Samuel Wilkeson told Hill he was one of the best reporters working. Gay recognized how important Hill's connections were to him and the *Tribune*.

Rancor for the Newspaper Business

While it may be true that Hill was good at newspaper work and may have even enjoyed it at times, Hill had reason to despise the way newspapers worked. Above all, he had good reason to despise the people who controlled the newspapers, especially newspaper owners and most especially Horace Greeley. Hill finally left the *Tribune* around December 26, 1863, and although he wrote Gay a final letter of resignation,[25] one can only speculate about what precisely caused him to leave, though it seems most likely he was fired at Greeley's insistence.[26] Hill despised Greeley, and Greeley (if he gave Hill any thought at all) despised him in return. The trouble began with one of Hill's dispatches during the summer of 1863, which stepped over the boundary from objective reporting to opinion, expressing an opinion Greeley objected to. As Gay describes the affair to Hill:

> Dear Hill . . . You "put you[r] foot in it" last night, & I blame . . . my self for permitting you to do it. My first impulse was to [cull?] out your dispatch on recruiting, & I should have obeyed it. Mr. Greeley to-day is very "wroth," & wishes me to write you several uncomfortable things—which, you can conceive. But in my own way, I may repeat what I have said before—stick to facts, leave us to unite [the] editorials. Mr. Greeley knows what he wants to say. I *ought* to know, & generally do. It is impossible for anybody to budge on this. . . . [If] Mr. Greeley was a *responsible* editor his head would have been safe on his shoulders at this moment. . . . If now you will take my advice in this matter you will say nothing to Mr. Greeley about it, but simply be careful in future not to commit the fault again. Write what you please to me—or telegraph it—but let your public dispatches avoid rumor, & opinions. In your capacity as

correspondent . . . have no opinions. (Gay to Hill, May 23, 1862, Duke University Archives)

A little more than a year later, something similar happened. About a month before Hill resigned, Hill had secured a "document he knew Greeley would not like,"[27] and the story was once again "killed." Hill wrote to Gay in disgust: "I think that the *Tribune* gains by giving all sides a hearing: and it seems justice to all. And this is no side but an apparently impartial statement of facts. Above all, it is *news*" (Hill to Gay, n.d. [November or December 1863], Gay Papers). One thing is certain: the whole matter filled Hill with rancor, as he felt unappreciated and believed he was fit for something beyond the life of a "newspaper hack":

> I was *not* aware of Mr. Greeley's unfavorable opinion of me, i.e. not specifically. I *was* aware that for nearly two years I had the responsibilities of night editor: unsubordinated after eleven o'clock, almost always & undivided without his protest: and that Mr. Dan frequently left the paper on my shoulders when Mr. G. was in California. (n.d. [ca. November or December 1863])

This rancor toward Greeley (as we will see when Hill reviews one of Greeley's books) and his embittering experience about journalism never subsided.

Whatever the reasons for leaving the *Tribune*, Hill would not remain unemployed for long, and this next experience in journalism would embitter him even more profoundly. In fact, Hill's high opinion of his journalism capabilities was probably well founded,[28] considering how quickly he, working with Villard and Horace White (then of the New York *Tribune* and subsequently the editor of the *Chicago Tribune* from 1866 to 1874), created and established the "Independent News Room."[29] This news-gathering enterprise enabled Hill and his associates to supply Western newspapers[30] with information less dominated by Northeastern seaboard concerns. Although these three journalists may not have seen their news room as an explicit competitor to the much-hated news monopoly of Daniel Craig, Craig considered it a brazen challenge to his newsbroking control. Through deceit, Craig succeeded in running the Independent News Room out of business.

Daniel Craig and his "six nations" associates in telegraphic journalism had by 1858 already secured control of the nation's telegraphy and newsbrokerage. Editors thought this monopoly a "menace" because it set the local agents of the press at the margins of news-gathering and -distribution.[31] Joseph Medill, who as editor of *The Chicago Daily Tribune* employed Hill as a "special correspondent" and was later a subscriber to the reports of the Independent News Room,[32] recollected in 1896 the unforgiving nature of Craig and his information monopoly:

> Mr. Craig was the boss and dictator. He had a short and effective way of enforcing discipline and maintaining his authority. If any of us grumbled at the lateness of receiving his news, or its quality, or talked back to his autocracy, he cut us off, stopped our news, and after we had begged his pardon and promised never to repeat our offense, he would let up, but fine us to the amount of the cost of the news as if we had received it. . . . When advertisers were slow in paying their bills, I had to "shin round" for the money with which to pay Craig, for to go to press without his news, thin and scanty as it was, would be to go broke and suspend publication.[33]

As news-gathering and news-dispersal were threatening to come under the monopoly of Craig, most everyone in the industry worried that the free flow of information was becoming substantially threatened.

In the context of my argument about Hill, it is important to note that Hill's resignation letter to Gay cites the issues of journalistic independence and of Greeley's intrusive, news-skewing political attitudes—Greeley's "chameleon editorial policy," which changed according to the public's demands. However long the idea of an alternative wire service had been in the works, Hill had expressed for some time a growing dissatisfaction with the newspaper's "killing" of his dispatches, and for his having to take a "back seat" to Greeley's whims. He objected to Gay's and Greeley's insistence that he "stick to the facts." Villard too saw independence as an important reason for forming the independent news bureau: "My position" with the news bureau, he wrote to Frank Garrison, "is very pleasant—independent (a thing which I value above all) and lucrative. I left the *Tribune* without regret. The crochets of Mr. Greeley never suited me."[34]

Whatever their reasons for forming the Independent News Room—whether from the desire for independence and money or from a sense of moral duty to see that all the news got out[35]—Villard, White, and Hill enjoyed surprising success. Although they were opposed and "handicapped by the monopolistic contract between the NYAP and the American Telegraph Company" (Reilly 239), they used the lines of the smaller, still-independent telegraph companies (which were soon to be swindled out of business by Craig [see Schwarzlose 2:1–29]), and succeeded during approximately five months of operation in scooping (and embarrassing) the NYAP (Reilly 238–45). As Starr has noted, Hill, with his numerous resources, was perhaps the best of the "Washington men" when it came to acquiring inside information about happenings in the government. White had a similar reputation (Logsdon 78–104) and Villard usually covered the war from the front lines. The Independent News Room was remarkably successful.

Therefore, press historians see it as no surprise that Craig used his influence to discredit the news bureau and portray Villard, White, and Hill as unpatriotic scoundrels. Craig got his chance on May 18, 1864, when two New York journalists fabricated the "proclamation hoax" in order to "cause such fluctuations in the prices of stocks, bonds and gold, as to enable [them] to make money" (Bates 230). With access to the telegraph lines, these two men were able to send a supposedly official proclamation from Lincoln and Secretary of State Seward calling for a day of humiliation and fasting and the conscription of 400,000 more soldiers for Grant's struggling Wilderness Campaign. Though the bogus proclamation was discovered and killed quickly, it managed to make its way into two widely circulating newspapers, the *New York Journal of Commerce* and *World* (the *New York Herald* discovered the hoax and had to recall and destroy 20,000 papers [Reilly 246]). Because the proclamation so embarrassed both the Lincoln administration and the NYAP, a quick and sweeping campaign was launched to find the perpetrators (with Secretary of War Edwin Stanton leading the pursuit). After determining the hoax did not originate with the AP, Stanton turned his attention to the Independent Telegraph Company and the Independent News Room, closing down the telegraph offices, imprisoning Villard, questioning White, and placing Hill under surveillance.

The entire episode was ephemeral from an historical context (the true perpetrators were discovered three days after the event), but Craig saw his opportunity in Stanton's suspicions of the news bureau, and he acted decisively, fabricating and sending over the AP wires a story that Villard, White, and Hill had played a key role in the bogus proclamation. After identifying this "body of news gatherers" by name and the papers they worked for, Craig asserts "either some member of the above Association was the author of the bogus Proclamation, or that some person connected with them, knowing the fact that a call was about to be made, wrote the Proclamation upon the predictions furnished by their dispatches" (quoted in Reilly 248–49).

Craig's most damaging charge, perhaps, was his unstated but unmistakable implication that the bogus dispatch was designed to aid the enemy. Loyalty, and especially the press's loyalty, to the Union was an extremely emotional and even dangerous issue during the Civil War, and especially during the "black spring" of 1864. Absolute support for the Union and hatred of the South were vital to any Northern newspaper that wished to have its news read and its buildings unburned.[36] It was common, for instance, to read in one newspaper that its rival held "Copperhead sympathies" and that this rival had surreptitious designs on its readers' patriotism.

Further, censorship on the press for reasons of security was accepted by Northerners.[37] At the outset of the war and again in 1864, there were rashes of violence directed at Copperhead and "peace-at-any-cost" newspapers. As Mott writes, "in 1864 . . . there were again scores of instances of mob violence against newspapers in the northern states. . . . So the mobs raged in the black spring and summer of 1864" (Mott, *American Journalism* 359).

While Craig's charge of disloyalty may have been implicit, the editors of the Western papers lost no time in explicitly defending the loyalty of the three men. Medill declared Villard, Hill, and White "gentlemen of unimpeachable character and integrity" who have not "turned from their sterling service in the aid of loyalty and the Government, to fabricate or be concerned in the production of a document exclusively in the interest of the enemies of the country." Murat Halstead of the *Chicago Tribune* explained the physical impossibility of their perpetrating the hoax and described them as "young men of good abilities and character, who are engaged in a perfectly legitimate business. . . . [T]heir occupation is fully as legitimate as that of MR. CRAIG."[38]

In the long run, perhaps the efforts of Hill, White, and Villard eventuated for the public good: their success may be partly responsible for the post–Civil War "successful revolt [by the Western Associated Press] against [Craig's] New York association"; White and Medill led the revolt (Reilly 259). But Craig's slanderous charges led to the embitterment of both Villard and Hill. Villard left his life in journalism permanently in September of 1864, journeying to his homeland of Germany (though later in life, after making a fortune in the Oregon railroads, Villard became benefactor to the *Nation* and the *New York Evening Post* [Villard 267–68; see also Reilly 258–60]).

For Hill the result appears to have been not only embitterment but exhaustion and perhaps a permanently besmirched reputation. His Harvard biographer says Hill suffered another breakdown in the summer of 1864; also, his known correspondence ends abruptly with a letter from E. F. Waters dated June 23, 1864, which suggests Hill discontinued his involvement with the Independent News Room around that time.[39] There is evidence, too, that his reputation was permanently sullied by his association with the Independent News Room. That is, Craig's accusation was either partly correct or it succeeded in painting Hill as unpatriotic. In any case, it seems plausible that a tarnished reputation—as irresponsible journalist who gave away state secrets during time of war—followed Hill throughout his life.

I make this suggestion about a sullied reputation because of an extraordinary editorial note placed immediately after a biographical essay on Hill in the *Report of the Harvard Class of 1853* (from 1913, three years after

Hill's death). These once-per-graduating-class documents have an almost hagiographic quality to them, and criticism of any Harvard graduate is rare (my searches through several of these reports revealed no criticism anywhere near as severe as that of Hill and the Independent News Room). But in an "editorial note," classmate Robert Samuel Rantoul stops just short of calling Hill a traitor to the Northern cause:

> [The Independent News Room's] relations with public functionaries must of necessity be close, and by astute manipulation it was very possible to discover, through methods not always patent, the very secrets which the Administration and its departments were anxious not to disclose.... [T]his new organization had already ensconced itself in sumptuous quarters on Pennsylvania avenue, where, with a wealth of books and maps and magazines and journals, and all the appliances for ease and comfort which lubricate that sort of work, its agents awaited, often with Hill in charge. Nothing was more natural than for a Senator or department officer, at the close of a weary day, to drop in to this restful resort, the very haven of late intelligence, and there refresh himself with a friendly conversation, with a glance at his home newspapers, with a harmless cigar and a cheering glass of wine. In such environment he was a born diplomat, indeed, from whose lips some little hint of the phase of the national problem which was next to his heart did not escape.

At the end of each day, the members of "this astute brotherhood," after individually gathering many "innocently" dropped "fragments" of "intelligence," would dine together and would synthesize "this mass of accumulated facts," which, "ingeniously put together, . . . revealed the whole."

> Few government departments could withstand the siege for many days. In this way, step by step, knowledge reached these headquarters, and ultimately the public which only sworn officials should have had.... *Hill and his confrères were largely editing, in this terrible hour, the press of the nation....Of such material are statements framed which affect the value of every day's work, and every barrel of flour, and every promise to pay value, on this continent.*[40]

What is enlightening here is not only the suggestion of Hill's aiding and abetting the enemy for personal profit, but also the proficiency with which Hill and his peers synthesized diverse facts into meaningful wholes.

The Independent News Room, then, supplied Hill with the freedom he complained of not having while working for Greeley's newspaper. In fact, it placed him and his associates in a position of enormous responsibility: not only were these men enhancing the freedom of the press by providing an alternative to the monopolistic New York AP, but they were also making editorial decisions about which news to pursue and send along to their subscribers.[41] In other words, they had transcended their roles as correspondents, which, due to the nature of Civil War reporting, was becoming an occupation of merely reporting the details with "objectivity."

Hill's experience in the newspaper business is important for at least two reasons. First, it helps explain why Hill would possess, like most intellectuals in the latter part of the century, a profound distrust of newspapers and their power to monopolize public discourse and what counted as news and, therefore, what counted as reality and knowledge. In Hill's case this distrust manifested itself in a profound rancor toward the newspaper business and especially the wire-services end of the business. It seems highly reasonable to assume that Hill, like most persons associated with the newspapers during the Civil War, hated Craig and his monopoly. This may explain why Hill often posed writing instruction as one antidote to the pernicious values instilled by America's newspapers.

Second, it reveals something about Hill's attitudes toward writing. Buffeted as he was by newspaper editors' comments to be more succinct ("DON'T WASTE THE TELEGRAPH"; "the news [you] sent might without detriment have been condensed one half")[42] and to provide them only with the facts ("stick to facts, leave us to unite [the] editorials"),[43] Hill understandably desired, probably for moral as well as personal reasons, the freedom to write *what he wished*. The letters written to Hill reveal that he was dissatisfied with the role of the reporter, as well as with the profit-motivated role that newspapers were assuming in public society. He was after all perhaps the finest investigative reporter of his day, but his editors—and then Craig's monopoly—silenced his skillful syntheses of news events. Hill's desire to write what he wished was both fulfilled and frustrated by his moonlighting for various other newspapers—the *Chicago Tribune*, the *Chicago Evening Journal*—as he was given the opportunity to write for various newspapers, but repeatedly warned not to editorialize. In such cases, Hill's response was invariably indignant. This desire was finally fulfilled, of course, when he, Villard, and White established their own news bureau to compete with the New York AP; it was frustrated by Craig's attempts to discredit the Independent News Room and Hill's subsequent breakdown. For his attempts to combat Craig's monopolization of public discourse, Hill was rewarded with more failed health and a besmirched reputation.

From Opinion Molding to Objective Reporting

Hill seems to have been a victim of the changing nature of journalism. In Channing's day, "respectable" journalism had traditionally been a career that afforded men the opportunity to express their opinions and to mold the opinions of readers via the written word. Certainly, the young Hill, who wrote his mentor James Walker about journalism's need for his "fine and vigorous style," was thinking in terms of such opinion molding. And even earlier in life Hill had such hopes. Although we can make no firm connections between the young Hill and the newspaper-worker Hill, his diary from the years 1849–50 reveals a young man desirous of entering the literary world of public discourse, quite desirous, as a sixteen-year-old, of entertaining and enlightening audiences. He became quite indignant when his efforts met with adverse criticism. For instance:

> Jan 28 . . . A composition of mine was read yester morn by the editor Johnny Barker on the Old woman who lived in a shoe. He murdered it most barbarously; left out the best and read the whole dreadfully, not understanding it at all and making it appear as silly as possible. . . . But it cannot be helped now. . . . I won't have another murdered in that fashion. Jan 31st. . . . My composition Ellen took and read to Fannie Wood and to her mother and they all praised it very much. Fannie Wood wanted a copy to show to her mother. Mrs. Blood said she had seen something like it in Blackwood's magazine and thought it very fine.

All teachers, it seems, would benefit from remembering their reactions to criticisms of their writing work; had Hill better remembered, perhaps composition might have taken a slightly different shape.

In any case, during the early part of the century, elite opinion seemed, at least, to dominate the public world. As the century progressed, however, new classes would become readers and voters.[44] Journalism was more and more becoming a career of news-*gathering* and less and less a career of *synthesizing* and overt opinion-molding. To put this another way, the content of the newspaper was rapidly changing from "criticism" to mere "intelligence," the reporting of one thing after another; facts and details had replaced criticism. In short, the ideal of objectivity was replacing explicit values and clear-cut partisanship.

More and more the human being within the newsprint was disappearing behind the mask of objectivity. To use Joseph M. Webb's helpful terminology, nineteenth-century America witnessed the transformation from "romantic" reporting to "rational" reporting. The romantic mode of journalism assumes that man is primarily a feeling, emotional, instinctual being, . . . that the Reality to be reported is primarily internal, inside human beings. . . . [I]nstead of an atomistic view of reality, it assumes a holistic view, assuming that life cannot be understood when it is cut up in little pieces. (39)

"Rational" reporting characterizes the nature of newsbroking (telegraphy-centered) journalism, which must supply copy that is suitable to a vast and variegated community of newspapers. That is, a news report must be palatable to readers in New York as well as in Chicago or Springfield, and the objective is to remove as much local color as possible—to become "objective." "Rational" reporting assumes that

Reality is essentially an external phenomenon understood via the senses; . . . human beings are fundamentally alike and it is their similarities that count; . . . to understand Reality it must first be cut up into pieces with each piece digested separately. (38)

According to Hill's classmate Rantoul and to press historian Starr, Hill was extraordinarily adept not only at uncovering the cut-up pieces of reality but also at putting "reality" back together, giving it coherence.

Hill, then, was a journalist caught between two worlds: he epitomized the new investigative reporter, but he seems to have longed to be that overt molder of a readership's opinions and values, which was the hallmark of the journalism that would fade quickly with the Civil War and the political and social changes it fostered. It might be said that Hill epitomized journalism itself, which itself was conflicted. On the one hand, as Schwarzlose points out, the Civil War witnessed the zenith of romantic reporting in the journalism of "war correspondents": those men, such as Villard and E. C. Stedman, who risked life and limb to gain eyewitness perspectives on battles, then galloped to the closest post office or telegraph office to report their impressions of the battle, the strategies, and even their opinions about what the general or president must next strive for. As Reilly points out, Villard's accounts of the Civil War were highly personalized, emotional, and moving. On the other hand, for the dozens of correspondents like Hill (Hill's one and only battle experience eventuated in humiliation), such romantic impressionism of daily events and government actions was not countenanced; editors wanted the "facts" and "the points" without opinion. Hill was caught in the middle of American journalism's great transformation from values to objectivity.

American press historians disagree on the precise timing and causes of this transformation, but all acknowledge that (1) it was primarily a nineteenth-century phenomenon, (2) it was propelled particularly rapidly during the Civil War, and (3), most important, it amounted to a fundamental shift in the nature of public discourse. Since Harold Innis's work of the 1950s, historians have acknowledged the important and complex role technology played in this transformation. Although few today adhere to his technological determinism, Innis argues that increased capacity, speed, and permanence of communication leads to sacrifices in communicative diversity. Also sacrificed are nonobjectivist epistemologies, for communication by telegraph or newsprint requires that information be "ground down to a convenient size" since "abstract ideas are less susceptible to treatment by mechanical devices."[45] James Carey, in an essay that tacitly criticizes the supposed objectivity of Vietnam War reporting, argued that the rise of objectivity came with the rise of the professionalization of journalism and that journalism maintained its objective frame in order to preserve its borders from interlopers ("Communications Revolution" 23–38). Michael Schudson argues that "a faith in 'facts,' a distrust of 'values,' and a commitment to their segregation" was part of the middle-class and market revolution against the aristocratic order; newspapers represented or sounded the clarion for a "new way of being in the world."[46] Dan Schiller makes several interesting and relevant points about "the rise of objectivity" in U.S. journalism, arguing that objectivity should be seen more as an effect than as a cause. First, argues Schiller, the path for news objectivity had already been cleared and laid by the popularity of positivist science and by photographic realism. Second, the penny papers gained their popularity because they defended the rights of the common person at "a time when those rights seemed to be threatened"; the penny papers also benefited from the republican belief that "knowledge, like property, should not be monopolized for exclusive use by private interests," and this belief was expressed by the penny papers' commitment to "cheap, value-free information," that is, to "objective fact" (10–11).

I suggest we should distinguish between at least two kinds of objectivity. The first—which might by called "immediate objectivity"—was popularized by America's cultural fascination with positivism, photography, and the newspaper; it was not valued by American intellectuals like Hill. The other—which might be called "contemplative objectivity"—goes beyond immediate physical perception, beyond everyday events and sensations; it involves the higher processes of *organizing* and *evaluating*, understanding the world in terms of higher meanings. Contemplative objectivity would not only perceive that an event has *occurred*, but also perceive the *meaning* of its occurrence.

While Hill adhered to American intellectuals' growing insistence that one search out the facts of any issue—an event, a natural phenomenon, and so on—the manner in which one *assembled* and *portrayed* the facts was crucial to the veracity of one's written message. Not just anyone in any situation could assemble, synthesize, and portray the world "as it is/was"; the kind of objectivity Hill wanted resulted from long and deep contemplation.

Furthermore, the ability to compose together facts into coherent, meaningful, and true wholes depended on the "higher faculties," which could be cultivated only by those who possessed a sound, "sincere" character. In other words, as Nan Johnson has shown, according to the "dominant" (she means dominant among intellectuals) view of rhetoric, only the man of sound character and developed intellectual powers could deliver sound critical writing; conversely, the writer who had not attained such stature was incapable of such critical writing. As Johnson writes:

> In [his *Lectures*] Blair popularizes the assumption that there is a cause-and-effect relationship between the cultivation of taste (through the study and practice of rhetoric) and the acquisition of intellectual, moral, and civic virtue. . . . The study of belles lettres and rhetoric supports the development of taste, intellectual ability, and moral virtue by defining how the principles of taste should be applied to the sense and form of conventional discourse. (45–46)

Obviously, these assumptions helped America's educated elite warrant their claim to possess what Pierre Bourdieu calls "cultural capital." It was a useful way for Harvard men and other educated leaders to proclaim their right and responsibility to lead the nation in its opinions, its civic and moral character, and its tenets of writing. There was more to writing sound public discourse than adhering to the facts, and then presenting them—*anyone could do that*. As Hill complained to Gay, any "hack reporter" could do that. Taste, among the foremost of the cultivated intellectual powers, was required in order to obtain a sound rhetorical sensibility. This intellectual capacity provided the writer with the power to compose myriad facts together. As Johnson explains, "the imagination serves reason in a special way because it allows the mind to apprehend aspects of truth (the sublime and the beautiful) that cannot be directly perceived by the understanding" (36). In other words, there was more to understanding the truth than merely "objectively" reporting the facts, which are indeed accessible to anyone; one needed the higher faculties in order to perceive and communicate the higher, moral truth.

As for what I am calling immediate objectivity, Schiller notes the popular acceptance of an objective world, which was seized upon and propagated by the newspapers:

> Positivism in science and history encouraged a general cultural acceptance of a reportable, objective world. News shared the same commitment. In the prospectus for his *Herald* Bennett wrote: "We shall endeavor to record facts on every public and proper subject, stripped of verbiage and coloring" (6 May 1835). Journalistic objectivity presumed a world prior to all imposed value, and the periodic construction of accurate and universally recognized copies of events in this world became the newspaper's fundamental business. . . . The newspaper ostensibly permitted a definitive separation of fact from fiction; indeed, the press itself testified to their disengagement. . . . [T]he newspaper generated and regenerated the very objectivity that it pretended only to display. . . . This is also evident in a ubiquitous contemporary metaphor, which called the newspaper "the historical photographer of national acts."[48]

Schiller points out further, arguing for cultural connection between newspaper objectivity and photographic realism, that the model for the newspaper reporter was fast becoming the machine; the reporter was coming to be seen as recorder of reality—a camera. Bennett's biographer, for instance, insisted in 1855, "A reporter should be as a mere machine to repeat, in spite of editorial suggestion or dictation. He should know no master but his duty, and that is to give the exact truth."[49]

Immediate objectivity devalues the human being, the "hack" reporter. As Schudson points out, "It was only in the decades after the Civil War that reporting became a more highly esteemed and more highly rewarded occupation"; only toward the end of the century would a college degree be worth something in newspaper reporting (68). When the reporter is likened to a machine, a mere recorder of events, there is little reason for the reporter to possess, say, a Harvard education or knowledge of moral philosophy and rhetorical theory. In fact, Horace Greeley, a self-made and self-educated man himself, thought that a college degree was an *impediment* to good reporting (a feeling that probably had much to do with the animosity between Greeley and Hill).

Hill's experience with Greeley's *Tribune* informed him that such machinelike objectivity was at best difficult, and it was impossible in profit-motivated journalism, where editorial policy was dictated by the reading public. And most of all, such machinelike work was not in any sense what Hill desired for himself. His education at Harvard—his rhetorical education, for instance, under E. T. Channing—told him that such immediate, photographic objectivity was not the kind of veracity that Hill or his contemporary intellectuals valued. Hill believed newspapers and newspaper persons should provide readers with insights that went beyond immediate sensation, impressions, and facts.

Horace Greeley and the Popular Culture of Newspaper Discourse

Composition historians puzzle over Hill's promotion to Boylston Professor, but Hill had earned his "man of letters" stripes with his essays on literary figures and, as I will stress here, on the shortcomings of American public argument. Similar to the way that Channing believed that portraying the world as merely "events crowding upon each other in a sweeping and wasteful tide" would endow the citizenry with alien ideas about reality, Hill thought that public and popular discourse needed more than presumably objectively stated facts, assembled together into dizzying wholes that change from day to day. There was also the importance of *vision*, which comes not from the immediate reporting of sensations, but from stepping back from the world, critically distancing oneself, contemplating relations, and then composing these multifarious events, ideas, and impressions into coherence, into an argument. This can be accomplished only by the person who has had time to cultivate the faculty of taste, who has been able to form himself or herself into a coherent individual—a healthy, integrated self. Not just any hack writer who secures a job at the newspaper can pull this off.

And not just any enormously influential, millionaire editor can do it either. In a remarkable essay appearing in *The North American Review* Hill would in one swoop criticize (1) his execrable, chameleonlike ex-boss, Horace Greeley (and his "class" of men), (2) the newspaper and its presentation of reality, and (3) popular forms of opinion-making, argumentation, and epistemology. Hill apparently never communicated with Greeley during the matter of his getting cashiered, but in the pages of *The North American Review* Hill could attain some measure of retribution.

On the surface, "Greeley's American Conflict" (January 1867) reviews Horace Greeley's *American Conflict*, a history of the Civil War published in 1866.[50] The title of Hill's essay plays on Greeley's title in a number of ways. First, the title suggests Hill's point that Greeley has written not so much about "*America's* conflict" as he has "*Greeley's* [biased version of the] American conflict." Second, Hill's essay has some remarkable things to say about Greeley's (and America's) ideas about the *nature of conflict*—how conflict is portrayed and resolved through discourse. This essay criticizes Hill's nemesis Greeley, but it also criticizes the popular rhetoric and popular ideas about pursuing the truth, a rhetoric that is exemplified by Greeley. Hill reveals his animosity toward the rhetoric that says the best reporter is the one who keeps his/her nose to (or in) the facts.

And since Greeley embodied (according to Greeley's own consciously created mythology) the new American newspaper, Hill criticized by synecdoche the discourse of an altered journalism. Greeley was a pioneer of the penny press and—to an extent even greater than his rivals James Gordon Bennett Sr. and Jr. of the New York *Herald*—made the daily newspaper a powerful influence over public opinion. A man of common origins, he came to New York with ten dollars and worked his way up from compositor to one of the most powerful editors in the history of journalism. Greeley, according to journalism historian Edwin Emery, "was like a character from a Dickens novel—so real that he appeared to be a caricature." Although he was a "professed Whig (the party opposed to popular rule), he worked all his life to bring a greater share of material and political benefits to the common man. . . . At a time when the democratic process was under great stress, Greeley 'put his faith in the unshackled mind' " (225–26). His first weekly received its main revenues from "lottery advertising, a circumstance his foes and rivals never let him forget later on" (227). During the Harrison-Van Buren campaign of 1840 he published the Whig campaign paper, the *Log Cabin*; Harrison's campaign discourse was considered by intellectuals the nadir of nineteenth-century political discourse.[51] With these political beliefs and with such an undignified biography, many intellectual contemporaries of Greeley "had nothing but contempt for Greeley"; William Cullen Bryant (also a "newspaper man") "refused to nod or speak to the *Tribune* editor even when they were brought together at social functions."[52]

Some of this contempt, certainly, is attributable to class enmity, but much was due to Greeley's enormous popularity and influence, especially among the increasingly literate and newspaper-reading masses. Joseph Buckling Bishop, editor of the *New York Evening Post*, wrote:

> The "Tribune" was a tremendous force in the country because of the personal faith of the plain people in the honesty of its editor. Every word the "Tribune" printed was believed implicitly because he was the man behind it. The power he wielded was not equaled by any editor of his time—neither has it been equaled by any editor since.[53]

Greeley, then, was synecdochically almost identical to the emerging and ever more influential modern brand of journalism. By criticizing Greeley's mode of public discourse, Hill was implicitly criticizing American journalism, as well as what seemed to be emerging as the American way of communicating, discussing, and debating the issues. Implicitly criticized also was Americans' credulity of the "facts" printed in newspapers like Greeley's.

Hill's letters reveal that he harbored tremendous personal animosity toward Greeley, criticizing his "chameleon [editorial] policy" for heeding public opinion and sales rather than the truth. Although such personal disputes with Greeley are not overt in Hill's review of Greeley's book, they are manifest in Hill's criticism of what he calls "the defects of a newspaper style of composition." Hill begins by considering and commending Greeley's writing style: "the narrative is condensed, the language plain and intelligible. . . . Mr. Greeley's power of condensed statement and his great skill in dealing with details are evident throughout its pages" (238). Furthermore, Hill compliments Greeley for his "thorough acquaintance with the minutest details of the conflict."

However, contends Hill, the substance of Greeley's history—his argument—is misguided and poorly reasoned.[54] Greeley's historical interpretations are guided by the kind of reasoning and methods employed by the newspaper editorial writer, not those of the historian. It is because of his position as powerful newspaper editor and as a key player in political circles that Greeley is able to muster his details, but these very advantages "become positive disqualifications" for writing accurate history, which requires nonpartisan distance from actual events. Whenever Greeley writes of issues for which he has a personal or political stake, he writes with unmistakable prejudice and inaccuracy, writing as an editorial writer rather than as an historian. Hill implicitly criticizes Greeley for writing a history with a political agenda, attempting to give undue credit to Greeley's friends and to pass over or misstate the noble actions of his political enemies. Hill's review, it might be said, strips away from Greeley's history the mask of objectivity.

Hill explains that Greeley's prejudices are typical of the new rational, or "objective," journalism, which pretends to be unbiased (writing only the facts), but subtly promotes a thoroughly political or profit-motivated agenda. Throughout the critique of Greeley's history, Hill evinces his disdain for the methods of the popular press and its capacity for influencing politicians and politics. In one instance he gives Greeley a backhanded compliment for "his familiarity with the working of the wires that, *invisible to the ordinary spectator, control the action of apparently automatic persons or assemblies*" (239, my emphasis)—a subtle jab at those politicians and chameleon journalists who take their cues from newspapers or from "the floating masses of voters." In another case, he cites Greeley's "newspaper provincialism" (245).

But to Hill, far worse than the politically biased interpretation of history is Greeley's belief in his *own* objectivity: Greeley, like his readers, has come to *believe* that reality can be reflected in the simplistic, biased, and money-driven discourse of newspapers. He has come to mistake opinion for fact, and he is unable to countenance the idea that more than one valid political position might exist. He believes his opinions stand for those of the nation and believes his opinions represent the facts: "This unfortunate habit of mistaking his own opinions and sentiments for those of the nation colors Mr. Greeley's views of men as well as of events" (244–45). Greeley's world, according to Hill, is the simplistic one that can fit within the pages of a daily newspaper, and that changes with each issue. Greeley believes that historical and political reality can be distilled down to the commonplaces that appear in his newspaper. He believes that one can deduce complex motivations—here, the motivations of a nation's voters—by examining bits and pieces of data. However, writes Hill,

> The truth is, that the feeling of a nation is not expressed in the returns of elections. Nothing lies like figures. The motives which determine men's action at the polls are too numerous and too complicated to admit being thus reduced to one simple term. But Mr. Greeley is too old a politician, . . . too old a political editor, too exclusively a political editor, to escape self-deception in this matter. (241)

In short, Greeley's habits of defective argumentation come from his editor's-eye view of the world, which by necessity sees the world in simplistic terms, atomistically, and as divided into two unequal segments, right and wrong. Hill attacks the now dominant mode of newspaper discourse and the epistemology it fostered. What Webb calls "rational" reporting—the idea that reality is external to human interpretation, that all human beings perceive reality more or less identically, and that detail, not integration, is the key to understanding it—is the very practice that so dismays Hill in Greeley's work.

We must not, Hill implies, allow newspaper discourse to infect other kinds of discourse. Such infection will lead, as it has already led, to the decay of real dialogue and reduction of complex issues into bipartisan politicking:

> [Greeley] is accustomed to regard the American people as divided into two great parties;—the one, on the whole, decidedly right, that is, of the same general way of thinking with himself; the other

decidedly wrong, that is, entertaining opinions diametrically opposed to his own. (241)

Greeley is both purveyor and victim of public opinion, which is the inevitable consequence of argumentation that pays heed to local, personal, immediate exigencies without benefit from information from higher truths or a higher ideal of a self. As is typical of Hill's early essays in publications such the *North American Review*, he concludes with a rhetorical flurry, this one decrying the power of public opinion and the predominance of passionate, specious, and partisan argumentation:

> "Greeleyism" permeates [*The American Conflict*]. In his editorial articles Mr. Greeley has frequently shown great skill in disposing of an adversary or an argument, without appearing to notice its existence; but many weapons which are effective in art or personal warfare have no place in the hand of an historian. He who would write a "History of the American Conflict" that shall be read by "our grandchildren"—as Mr. Greeley hopes that his will be—must not only avoid the defects of a newspaper style of composition, but he must still more carefully refrain from regarding persons or events from the stand-point of an editor, or a politician, or of a partisan. (247)

These arguments—about the newspapers, the decay of public discussion, and the need to reform both—will be returned to by Hill throughout his life, especially as he describes his rationale for the teaching of writing.

Anti-Intellectualism, Intellectual Martyrs, and the Culture of the Newspaper

As I argued in chapter 2, a predominant theme running through composition history posits that the professors and administrators of the modern university were willing participants in the growing predominance of managerial capitalism. According to this argument, current-traditional rhetoric—with its emphasis on mechanical correctness rather than the time-honored mission of rhetorical training for developing sound reasoning, argumentative skills, and civic virtue—was part of the effort to train managers who would assume their managerial roles in this new society, which needed an educated class that would not question or transform reality, but fit themselves within it, taking their orders and passing them on to those they managed. However, this neat cause-and-effect relationship between the dominant business world and the new university assumes a pan-societal ideology that is far too isomorphic to be of much help. Such a paradigm does violence to the subtleties of cultural change and allows historians to pass over the subtleties of composition theory and the culture within which it was formed.

In fact, American intellectuals—especially those who were the architects of the modern university—*perceived themselves* (at least) in a role that decidedly opposed the ideologies that were offered by the moneyed classes and that were foisted upon the public. Intellectuals saw themselves residing within an imposter culture that badly needed their cultural and political contributions, but that ignored them and thereby ignored their own best interests. Richard Hofstadter traces roots of cultural alienation of intellectuals as far back as the revolution, but notes that intellectual disenfranchisement became particularly pronounced after the Civil War:

> As the grim shape of the new America emerged out of the smoke of the war, there emerged with it a peculiar American underground of frustrated aristocrats, a type of genteel reformer whose very existence dramatized the alienation of education and intellect from significant political and economic power. The dominant idea of the genteel reformers was public service, their chief issue, civil-service reform; their theoretical spokesman, E. L. Godkin of the *Nation*. . . . Their towering literary monument proved to be that masterpiece in the artistry of self-pity, Henry Adams's *Education*. (*Anti-Intellectualism* 174; see also Trachtenberg 153–60)

I will not address whether intellectuals actually succeeded in transforming American culture and politics or whether they merely succeeded in subtle accommodation. But intellectuals saw themselves as "countercultural" reformers. They opposed what American culture, politics, and economics had become: politicians and other civil servants were corrupt and driven only by the desire for reelection and the rewards of public office; moneyed interests (the hated "plutocracy") had succeeded in establishing greed and individualism as the principal motivations for all social action. The quality of public debate had decayed into newspaper drivel, which excluded the kinds of complex arguments and the kinds of serious questioning that intellectuals hoped to inject into the forum. "Wherever men of cultivation looked," Hofstadter says, "they found themselves facing hostile forces and an alien mentality. They resented the new plutocracy which . . . they considered as dangerous socially as it was personally vulgar and ostentatious." They were excluded from public debate and thereby "condemned to political ineffectuality"; any full-fledged "frontal assault on any major citadel of politics or administration" was impossible, so they "content[ed] themselves with the hope that occasionally they could get their way by acting 'on the limited number of cultivated minds.' "[55]

In his criticism of Greeley and his argumentative methods and in his other *North American Review* publications, Hill was clearly writing within the intellectual tradition described by Hofstadter. In his essay "Life of Grimes"—appearing in *The North American Review* in 1876, the year he was promoted from Child's assistant to Boylston Professor of Rhetoric and Oratory—Hill assails the decayed character of American public discourse and the frightening power of public opinion. This essay might be considered a companion essay to his review of Greeley's history. Whereas the review of Greeley's history attacked the kind of discourse fostered by newspapers, this essay commends the life of a man who embodied responsible public and political discourse and who heroically resisted the force of public opinion. His argument is interesting also in the way it critiques, co-opts, and then appropriates some of the rhetorical strategies of anti-intellectualism.

On the surface the essay reviews a biography of James W. Grimes, governor of Iowa (1854–58) and U.S. senator (1859–69). Just below the surface, the essay eulogizes Grimes. And a little further below, it eulogizes public discourse and brave political action in America. Hill portrays Grimes as a political and public hero who strived to preserve America and American politics from its own worst habits.[56]

Historically, Grimes is best known for joining seven other Republicans who broke ranks with their party and voted against Johnson's impeachment, which failed by a single vote. Of these seven, only Grimes and his close friend William P. Fessenden were returned to the Senate by their state legislatures. The others, as Hill portrays it, were martyred to the vagaries of political turmoil and public opinion. Hill portrays Grimes as a symbol, the public figure who refused to give in to such political pressure and public passion. Grimes was a symbol of the man who always endeavored to see past the emotional and the ephemeral by marshaling common sense and character. He stood up to the press and its habit of molding, then exploiting, public opinion, and he refused to compromise his beliefs either for public office or for the esteem of the public.

In portraying Grimes, Hill brings to his pro-intellectual argument many of the standard nostalgic and homely characterizations that were common to anti-intellectual hagiography as well as to the rhetoric of populism—that is, the hagiography of men like Davy Crockett and Andrew Jackson, popular favorites who made their mark by bashing intellectual Americans. This kind of anti-intellectual rhetoric had become a fixture in American hero-building during the 1830s' populist political campaigns, which heroized and secured the elections of such men as Davy Crockett and William H. Harrison. Crockett, when asked whether he would be afraid to address the House of

Representatives, with all its educated and cultured members, replied, no, because he could "whip any man in it." The man who enjoyed leisure, comfort, or ornament had also become ineligible for herohood with the rise of populist political campaigning. One of the principal issues during the 1840s campaign was Harrison's lowly log cabin and Van Buren's installation of some bathtubs into the White House (see Hofstadter 161–66; and Antczak 12–54).

To counter such anti-intellectual appeals, Hill, it might be said, was engaging in "anti-anti-intellectual" rhetoric. That is, he was responding to the ubiquitous anti-intellectual rhetoric, appropriating its terms and assumptions, and arguing that it was in fact the intellectuals—not the capitalists and other self-made philistine imbeciles—who were the true masculine men of action and decision. Grimes, argues Hill, was a plain man of plain speech; he possessed character and he spoke and abided by the truth.

> Mr. Grimes belonged to a class of public men, happily not yet extinct, but peculiar to the earlier days of the Republic rather than to ours. Gifted with no extraordinary intellectual powers, armed with few of a scholar's weapons, with little taste for the ornamental part of life, he was pre-eminently a man of character. . . . He prized action above speech, speech straight to the point above *speech rhetorical*, and speech to the audience nominally addressed above *speech to the galleries or the newspapers*. (108, my emphases)

It is important to see, first, how Hill deploys "rhetorical" as a disparaging term, placing it alongside "unmanliness." He also places it in a parallel relationship with "speech to the galleries of the newspapers": Grimes preferred face-to-face ("man to man") debate over speeches designed to read well in the newspapers.[57] Later in his career, in his lectures and his rhetorics, Hill would denominate the newspaper writing style as effeminate.

Hill addresses and reverses another aspect of anti-intellectual rhetoric: the popular charge that the unselfish civic concern—the role of the reformer—was an effeminate task and revealed a lack of self-integration. Hofstadter characterizes this particular aspect of anti-intellectual rhetoric:

> As the politicians put it, they, the bosses and party workers, had to function in the bitter world of reality in which the common people also had to live and earn their living. This was not the sphere of morals and ideals, of education and culture: it was the hard, masculine sphere of business and politics. The reformers, they said, claimed to be unselfish; but . . . [in] the hard-driving, competitive, ruthless, materialistic world of the Gilded Age, to be unselfish

suggested not purity but a *lack of self*, a lack of capacity for grappling with reality, a *lack of assertion, of masculinity*. (186, my emphases)

Anti-intellectual rhetoric, then, employs as its key terms manliness, action, and self-integration through self-interest. It paints intellectuals and social reformers as effeminate sophists who would rather make fine distinctions and fine speeches than take action, and who are without core beliefs or a core self. Hill tries to turn such rhetoric on its head by pointing out that (1) it is public opinion—especially as ballyhooed through the newspaper— that has no core and that alters itself with the winds, (2) that real manhood[58] and real struggle (perhaps even real agonia) lie in facing down the politicians and the public, the most fearsome of all opponents. Grimes, Hill says, is one of the very few "men that can stand four-square against all the winds that blow," resisting "the behests of party newspapers . . . or the howlings of a partisan mob" and choosing instead "self-respect."[59] As in the Greeley essay, Hill again concludes with a rhetorical flurry, employing accumulation and anaphora to provide a sense of dramatic closure.

> By the winds that blew in Washington during the three months of the [Johnson impeachment] trial, a man of ordinary courage might easily have been daunted. . . . To stand up to an opposing party, however violent its attacks, is comparatively easy: but to be made to feel that you are considered a traitor; . . . to be called a lost leader . . . to receive by every mail scores of newspapers, which have hitherto supported you, but are now your bitterest assailants; . . . to feel, in a word all the currents of public opinion . . . now setting against you,—such things as these it requires unusual courage to meet. Such a trial Mr. Webster passed through after his 7th of March speech; and such a test was successfully endured by Mr. Grimes, though not without a great strain on his powers of endurance, as was evinced by the stroke of paralysis by which he was prostrated two days after he delivered his opinion that the President had not been guilty of an impeachable offense. (192–93)

This passage, like the rest of the essay, blends together the themes of manliness, struggle against popular sentiment, and exhaustion/martyrdom. (Such a model of heroism resonates with the persona Hill often assumed in his letters to Gay, as he described his battles with Greeley's popularity-driven policies and how it was taking its toll on Hill's mental and physical health.) In an earlier passage, after describing Grimes's "manly and tender" friendship with Senator Fessenden, Hill concludes "they foresaw the still darker days that have since come upon us; and they were alike fortunate in dying when they did" (187). At this point, Hill swerves into the theme of the public martyr, which he has flirted with throughout the essay.

It is interesting to note how Hill lines up the various heroes and villains in this essay. On the virtuous side, there are (1) Webster, Fessenden, and Grimes, (2) self-respect and ability to resist fickle public opinion, (3) speech that is unornamented, old-fashioned, face-to-face[60] ("speech straight" and "speech to the audience nominally addressed") (4) manliness, and (5) a losing but noble cause. On the other, less-than-virtuous, side are (1) the partisan mobs, parties, public opinion, and newspapers, (2) whatever opinion that sells newspapers, pandering to the public, (3) speech not intended to persuade the person or assembly addressed, but intended to win the approval of those who, through the newspapers, are listening in, (4) effeminacy, and (5) a sordid victory.

Hill's arguments with Greeley, the newspapers, and public (popular) culture address the unstated questions, "Who is allowed to interpret public life?" and "Whose discourse will count as legitimate?" As I will explore in the next chapter, this was also one of the questions the new university sought to address.

The Power of the Press versus the "Trickle-down" Power of Intellectuals

With the explosion of print and of literacy coupled with the technologically enabled capacity for journalism to reach the masses privately—each day— Hill and other members of the gentleman class had been displaced as speakers for American society. Whereas Channing had applauded literacy for its capacity for quelling the passions of debaters, Hill saw literacy boost the power of the few who controlled the nation's journalism. This new class did not itself supplant the elites, but they enabled popular opinion ("the floating masses of voters," as Hill called them) to supplant them.

Although today it is common to regard the newspaper as a relatively positive public force—far less menacing, for instance, than the television— for Hill and other disenfranchised elites of the nineteenth century, the newspaper had redefined society by altering what counted as public discourse and who counted as public discussant. Press historian Michael Schudson provides an ethnographic view of the nineteenth-century newspaper, illustrating how it succeeded in positioning itself as interpreter of public life and how fundamentally it altered the worldview of a nation. This was inherent in the very nature of "the news," the idea that the world might change enough each day that it warranted an entirely new six to ten pages of fine newsprint to understand it. As we saw in Channing's reaction to the news in 1817, it upset the aristocratic, Scottish Enlightenment idea of a fixed but progressing order, and it was harmful to the masses, who would only be excited by it and distracted from concentrating on more important matters. In fact, for Channing, the "news" was so novel a public-discourse phenomenon that Channing had no name for it, resorting to metaphors in order to make his definition. Channing had warned that certain forms of communicative media (specifically, oratory and "the news") fostered pernicious "habits of thinking." Hill too is concerned about what the new media of public discourse had done to Americans' "habits of thinking."

By the time Hill assumed the Boylston Professorship of Rhetoric and Oratory in 1876, it had already become a cliché that the newspaper had replaced the rostrum and the pulpit. The newspaper had become the center of public discourse. Furthermore, the content of the newspaper had changed from "criticism" to mere "intelligence," the reporting of one thing after another.[61] For Hill, then, the warnings sounded by Channing are not looming on the distant horizon; pernicious habits of thinking and of argumentation had *already* become securely embedded into American thought. Also, Channing had been involved in journalism at a time when it seemed, at least, that elite opinion dominated public discourse; his objective, therefore, lay in conserving that elite domination, whose influence seemed at worst in danger. For Hill, such elite influence had become a matter of nostalgia. His objective lay in ensuring that a limited but stable segment of the citizenry forge an "immunity" against harmful forms of discourse. The "public" of Hill's public discourse had been reduced from "the citizenry" to a small coterie of intellectuals who might transform America in a "trickle-down" fashion.

And as the century progressed, the newspaper, with its changing conventions of communication, was beginning to transform the definition not only of a "reading public" but also of "a public." As Schudson explains, the advent of the "summary lead" and the interview altered the perceived (and thus the actual) importance of the reporter and the reader. The summary lead was "a literary invention that asserted the journalist's authority to define for readers the most important elements of a news event." The interview

> promoted a novel form of communication ... in which the most important auditor, the public, was present only in the imagination. That imaginative construction of a public for whom the words of the interview were designed, helped construct and define the concept of the public itself.... [Interviewers and interviews] flatter the public, provide it an overinflated sense of its importance, encourage in its leaders not only sensitivity to public opinion but sycophantic submission to popular prejudice.[62]

Intellectuals despised and absented themselves from such journalism. While it is true they had their own publications, none of them achieved readership numbers anything like those of the dailies. Intellectuals had no place in the pages of the dailies, it seemed. Therefore, they concentrated on criticizing the cultural consequences of such discourse.

Journalism as Entertainment and the Infantalization of American Readers

I argue that Hill, in striving to expose and thereby diminish the power of the press and of popular opinion, was engaging in, as today we call it, *cultural criticism*. He wanted to "unmask" the mystery of journalism. In doing so, Hill was not in any sense alone. E. L. Godkin, the enormously influential editor of *The Nation* and of *The New-York Evening Post* (and a coauthor of the famous Harvard literacy reports), led the elite charge against newspapers (from 1865 to 1900) and sounds so thoroughly familiar to the modern ear as to be both humorous and haunting. As early as 1865, Godkin was criticizing the nation's newspapers for, in effect, altering the nature of American consciousness, for impoverishing, as we might call it now, Americans' critical literacy.

Godkin's influence among American intellectuals can hardly be overstated. As Charles Eliot Norton wrote to his friend Godkin (a quotation that seems ubiquitous in cultural histories of this era), "the *Nation* & Harvard & Yale seem to me almost the only solid barriers against the invasion of modern barbarism & vulgarity.[63] As William James wrote of Godkin, "To my generation, his was certainly the towering influence in all thought concerning public affairs, and indirectly his influence has assuredly been more pervasive than that of any other writer of the generation, for he influenced other writers who never quoted him, and determined the whole current of discussion" (quoted in Stewart and Tebbel 79). As Frank Luther Mott described the influence of Godkin via the *Nation*, though it had a modest circulation,

> the power of the *Nation* came not from the number of its readers, but from their station and influence and from the frequency with which it was quoted. And a power it rapidly became, indubitably, in both politics and letters. . . . [T]he paper stood unsupported and almost alone, an authority among the intelligent few, and an influence among newspapers, but without a powerful circulation or a remunerative advertising patronage. . . . [I]t was intellectual, critical, but not bellicose. (*A History of American Magazines* 3:339, 341)

Tebbel and Zuckerman, in their more recent history, concur: The *Nation* had "a trickle-down influence on large numbers of people. It was quoted frequently in pulpit and press, and its ideas were sometimes the subject of debate in Congress" (122).

I quote at length two passages from Godkin's press criticism that resonate particularly well with some of the current criticism of the mass media because I want to punctuate the similarities between Channing's media criticism, this middle- and late-nineteenth-century media criticism, and the media criticism of our own age. Newspapers, argues Godkin in 1865, are *creating* a new kind of reader, one more interested in entertainment than in enlightenment and increasingly incapable of critical engagement. These readers were passive in character and increasingly demanded—and received—spoon-fed intelligence, which was becoming difficult to distinguish from (as today we call it) "entertainment."[64] Newspapers were participating in the creation of an infantilized citizenry.

> We find that one large class objects to the *Nation* on the ground that it requires them "to think"; and this is invariably spoken of as a great hardship. . . . [T]he habit of reading or talking at all except for amusement, and any demand on their reflective powers they look upon as a species of extortion. They like "light stories," "pleasing anecdotes," and would like to have all the great questions of the time disposed of in at most half a column. . . . The glimpse we get of the feelings of this class on this subject gives one a tolerably fair idea of the influence of the daily press upon them. ("The Newspaper and the Reader" 165)

Thirty-four years later, in 1890, Godkin continues his attacks, blaming the newspaper for diminishing the *attention span* of Americans so that novels are the only thing they can read:

> Now, nothing can be more damaging to *the habit of continuous attention* than newspaper-reading. . . . [I]t never requires the mind to be fixed on any topic more than three or four minutes, and . . . every topic furnishes a complete change of scene. The result for the habitual newspaper-reader is a mental desultoriness, which ends by making a book on any one subject more or less repulsive. ("Newspapers Here and Abroad" 202, my emphasis)

He concludes with typical intellectual resignation: "The new generation which the public schools are pouring out in tens of millions is getting its tastes, opinions, and standards from [newspapers], and what sort of world this will produce a hundred years hence nobody knows."[65]

As Godkin's criticism suggests, what intellectuals feared about the newspaper was its cultural *infectiousness*. That is, the newspaper not only *appealed* to readers who are habitually passive and disengaged ("ignoramuses" and "idiots," as Godkin calls them), but it also *created* such readers. As Hill would later argue, not only was the public at large suffering from such infected habits of discourse, but so too were incoming university students. Therefore, the struggle with profit-driven public opinion and public habits of thinking would be taken into the classroom.

Both intellectuals and the profit-driven philistines of journalism (to use the intellectuals' terms) had vied for public opinion, and, in the popular public sector, it was the philistines clearly who had triumphed. What is more, patrician intellectuals were, as Hofstadter and Trachtenberg observe, painfully aware of and frustrated at their marginalization from society and from decision making of all sorts. One of their principal strategies for regaining, or conserving, some social power lay in the modern university. As I will suggest, the composition classroom played an important role in rescuing the citizen/student from the uncritical immersion in the unhealthful journalistic rhetorical practices of his day.

5

A. S. Hill (ii)

Reforming the Public and Its Discourse at the Modern University and in the Writing Course

We are now dealing with a generation which has grown up under the newspapers, and the "Americanism" of the schoolbooks. . . . The newspapers stand between this generation and the light and make it hard to get at them. . . . College culture somehow does not get down among the masses quickly enough to affect politics.

—E. L. Godkin

The best teacher of English composition is he who stimulates his pupils to put their natural selves into all that they write.

—A. S. Hill[1]

The Modern University and Social Reform

Postbellum Harvard had a new, high-profile, progressive-minded president in Charles W. Eliot, who, more than anyone else, emblematized and led the way to the revolutionary changes occurring in American higher education. He happens to have been a classmate of Hill's from the Harvard class of 1853. This German-educated professor of chemistry, who had taught at Harvard for several years and had become well known for his innovative ideas about education,[2] was elected president in 1869. His inaugural address is generally considered (and it was certainly considered by Harvardians and other close watchers of the contemporary educational scene) the bell-wether address in the transformation of the American university: higher education in America would move away from the classical and liberal-arts curriculum, which had been designed for producing gentlemen who would take positions at the bar, the pulpit, and the lectern; it would move toward elective-system and disciplines-oriented curricula, which were designed for producing graduates who could enter an increasingly professionalized world and guide the nation into a new century. This new era would be guided by objectivity, reason, scientific inquiry, expertise, and practicality. The new American university was moving away from the ideals of so-called "liberal culture" and the "well-rounded man."

Eliot did not pull these ideas out of thin air, of course. For decades, there had been significant debate about what a college should look like, what it should do, how it should prepare graduates, and who should do the preparing. As Frederick Rudolph explains, educators felt the time was right for changing the character of the American college and university. There was a sense that the public mind was at that moment in a "plastic, impressionable state," ready to accept new ideals and practices of education (241–63). The passage of the Morrill Federal Land Grant Act of 1862 was in part a response to the growing sentiment that the new age would require new kinds of practical training, including scientific, agricultural, and technical preparation and research. The year of Eliot's inauguration is also the year that Cornell University opened its doors, a university explicitly committed to uniting practical and liberal learning. Cornell's first president, Andrew D. White, convinced Ezra Cornell that the university ought to do more than train citizens in various trades, but must "train what White later referred to as 'captains in the army of industry' " (Rudolph 266).

Eliot, in similar fashion, wanted Harvard and other institutions to prepare graduates who would make an impact on the public world beyond the academy, a newly educated elite that would guide the nation not only in its moral and ethical affairs but also in its practical duties. Forever changed in America was not only higher education, but also what counted as knowledge. Forever changed was the relationship between university culture and American culture in general. Hill, like most of those involved in the modern American university, faced the challenge of making his teaching relevant to the needs not only of the student but also of society.

So it is true, certainly, that Eliot's Harvard would no longer turn its back on society but engage with it in meaningful and socially useful ways, even to the extent of preparing a corps of business leaders. However, this ought not imply that Eliot or other leading thinkers and teachers at Harvard wanted their ideas and their students *merely* to fit in with society. The "manly ideal" at Harvard, as Kim Townsend has argued in *Manhood at Harvard*, meant

above all *grappling* with real social problems, most often resisting the commonplace beliefs and attitudes of American culture rather than accommodat-
ing oneself to them wholesale. Nonetheless, *some accommodation* was
essential if Harvard's "messianic mission," as Townsend calls it, of social
reform were to be effective. Independence of mind and "mental resistance"
were crucial. Furthermore, for William James and others, one achieved such
mental toughness through an act of sheer will and by cultivating "habits"
that would allow one to take full control over one's life. However, insularity
from the public and obsession with abstractions over practical affairs were
just as problematic as being overrun by public sentiment. Real men grappled
with the public in the public sphere. In spirit at least, and probably in effect,
the ideal Harvardian scholar would shed the role of disinterested spectator for
the role of active, critical public participant.[3]

This manly ideal of the scholar is reflected in a late essay of Hill's, "The
Influence of Emerson" (1896). Here he holds up Ralph Waldo Emerson as
an ideal scholar who simultaneously remains independent of public sentiment and engages it directly. For one thing, Emerson succeeded in
influencing American culture. When Emerson began his career America
was indeed "unlovely": "we were a vulgar people, pursuing vulgar ends in
a vulgar spirit" (36). But Emerson changed that: "If Americans worship the
Almighty Dollar a little less than they do, the change, though coming no
doubt from many causes, is to be credited to Emerson more than any one
person" (38). He accomplished this by speaking to all Americans, not only
holding up lofty ideals but by addressing "plain people [with] . . . his good
sense" (28). They were "drawn toward Emerson by his manliness": "The
public never confounded him with the weaklings of culture, whose selfishness
differs from that of ordinary men chiefly in the fact that it has less muscle:
With Emerson culture meant true manhood" (27). That is, Emerson did not
undertake the "effeminate" act of remaining in his library or addressing
only high-brow audiences. In a formulation resembling Frederick Jackson
Turner's "frontier hypothesis" (1893), Hill says Emerson brought intellectual life and practical life together and brought about a synthesis: "Emerson's
originality," which defines the best of American character, "lay neither in
his old-world philosophy nor in his new-world shrewdness, but in the union
of the two" (26). If the "current sneers at 'literary fellers' . . . [and] college
professors" (31), are to be dealt with, if contemporary scholars are to enjoy
"the influence of Emerson," Hill suggests in this article published in *Studies and Notes in Philology and Literature*, they too must effect such a
synthesis.

And even beyond Harvard, for patrician intellectuals, nothing would
have been more distasteful than joining, as Tocqueville called it, "the tyr-
anny of the majority." Rather, men like Eliot, Godkin (second author of the

Harvard "literacy reports" of 1893), Charles Francis Adams (primary author of the "literacy reports"), and A. S. Hill wished to challenge the popular public sentiment. Although their instincts may have been to merely ignore such sentiment, most often they strived to confront and oppose anti-intellectual sentiment, which distrusted serious argumentation and distrusted inquiry that strived always to remain detached from the hard and hearty world of commerce, politics, and action. As Hofstadter describes intellectual/academic culture during the Gilded Age, it was "estranged" not only from power but also from "public opinion." Freedom of inquiry and scientific objectivity (though men like Eliot used the term "neutrality") were absolutely vital to the universities' new mission. The "freedom" aspect of higher education—as in "academic freedom"—implied freedom *from* politics and public opinion. As Walter P. Metzger writes:

> Indeed, from Tocqueville to Lippmann, no group was more critical of the workings of public opinion than the theorists of academic freedom. . . . In sponsoring the public interests, therefore, American theorists were sponsoring something that transcended all the current and ephemeral forms of its expression. Like Rousseau, they found the true will and need for the public to lie not in the public's own transient notions, but in something more nebulous and abstract. (Hofstadter and Metzger 399–400)

Hill's popular writings on college composition and literacy reveal that he concurred with Harvard's manly ideal and with general patrician intellectual attitudes about society: the composition course, for Hill, was not intended to prepare students to fit in with, for instance, the new "managerial capitalism," but was to oppose a pernicious popular culture that had seized control over the nation's reading material—and thus the citizenry's reading habits. Sound rhetorical training, thought Hill, might endow students with the resistance they needed to oppose an all-too-enticing culture of the newspaper and the dime novel.[4]

Hill's "popular writing" on Greeley and Grimes (chapter 4) is important to my argument because it demonstrates that Hill was not simply some Harvard alumnus—a friend and classmate of the new president—who had journalistic experience and who could thus teach Harvard students to become proficient in various forms of professional writing. Hill's writings grapple with and *criticize* popular forms of public discourse. In criticizing the habits of communication of Greeley and of Grimes's detractors, Hill is calling for forms of public discourse with different, *higher* standards. With this in mind, Eliot's appointment of Hill to the Boylston Professorship becomes more understandable: Hill had been in the trenches of the rough-

and-tumble world of journalism and politics and had tried in his own ways to alter its course.

The Public Health of Learning to Write: Resistance to Public Discourse

In documenting Hill's ideas on these matters, I turn to his collection of popular writings, *Our English*, which consists of five essays that originally appeared in *Harper's*, *Scribner's*, and *The Christian Register*. It is here—and not in his influential textbooks—that Hill discusses the relationships between writing and reading and American culture. Here Hill expressed the *ideal* role for composition and for the university, as a kind of protector of student health—linguistic health, which is closely related, for Hill, to the moral health of the individual and of a society. (Whether Hill practiced these ideals in the classroom or in his textbooks is a problem I address later in this chapter.) By analyzing Hill's published work through the lens of its cultural and biographical contexts, we might find that many of our basic assumptions about Hill and his ideas about composition are problematic.

One issue of composition historiography complicated by *Our English* is "the doctrine of mechanical correctness." For one thing, the issue of rhetoric's fetishization of prescriptive grammar was a much-discussed issue among Hill's contemporaries, and Hill (as well as others) perceived his mission as directly opposing such arid instructions, devoid of larger rhetorical contexts. As one reviewer of Hill's *Foundations of Rhetoric* put it, Hill's textbook, unlike many of its competitors, does not "suffer from the reproach of arid technicality" ("*The Foundations*" 294). On the other hand, some contemporaries thought Hill's textbooks were among the offenders. A review of *Foundations of Rhetoric* appearing in *The Nation* faults Hill's textbook for making such "fine distinctions, such prohibitions of words in current and, in some cases reputable colloquialism and written use" that the book is in danger of "repel[ling] the young student's confidence, [and] perhaps mak[ing] him mistrust the authority of principles administered so rigidly." The reviewer then advocates the "incidental method," which urges the young writer to regard the conventions of language as tools for effective expression as he or she uses language for communicating some thought that he or she finds interesting enough to take seriously.

It must be noted, however, that these suggestions for teaching rhetoric incidentally reflect almost precisely those made by Hill himself and by the authors of the Harvard "literacy reports." As Adams and colleagues put it in 1897:

> The problem is to increase to a very great extent the work in
> written English now done in the preparatory schools, and at the

same time largely to change its character. . . . The solution seems
to be simple;—English should be taught in the preparatory schools
not, as now, altogether objectively, but incidentally, and in connection with other studies—mathematics, geography, history and especially, foreign languages and the Classics. . . . In this way, the
scholars would be accustomed before entering college to use written English as a means, and not merely as an end. (Adams et al.
113–14)

It is worth noting as well that the literacy reports do not resort to a nostalgia for a time when college students could write well (as has been suggested by Russell 3–10). To the contrary, the authors were well aware that
a shift in communications—changes in technology are explicitly men-
tioned—had radically altered the exigencies of college education, creating
new demands that had not *yet* been addressed. In fact, one of the lifelong
missions of the reports' principal author, Charles Francis Adams, lay in
reforming the old systems of English instruction, which he found worthless, dull, and incapable of preparing students for the world they would face
after college (see Lodge; Adams, "A College Fetish"; Kirkland 187–200).

Hill, too, advocated "the indirect method of teaching the rudiments of
English" (*Our English* 42). As he put it, good English should be treated
"not as a thing by itself, but as part and parcel of every study in which the
mother-tongue is used" (40).

The English of a boy's formal essay . . . may be, and often is, merely
words that serve no purpose, and seem to him to serve none,
except that of filling the prescribed number of pages . . . ; in the
formal essay he has, or thinking he has, nothing to say on the
subject given out, and he is usually supplied with nothing definite
to guide his mind and steady his steps. (43)

For Hill, the goal of the incidental method was not merely to help students
write grammatically flawless prose that possessed clarity and succinctness.
"Many teachers . . . act as if they thought it more important that a boy
should spell and punctuate correctly than that he should write an essay
which is a pleasure to read" (8–9). Rather than concentrating on a "frigid
correctness," the "teacher should leave free play to individuality, remembering that an opinion which is a boy's own is worth more to him than the
most orthodox dogmas taken at second hand" (31).

Indeed, it is ironic that Hill would be labeled as one of the great pro-
genitor-villains of the "doctrine of mechanical correctness." (This is not to
say that Hill should be absolved of all responsibility, only that his *intentions*

appear to have been much different.) For Hill, poor grammar and lack of clarity and cohesion were *symptoms* of a larger, more important issue. There was something else, contended Hill, that caused "the touch of a pen or pencil [to] paralyz[e] [students'] powers" (14). One problem was *too much* dry, uncontextualized grammatical instruction. The other more important problem was the homogeneity of student compositions—as Hill puts it, a "tedious mediocrity" (13). "[T]here is a dead level, rarely varied by a fresh thought or an individual expression. Almost all the writers use the same commonplace vocabulary—a very small one—in the same unintelligent way" (13). Hill wonders what could have brought about this low(ly) order of homogenization among "the picked youth of the country, . . . all with blood in their veins, and brains in their heads, . . . [m]any of [whom] came from the best families in point of culture and breeding, and from the best schools we have" (14).

This tedious mediocrity—its causes and its remedies—is a principal focus of *Our English*, which addresses, far more explicitly than anything in Hill's textbooks, the methods and the goals of learning to write. The book's opening page, a single epigraph from Coleridge, illuminates how Hill desires his work on elite literacy to be taken: as an effort to directly engage and counteract the powerful influence of popular discourse.

> In prose I doubt whether it be even possible to preserve our style wholly unalloyed by the vicious phraseology which meets us everywhere, from the sermon to the newspaper, from the harangue of the legislator to the speech from the convivial chair, announcing a *toast* or sentiment. Our chains rattle even while we are complaining of them. . . . Much, however, may be effected by education. (S. T. Coleridge, *Biographica Literaria*)

"*Our* English," then, is the English that is threatened by the "vicious phraseology that meets us everywhere," an imposter English, an imposter means of communication. "*Our* English" will serve to countervail those forces of popular culture.

The "tedious mediocrity" of student compositions is caused by students' efforts at emulating the discourse they find in newspapers and in the other trash they read. By immersing himself or herself so fully in popular writing, the student loses touch with his or her individuality and thus reproduces the cultural verities and cultural forms of writing. The most important goal for the teacher of writing, then, is helping the student to rediscover this real self: "A wise teacher of English will try to make his pupils put their *real selves behind the pen, and keep them there*" (46, my emphasis). In other works on composition, Hill consistently (in fact, repeatedly) traces problems in student writing to problems that students have in knowing *who they are*. For instance, in an 1899 work for the *Educational Review* within a passage that discusses students' vocabulary, Hill writes:

> The quality of language which pervades the mass of the examination books is commonplaceness. . . . Much of the writing is characterized by what I have termed in my notes "a mixture of boy and book." By this I mean that the writers do not *put their real selves behind the pen and keep them there*. They make sudden attempts to be Shakspere, or some other writer, and as suddenly fall back into their own personalities. The resulting combination of bookish and boyish expressions is often very amusing. ("Sub-Freshman English" 479, my emphasis)

And as he says in the second chapter of his preface in *Beginnings of Rhetoric and Composition* (1902, a textbook for secondary students), "The best teacher of English is he who stimulates his pupils to *put their natural selves into all that they write*" (3, my emphasis).

Hill wants his students to think and to write in more sophisticated and complex ways. The means for accomplishing this are, for Hill, simple—and for us, simplistic. And yet Hill shares a sentiment that is similar to contemporary arguments about contemporary students' tendency to move to premature closure and to remain satisfied with solving a pressing problem with a mere comment. Hill sizes up the most pressing problem for composition this way:

> [The teacher] should discourage his pupils from announcing platitudes as if they were oracles, and from apologizing for them as if they were original sin; from dealing with a moral question either as if they had long ago lost their relish for cakes and ale, or as if there were nothing but cakes and ale worth living for; from writing stories that strive to be original, and succeed in being morbid or grotesque, or that outrealist modern realists in the trivialities they photograph and in their ostentatious lack of plot and *dénoument*. (91–92)

Thus students do not *lack* the mental powers that are necessary for such complex forms of thinking. Rather, because they have learned to emulate the discourse of popular culture (trying to "outrealist modern realists"), their natural powers have merely gone dormant, have been overwhelmed by contemporary models of public writing. To awaken the students' critical faculties from the culturally induced slumber, the teacher should "stimulate their minds, so that they may put forth their full powers when they write, and put them forth naturally and with the force of their individuality" (93).

Notice how Hill portrays these writers' powers as having been weakened by newspapers and other cheap reading materials. What should be natural to them, what he called a strong and masculine style, has become infirm and debilitated. Note how Hill suggests that what students need is training to make their moral and stylistic health more robust, which will protect them from such assaults on who they are naturally or should be.

This was a problem not only for the writing classroom but also for the classroom of life, for healthy citizenship. As early as 1865, E. L. Godkin had criticized contemporary newspapers on similar grounds, explicitly condemning newspapers for their part in creating unreflective readers.

> We find that one large class objects to the *Nation* on the grounds that it requires them "to think"; and this in invariably spoken of a great hardship. . . . [I]n the daily press, . . . the weightiest questions of morals and politics are settled in from three to five lines, or an opponent [is] squelched by some pleasant thought. . . . [I]t would puzzle one to make out how a community can get along in which thinking is so carefully avoided by so large a proportion of it that it has become painful . . . [I]t is impossible not to conclude that there is a much larger portion of the community than any one who is interested in its highest welfare would like to believe, who do deliberately cultivate both in themselves and in their children the habit of avoiding reflection. ("The Newspaper and the Reader" 165–66)[5]

Newspapers and novels, writes Hill, are the primary culprits in weakening the capacity for critical thought and expression. The predominance of such reading has homogenized the American mind, and more specifically the minds of college students. "To read nothing but newspapers and second-rate novels," warns Hill, "tends to weaken the powers of attention and of concentration, to diminish, if not to destroy, freshness of thought and individuality of expression, and to relax the mental fibre" (*Our English* 106). Again, this was a common complaint. As Godkin writes in 1890, "The result for the habitual newspaper-reader is a mental desultoriness, which ends by making a book on any one subject more or less repulsive" ("Newspapers Here and Abroad" 202). Sound rhetorical training, for Hill, should counteract these powerful culture models: "Therefore," rather than relaxing their critical faculties, "educated men should *arm themselves* at all points against the numerous foes that beset pure English on every side, in these days of free speech and free press. *Noblesse Oblige*" (78, *Our English* first italics mine).

In fact, writes Hill, newspapers are defining an entirely new philosophy of composition, one that values conformity, rapidity of composing, and grandiloquence over individuality, thoughtfulness, and concision. Hill identified lack of concision with newspaper writing and called it "feminine." "Manly" writing used Anglo-Saxon words and reigned its passions and its copiousness to the concise minimum. The newspaper reporter (the "news-*gatherer*") and the modern novelist were defining—for American culture and thus for students—the nature of composing and of the composed prod-uct. The egregious grammar and use of slang used by these writers is pernicious, but to criticize these things, comments Hill, "would be to go into minutiæ foreign to my purpose" (120). Most harmful are their *models* of composing. Such ubiquitous and enticing models lead students to their habitual pronouncement of clichés and their abandonment of individual expression and thought. The articles one reads in newspapers "smack of the mill, the writer sinking his individuality in that of the journal to which he contributes. Even if he had the desire, he has not the time to be himself, as he has not the time to be concise" (118–19). The novelist has a "better chance" of expressing individuality, "but he also is in haste to get his wares to market, and is inspired by the idols of the market-place rather than by the spirit within" (119).

However, newspaper work—like newspaper English—poses a "special" danger to the moral and linguistic health of even the most cultured of individuals. College must prepare such students to enter this unwholesome environment, so that students might inhabit it without suffering its ravages. Such preparation should endow the student with resistance, which is especially important at this time, Hill says, because more and more students are entering journalism as a profession—"because of late years large numbers of them have taken to the pen for a living, and because they are *exposed to special dangers*" (138, my emphasis). The temptation to resort to the lowly standards of newspaper English are enormous. Even the

> "liberally educated" youth, who knows all that Murray and Blair can teach him, is tempted, when he discovers (as he is pretty sure to do) his inferiority in some respects to the self-educated reporter at the desk by his side who began life as an office-boy, but who has "the newspaper sense," and has mastered the tricks of the trade— is tempted, and sometimes yields to the temptation, to sacrifice his English to his desire to attract attention. (138)

Such a youth can withstand "the chilling influences" of the news room only if "his English is hardy" (137–38). Then the young reporter might use his English, "not as an end in itself, but as a means to something more important[:] . . . [his English may be] felt in his little world as a *purifying and inspiring force*" (139, my emphasis). Young writers must not only be given the *ability* to write well, but must also be endowed with what Hill calls "moral stamina" (107). Moral stamina is necessary to resist the temptation to allow one's writing to suffer from a kind of disintegration—and disintegration of language was intimately connected, for Hill, to the disintegration of "individuality," of the self. When writers fail to put "their real selves behind the pen," they become *not* themselves, but products of their culture, spouting forth the empty-headed clichés of an empty-headed culture. American culture, for Hill, had little to do with one's genuine self. "To the extent that [a writer] fails to put himself into his work," writes Hill, "he becomes what is known as a hack writer, a mere beast of burden that serves as a common carrier for the thoughts of other men."[6] As I will discuss later, while the profession of journalism is potentially a noble calling (a kind of civic virtue, even), it poses special dangers—loss of, or invasion of, the self.

For Hill, as for the Scottish Common Sense rationalists and for other nineteenth-century American composition theorists, the ability to write well involved more than erecting a facade of language, but signified something much more fundamental and much more important. Good, coherent, moral writing signified a "good," "coherent," "moral" "self" behind the pen. Thus, Hill insists—he seems, in fact, obsessed with the point—that the writing teacher must allow writers to offer forth their *true* selves, not some imposter self that serves merely as the "beast of burden of other men's thoughts."

According to the Common Sense school, as for Channing, for Hill, and for English-department apologists, "human nature" was universal among humankind, and the best way to enable students to understand that human nature was to expose them to the great works of great minds. By coming into contact with the works of genius—the most beautiful productions of the "natural aristocracy"—persons not only strengthened and refined their faculties of taste, but also discovered their "true" nature—"human nature," their "true self." One becomes *more* oneself by coming into contact with the genius of eras past. In turn, one becomes *less* the product of one's current society, which, for Hill, had everything to do with profit-making and popularity and almost nothing to do with the universal standards of taste propriety, reason, and virtue.

For Hill, as for his teacher Channing, students become more "themselves"—they are "carried beyond [themselves]"—by examining great writers.

What the text-book helps him to do consciously, familiarity with superior writers ought to help him to do unconsciously. Surrendering himself to the influence of genius, he will be carried beyond himself, his mind will work more freely than usual, and his sentences will reproduce his thoughts in more perspicuous and more telling language. . . . [C]ontact with greater minds . . . feed[s] the powers of thought and the powers of expression at the same time, and thus enables one to think, to talk, and to write to more purpose. (82–83)

In this sense, then, Hill sounds more like a Ken Macrorie or Peter Elbow than the Hill that has been portrayed in composition historiography. In theory at least, Hill wanted the writing student to strive for "natural" expression, to "forget himself in what he is writing" (6), "surrendering himself to the influence of genius," which is within him, as it is within all persons. Helping students get to this place, teachers help "students put their real selves behind the pen."

Composition as Preparation for Civic Virtue: The Importance of "Efficiency" for Accommodating Writing to the Demands of the Age

But "mental resistance" could only do part of the work for bringing about what Hill thought was the social mission of the college educated and the intellectual. In order to engage and reform the world, the writer had to make the world *listen*. Writing instruction and the writer had to strike an accommodation between the lofty ideals of the university and what the public, with its new attention structures, would hear.

Hill recognizes "people will not give up reading ephemeral publications" (135); in fact, such reading will most likely continue to grow in degree and in cultural influence, owing to changes in the technologies of communication, in hierarchies of literacy, and in the nature of authorship and readership. The newspaper was both seductive and dangerous because *anyone* could read it. In fact, among the most common of the intellectuals' complaints was the lamenting that newspapers were targeted to the lower classes of America, and newspaper reading was therefore pulling down the entire nation. The "lowest common denominator" argument was widespread during this era, and not only in Hill's and Godkin's criticism. For instance, James Bryce—"the most famous English visitor in the later nineteenth century" (Bledstein 48)— wrote in 1895:

The cause of [American newspapers'] deficiency is probably to be found in the fact that . . . American journals were . . . written for the bulk of the people. . . . [Newspapers] had attained no high level of literary excellence when some forty years ago an enterprising man of unrefined taste [i.e., Horace Greeley] created a new type of "live" newspaper, which made a rapid success by its smartness, copiousness, and variety, while addressing itself entirely to the multitude. . . . [T]hey still think first of the mass and are controlled by its taste, which they have themselves done so much to create. (775–76)

Even worse, almost anyone could *write* for newspapers; too many with too few qualifications are "at liberty to publish."[7] Hill quotes Englishman Thomas Frost ("Reminiscences of a Country Journalist," 1886) at length:

"The diffusion of elementary education . . . which flooded mercantile offices with clerks whose qualifications were limited to the ability to write legibly and add up columns of figures, has, for several years past, had the result of overrunning the reporterial [*sic*] . . . market with lads whose sole qualifications for reporting is the knowledge of short-hand. As a rule, these young gentlemen are ignorant of grammar, in many instances cannot spell correctly, know little or nothing of modern history, the knowledge of which is essential to a journalist, and whenever condensation is required are apt to make their sentences unintelligible." (*Our English* 108–9)

Therefore, argues Hill, intellectuals should not turn their backs on the American press, wishing it away, but, engage the problem at its very foundations. Hill advocates that "[m]en and women of culture and of high aims must be encouraged to write for the public" (137).[8]

As Nan Johnson shows, this sentiment of civic virtue—that the capable person uses his or her abilities to promote the social good—was at the foundation of Scottish Common Sense rhetoric and of American rhetoric as well. It was at the heart of Harvard's "messianic" social mission. Persons who had cultivated the faculty of taste were best able to envision civic virtue and it was their civic duty to help the rest of society to comprehend that vision. Hill, in his own way, confused and probably unsuccessful, adhered to this civic vision.

What Hill did not do, I think to his credit, was to simply turn his back (or ask students or his fellow scholars to turn their backs) on popular forms of public writing. In fact, Hill called for an accommodation of scholarly and student writing to the new forms of "attention," which had been created by new forms of writing, most notably the newspaper.

But for Hill—one of the disenfranchised, frustrated, patrician intellectuals of late-nineteenth-century America, who felt very much at odds with dominant American culture—there were other factors to contend with. Hill feared that American youth was becoming lost to the alluring ideas and attitudes pandered by newspaper and low-order novels—even the youth from his class, coming "from the best families in point of culture and breeding, and from the best schools we have." But Hill and his fellow patrician intellectuals were painfully aware that they had lost access to the majority of readers, whose tastes had become warped by the crass, profit-motivated institution of the newspaper. As Hill laments:

> Most of us would probably find it difficult to induce the editor of a newspaper to put our thoughts . . . into type. . . . Our contributions to a newspaper would probably lack the very qualities that give success to editorial articles, which, though far from being models of good English, suit, nevertheless, the intelligence and taste of their public, . . . written in language that would make Addison turn in his grave, containing the facts which people want to know, and stating them in such a fashion that a hasty reader understands them at once. (112–13)

The newspaper had become the center of public discourse, and there was no place for the intellectual in its columns—at least not the traditional intellectual who merely disdained the masses. Whereas Channing had been fairly satisfied with merely turning his and his students' backs on society (finding the two worlds incommensurable), Hill acknowledges the difficulty of intellectual reform but also anxiously desires some sort of influence on popular public discourse. Composition ought to prepare students to enter these new forms of discourse.

Engaging Popular Public Discourse While Still Resisting It

Hill's desire to protect his students from the popular press may lie behind the obsessive attention to grammatical improprieties (despite his insistence in *Our English* that they were not really so important to him). Historian Donald Stewart says Hill "was obsessed with these mechanical matters. . . . [and] the doctrine of correctness won the day" ("Some History Lessons" 17). But even if it is true that Hill was something of a linguistic fussbudget, he was at least not a nostalgic fussbudget. He believed that in some senses the nature of public writing had *improved*—even some of the writing and reading habits that had come from or had been reinforced by the American newspaper. (He could not or would not reject *all* that he learned from those men he admired in journalism.) Throughout *Our English* Hill speaks of students' (and the citizenry's) "exposure" to bad English and how we must be "on guard" and "hearty" if we are to resist. But we must do more than merely endow our students with a linguistic constitution that would help them resist what predominates (badly) as public discourse; public discourse itself must be reformed. At one point he calls "English in newspapers and novels" a "poison," but asks further, "Can we do nothing but provide an antidote? Is there no way of keeping the poison out of the system?" (135)

Because "in these days of free speech and free press" men of Hill's class no longer have the power of censorship, they must engage with the public on its own terms. If their writing and their students' writing are to mean something—if their writing, to use Susan Miller's term, is to be "transitive" rather than "intransitive"—it must engage the public with all its current tastes (good or bad) and address topics of public interest, and in a *form* that appeals to that public.

The public has changed, and in fact changed, in some senses, for the better. Specifically, readers now desire directness, clarity, and above all brevity. This "movement towards this ideal" (222) can be witnessed, he suggests, in writing since Dryden's times: "When . . . the reading public came to include many persons of both sexes who were far from being scholars, writers [such as Johnson, Addison, Swift, and Defoe] naturally adapted themselves to the tastes of the majority" (233–34). More recently, Hill writes, in America, discourse has progressed from the "highfaluten" to the "colloquial," at political rallies, the bar, literary festivals, and college commencements (222–25). There is, apparently, no sin in a little conformity; in fact, it can be a virtue (and even manly) when the writer conforms in order to have an impact on an audience.

In his chapter "English in the Pulpit," Hill explains why the clergy has been marginalized by society, why nobody listens to them anymore: they cannot speak *to* their audience's tastes. Audiences today value efficiency, and this, for Hill, represents progress. Therefore, he gives to preachers the same advice he gives his students: be brief and clear *in part because* you are speaking to an audience that is accustomed to and desires concision and directness.

> [An effective] preacher knows that, if he would hold his own against the platform, against books, magazines, and newspapers, he must be short and to the point, must in his first sentence strike the keynote of his discourse, and must keep that note ringing in the ear. . . . [H]e must not only have something to say, but he must say that something as briefly and vigorously as is consistent with perfect clearness and perfect taste, and in as orderly a manner as is consistent with ease and flexibility of expression. (163)

In part, then, American speakers must adapt their discourses to their audiences, whose tastes and attention structures have changed.

An economic, efficient style was more affective in public discourse, just as more prolix styles had been effective in the past. But Hill must make a careful distinction between *present* and *reputable* linguistic use. In terms of what counts as good usage, Hill echoes precisely George Campbell's *Philosophy of Rhetoric* (1776), in fact, duplicating his word order and italics: good usage is defined by what is *"reputable, national,* and *present"* (Campbell 151; Hill, *Principles* 6). Both authors are particularly careful in distinguishing "reputable" from "present." Campbell admonishes his readers from suspecting good usage can be reliably found in "the lower walks of life" (142): "Use in language requires firmer ground to stand upon. . . . It is important to have some certain, steady, and well-known standard. . . . And this can be no other than the authors of reputation." And "reputable authors" themselves cannot be defined according to "the esteem of the public" but only by their "intrinsic merit" (144). Hill follows Campbell's guidelines precisely, though far more concisely:

> *Reputable use* is fixed, not by the practice of those whom A or B deems the best speakers or writers, but by that of those whom the world deems the best,—not the little world in which A or B moves, but the world of intelligent people. . . . The practice of no one writer, however high he may stand in the public estimation, is enough to settle a point; but the uniform, or nearly uniform, practice of reputable speakers or writers is decisive. (6)

Hill recognized that language, usage, and sound rhetorical practice changed: Johnson was more direct than Milton, and that represented progress. The age—any age—demands change, but that change must not be dictated by the unschooled.

The question for Hill is, how can public speakers and writers communicate in ways that their audiences will respond to without slipping into the unwholesome habits of popular public discourse? On the one hand, he says newspapers are destroying English and the American citizenry's habits of attention, but on the other he says intellectuals should follow something like the newspaper style of brevity if they are to communicate effectively. He says, we should speak to audiences in "their" terms but only in the "best of" their terms.

> [A] preacher cannot hope to interest and impress his hearers unless he uses language which they readily understand, language with which they are familiar in the best books they read and the best speakers they hear. (151–52)

However, Hill has said just previously, educated persons must face and respond to the enormous responsibility of influencing, but this is difficult when the public's tastes have been so contaminated by newspapers and other "ephemeral" reading materials: the public can no longer be reached by sound argumentative methods. Here, the best he can suggest is a middle road for intellectuals, the clergy, and college graduates, neither too "highfalutin" nor too "colloquial."[9]

The depth of this problem was, it seems, invisible to Hill, perhaps, because of his great faith in the power of clarity and force, or perhaps due to his nearsighted Harvardian insularity. My argument, then, does not significantly conflict with Crowley's argument that nineteenth-century text-book writers could reduce composition to methods of clarity and organization, because all minds (at least all minds worth addressing) functioned alike (*Methodical*), that in fact the role of the current-traditional "method" was to ensure that all minds continued to think alike. While Hill insists that students write about matters that interest them and that preachers address issues that concern the public, Hill can offer only meager unhelpful advice for determining what arguments will be of interest. Invention is still not a social act, but it *is* an act that must somehow engage, interest, and change society. Whereas he has argued earlier that too much of the public no longer *can* respond to intellectual discourse, here he seems content to say the public will respond because they should be able to respond.

Hill's advice to preachers, intellectuals, and others who wish to sway the public is simple: be clear, concise, and organized. Much like a good schoolboy's theme, good public discourse "deals with one definite subject, and only one, deals with it methodically, and in language like that used by lay writers and speakers of the best class, and dwells upon the central idea of it long enough and strongly enough and warmly enough to make it felt as well as understood" (171). Well-composed individuals (linguistically and morally healthy individuals) will compose discourse that naturally appeals to their audiences.

Hill believed also that such a style was simply better—naturally, truthfully (but note, not transhistorically) better. To invoke Crowley's argument once again, such discourse best engaged the universal human mind. There-fore, the effective, moral writer does not "change registers" (as we say today) when speaking to "lower" audiences; rhetoric for Hill is not, as Jasper Neel suggests of Aristotle's aristocratic public rhetoric, a method that superior intellectuals adhere to when entering the messy world of actual public prac-tice ("the prophylactic that demonstration and dialectic wear in order to protect their identities and their processes from the free play of linguistic transfer," 179). The strength to resist the pernicious effects of public rhetoric comes from within the writer herself, from habits of good English developed in the classroom and from the immunity provided by exposure to great genius. So, rather than "prophylaxis" (a general term for all sorts of disease prevention, including devices, hygiene, nutrition, etc.), "inoculation" seems to better describe how composition prepares the student-citizen for the un-wholesome atmosphere of public discourse.

But I think we can be somewhat generous here. Hill had trouble making this argument cohere because intellectuals were entangled in a terribly difficult predicament, just as it is difficult for us today to work out our own similar problems about the relationships between public writing and the composition classroom. In order to engage the public, we must adopt public forms of argumentation, but it is difficult to address the public in the forms we know and admire, those we tend to believe are superior—those forms we consider to be productive of fair and healthful public discussion.[10] It is difficult to think and argue with forms and methods that are foreign to us, or that we fear are somehow beneath us. Hill's civic nearsightedness should remind us of our own insularity and of the difficulties academics still face in striving to make composition studies engage with the civic sphere.

Hill's Classroom and His Textbooks: The "Habit" of Self-Mastery

In chapter 3 I noted how Channing had too cleanly separated the ideal world of discourse from the real world of public discussion. Channing recognized the difference, wrote about it in his *North American Review* essays, and made frequent passing references to the difference in his *Lectures*. But Channing felt more "at home," as he put it, in the ideal world—Harvard Yard rather than the Boston Common, in the Senate rather than on the stump, arguing before a judge and other advocates rather than before a jury, belles lettres (generally conceived) rather than popular or even mainstream public discourse. Both Channing and Hill believed the world of journalism was posing special hazards to the American citizenry, but Channing's generation did not face the intense anti-intellectual animosity that Hill's faced, nor were students quite so ill-prepared as those Hill would teach. Therefore, Channing, unlike Hill, could indeed "turn his back on society" once he was settled into the Boylston Professorship.

Hill either could not or would not regard the university as a place *entirely* apart from the public world. Composition had its place in reforming the world. True, Hill's civic virtue is a far cry from Isocrates' denunciation of idle philosophy's search for transcendent truth, and from the Neo-Ciceronian ideal of the citizen orator. Nonetheless, Hill suggested that composition might indeed change the world for the better, in "trickle-down" fashion.

It is difficult to square what Hill put in his textbooks with, as I have hazarded to call it, his mission of civic virtue and engagement. Indeed, many composition historians have pointed out that Hill's textbooks (like competing texts of the period) are suffused with a spirit of "correctness" of all sorts. Student notes from lectures of "English A" and "English 22" also suggest that a great deal of time was devoted to matters of grammar and propriety with only occasional mention of public discourse and how the composition course might prepare students for that world.[11]

But Hill thought that the "mental discipline" endowed by exercise in writing had a social value. It gave students the inner strength—a "moral stamina," a sort of "immunity"— they needed to maintain their moral and linguistic health in an environment of unhealthful public discussion. This aspect of mental discipline, as Crowley and Kitzhaber have shown, surely had roots deep in Scottish realism and in the faculty psychology it encouraged, where the reasoning and other faculties might be "strengthened" (like a muscle) by consistent exercise. And as Johnson has argued, rhetoricians of this period "assumed without question the claim that the study of rhetoric confers mental discipline as well as the powers of eloquent expression" (236) and that such discipline was crucial to the social health of a society.

> From the nineteenth-century point of view, the advance of culture and the stability of society relied on the attainment of mental and moral development by each individual. . . . The nineteenth-century rhetorical tradition corroborated one of the most ernest beliefs of nineteenth-century North American society: that the productive exchange of ideas between rational minds furthers the progress of democratic society and protects the fortunes of all. (245–46)

However, in addition to these philosophical and republican-inspired sources, there was simultaneously at play a more immediate cultural exigency—the importance of maintaining a unified, coherent, and healthy self, which was necessary for striking out into the world and remaining inviolate against the vagaries of a dangerous popular culture. As public-health historians Fellman and Fellman argue, such discourse about self-mastery was everywhere in discussions of physical and mental health. "Will was the chief mechanism for freeing the self from the domination of determinist forces," such as heredity and environment. Individuals were responsible for their own health, both mental and physical, and this applied especially to diseases of the "nervous system," such as "nervousness" and "neurasthenia." In this era, many (perhaps most) intellectuals conceived society to be a fragile thing and at the brink of chaos; they also had "the haunting fear that the body and the mind are fragile structures" (138). But the body and mind could be made hardy and resistant to disease by sheer acts of the will. However, in a world that was apparently becoming increasingly undone and dominated by chaos (produced, for instance, by telegraphic journalism, rapid transportation, and information overload [e.g., see Lears]), "individuals could not be expected to expend their limited fund of time and energy on every little choice that life presented" (Fellman and Fellman 123). Therefore, they had to find ways to make such acts of will and self-determination automatic.

The prescription for making the will operate automatically, for enabling the individual to retain self-control, lay in "habit." By cultivating healthful habits at an early age, moral behavior would be "systematized" and would "lead to that lifelong self-control and self-improvement the [American] late Victorians considered so essential" (123). "Habit" was the subject of William James's most popular lecture and the subject and title of an essay appearing in *Popular Science Monthly* (1887, and reprinted again and again in James's collections). For James, early acquisition of healthful habits gave one resistance to the epidemics of "nervousness" and "neurasthenia" (from which both James and Hill suffered), which were typified by morbid self-consciousness and the inability to take any action. Individuals fortified themselves against such afflictions by engaging in exercise, both physical and mental. This produced, said James, "habits of concentrated attention, energetic volition, and self-denial." An individual who had been endowed with self-mastery through habit would "stand like a tower when everything rocks around him, and when his softer fellow-mortals are winnowed like chaff in the blast" (quoted in Townsend 173–75). If the individual were to maintain a "manly independence" coupled with active engagement, if the will were to remain strong in a world that everywhere conspired against the individual, the cultivation of sound habit (the earlier the better) was crucial.

Composing the Habit of Self-Unity

Hill's approach to teaching writing demanded the habit of maintaining "unity," of subject and of self. Of Hill's four canons of composition—"unity, clearness, force, ease"—he stressed unity above all others. "The importance of unity can hardly be overestimated," he wrote in *Beginnings of Rhetoric and Composition*. "Other qualities are useful to a writer, but this one is essential to the achievement of the highest success" (415). Writing a theme that possessed unity was an exercise in unity in general—a means for acquiring the "habit" of unity.

The importance of consistent habit was passed on to Hill's composition students. Wilhelm Segerblohm, in his notes for English 22 (1893–94, for which Hill was the teacher of record, if not the actual teacher), transcribed the following instructions, strategies, and rationales for the daily theme:

> daily must be deposited at right of Sentry in box, in Matthews before 10 o'clock A.M.. . . . Never write more than one page, criticism concern spirit of work not tecknical errors. Impossible to make up dailies. Regularity of dailies is very important. Daily facilitates ready & rapid writing. Fortnightlies & dailies supplement each other. Write dailies rapidly after thinking it over all day. Dailies make one sensitive to outside influence. Chose subjects from everyday life. . . . Write about incidents of today and not from far past. 1) Look out for unity 2) Avoid surplusses, 3) Daily should have a point. 4) Use principles of suspense. 5) Be specific and find out where individuality of the thing lies. 6) Study your attitude.

In order to ensure that every theme (both daily and fortnightly) was an exercise in unity, the subject of a theme, above all else, had to be manageable, something an eighteen-year-old could control and master. Therefore, Hill, like most of his contemporaries, assigned personal, almost always simple, essays. Certainly, this move from general to personal and concrete topics represented a general move away from classical forms of invention (Crowley, "Invention"), was influenced by Romanticism and Emerson (Veeder), and responded to the necessity of dealing with students who did not have a large storehouse of information and commonplaces to bring into their discussions (Connors, "Personal"). But I suggest it might have also represented, for Hill at least, an ideological effort to restore a sense of self in a world that imperiled the unity of the self or encouraged individuals, with frightening effectiveness, to adopt modes of being and thinking that were not of themselves, but of an impostor culture.

In response to all this, Hill's theory of invention is both simple and simplistic: read great works of genius, discover (in a largely mysterious fashion)[12] who you are, and write "naturally," as he often put it; put that real self into the argument. Thus, when Hill speaks of "unity" in a composition, he means not only "unity of expression" but also "unity of self." For Hill—and this goes directly against the standard depiction of his theory of language—it was impossible to separate thought from expression or self from expression. One *is* what one writes. As he stated this idea in *Foundations of Rhetoric*:

> Unity in expression grows out of unity in thought. A writer who is in the habit of keeping together in his mind things which belong together is more likely to form his sentences on a similar principle

than one whose mind is a scene of confusion. He, then, who would
secure unity in expression must have it first in his thought. (270)

Unity of expression grows out of unity of thought and of self. It is in
this sense that William Coles Jr. is precisely right in saying that for Hill,
good writing was intimately connected with "moral rectitude" (*Plural I*
281). Moral rectitude, like physical and mental health, requires a consistent
regimen—a daily habit, as in the "daily theme"—of exercising the will to
predominate over deterministic social factors.

Hill does not claim (as do most contemporary compositionists) that
invention is a way of knowing, that one can achieve unity of thought *by
way of* unifying expression. Writers do not discover or create their ideas
through writing. Before one begins writing, one must know precisely what
one's idea is, then present that stand, full force, unflinchingly, presenting
to the world an autonomous human being—a real, unified self—behind the
pen.

Hill's invention is clearly not a "social act" in our current sense of that
phrase. But the process of composing, for Hill, was indeed social. "Human
nature" is *not* the product of society, as social constructionism, for instance, would insist. Society is—or at least it should be—the product of
human nature. Therefore, the writing teacher must enable students to
uncover what really is their universal, human nature, their "real selves."
The writing teacher helps students "wash off," we might say, popular culture, which covers the citizenry—and thus college students—like a patina.
Then, by endowing students with a "hardy English," a "moral stamina,"
teachers provide students with the resistance to subsequent assaults on
their true selves. In this sense, Hill's invention was social: it helped individuals (again, in a mysterious fashion) understand what the self and what
society *should* be. Examining great works of genius and expressing one's
individuality helped "demystify" (as we say today) cultural constructions of
what one has become and what society has become. Today "cultural studies
in composition" might be said to help a student understand "what made me
me"; for Hill composition helps a student understand "what made me *not
me*." This uncovering of the true self remains for Hill very mysterious,
almost magical. But then again, the demystification of consciousness has
always been—and remains—at its core mysterious.

With presentation of an autonomous, unchanging self as a primary
goal of student writing, then, there is little wonder that Hill's principal
criterion for assignment-making states that it must be interesting to the
student, something the student can engage with. The writing assignment
provides students with the occasion for composing a writing self that is
absolutely secure and stable, certain of itself as well as its argument; a self

that knows just what it wants and believes, and comes forward confidently to say it. The teacher provides assignments that are straightforward enough to enable this composing of a stable self—a self that can, after graduation, reenter the world of newspaper- and novel-production and "raise . . . the quality of those that are produced" (*Our English* 137). The writing assignment enables the student to present to the world his or her sincere self. As Hill put it:

> To write as we talk in our best moments is to write simply, natu-rally, sincerely. . . . Thus, and thus only, will what we write be the exact and complete reproduction of what we think and feel in our sanest and most fruitful moods. (245)

Therefore, I do not wish to lionize Hill, but I would suggest we miss an important factor in the origins of modern composition when we assume that rhetoric was conceived as a deliberate divorce from the student's social setting. Rather, composition instruction was conceived indeed as preparing the minds of a citizenry to become healthy, critical consumers of public discussions, which were anything but healthy or healthful. And although Hill thought that students might go out into the world and, armed with their fortified critical capacities, alter public discourse in trickle-down fash-ion, the primary goal lay in rendering the student-citizen aloof, critical, distant. When Hill encourages teachers to help students discover their true selves, he is engaging in countercultural discourse. He believed that such instruction would lead his students to resist—rather than conform to—the cultural norms he and other patrician intellectuals so despised.

Hill tried to remedy this assumed society-wide imposition of self by supplanting into his students his ideas of what a natural, whole, unified self ought to be. If students were to do any thinking about their unique back-ground and personality, their response to their culture, it was to be on Hill's terms, in the straitjacket format of a unified essay. There was no room for wondering out loud in such an essay. There was no room in Hill's classroom, as Oswald Garrison Villard suggests, for responsible and sensi-tive exploration of a student's unique response to his or her world.[13] What was important (as Crowley [*Methodical*] has argued of current-traditional rhetoric in general) was adherence to already-laid-out thinking and writing processes that would bring students to a new view of themselves and their world. The purpose of writing instruction was consciously ideological, a shift to the ideology of the teacher and his or her class.

And *this* is the legacy of Hill's that still survives and that we need to continue questioning. Contemporary compositionists, have, for the most part, dispensed with much of the current-traditional claptrap—mechanical correctness as an end in itself, the four forms of discourse, simplistic theories of invention—but some remain timid about presenting students with writing situations that might challenge their very notions of a stable self, so that students could see themselves as writers who recognize and engage difficulty, and who, in doing so, create a writerly self—a self that consciously is the product of the rhetorical situation, of the "community" for which the assignment is completed. And this is the legacy, perhaps, that continues to make teachers of composition uncomfortable with student compositions that "wonder out loud," that in striving to deal with difficulty and ambiguity, fall apart in several ways: formally, grammatically, and even ethically. That is, the ethos of the writer flutters, fades, becomes disjointed, or seems unsure of the argument or who the writer is. Such wondering out loud, such diffusion of self may come from striving to understand and incorporate disparate ideas, values, and beliefs.

But such wondering out loud—and the inevitable insecurities such wondering would reveal or elicit—might also be considered a *potentially* healthful sign of development. Perhaps the goal of the writing assignment and the writing course should be to make student writing as well as the writerly ethos "fall apart"—for a while at least. To put this another way— in the terms I will be discussing in the following chapters—perhaps we need to help students shift the definition and the focus of their "argumentative responsibility," from responsibility to oneself, one's integrity, and one's argument. I will argue we need to help them move beyond the idea that the goal of the finished essay is to convey an autonomous, mechanically flawless human being behind the pen. Instead, we need to help them cultivate a responsibility to communicating to others within a community, responsibility to the conflict at hand and to its resolution.

Part Three

Contemporary Pedagogy

6

Classroom Argument, Responsibility, and Change

Responsibility—exerts a high level of effort and perseveres towards goal attainment.

—U.S. Department of Labor Secretary's
Commission on Achieving Necessary Skills

I don't think we accept things at face value like your generation did. Generation Xers (of which I'm proud to be a member) are critical thinkers.

—20-year-old student in a writing-class journal

Since rhetorical proof is never a completely necessary proof, the thinking man who gives his adherence to the conclusions of an argumentation does so by an act that commits him and for which he is responsible. . . . This role of argumentation in decision-making is denied by the sceptic and the fanatic. In the absence of compelling reason, they both are inclined to give violence a free hand, rejecting personal commitment.

—Chaim Perelman and Lucy Olbrechts-Tyteca

Lively Discussion. Healthy Debate.

—Promotional slogan for the TV show *Crossfire*[1]

Habits of Argument: Nineteenth Century and Contemporary

Channing and Hill, like many other patrician intellectuals of the nineteenth century, engaged in a kind of cultural critique. They examined systems of popular discourse, demystified them, explained the "habits of thinking" fostered by them, and advocated educational processes they believed would counter the cultural and psychological force of such discourse. A citizenry's habits of thought, they recognized, were created in large part by the forms of discourse that society embraced and used. For both men, there was a tremendous and, it seemed, growing gap between the ideal discourse of intellectuals (analogous in many ways to our current "academic discourse") and the real discourse of the popular public sphere. Channing did not seem to worry much at all about the connection between intellectual and popular discourse. The world of intellectuals, in his day, perhaps still seemed big enough and insular enough that popular public discourse could be commented upon as a danger to the masses but posed little danger to men of his class or to Harvard students.

But Hill could not get away so easily from this gap between the ideal and real. For Hill, Harvard undergraduates and America itself had changed dramatically. For one thing, the unprecedented expansion in the number of undergraduates and of undergraduate colleges meant Harvard no longer laid hold on the "cream of the crop" of American boys (Brereton, *Origins* 7; Connors, "Modern University" 80–81). America's habits of communication had produced crops of incoming Harvard boys who not only could not write very well but also could not distinguish themselves from their culture, one's ability to write and one's character being part and parcel of the same problem. In order to help students distinguish their "real selves" from their culturally induced imposter selves, Hill advocated a *kind* of "critical thinking," but it is difficult to say how well or even whether Hill carried his theories for countercultural amelioration into the classroom and into his students' consciousness. Hill, like his contemporaries, may have been overly confident in the benefits of "habit" for making the will strong and impervious to disease, and that he could therefore assume that habit-forming exercises in "writing with unity" would help make his students more unified (more "whole"), impervious to dangerous popular public discourse—just as habitual exercise of the will might make late Victorians impervious to diseases such as neurasthenia, also thought to have had their origins in the confusions and stressors of modern life. In fact, his students seemed never to have realized that they might be undergoing such countercultural "treatment"; that is, the connection between Hill's approach and student change (how they change, whether they change, and whether they stay changed) was undertheorized. It just happened, apparently, just as one acquires a habit of good sense, good writing, and proper thinking.

The problem of theorizing how students change, I suspect, remains our problem. How is it that students change at all, and what practices should we engage in to foster change? Some of Hill's goals for composition resemble the current goals held by many of us today. His methods and his epistemology were, of course, very different from "critical pedagogies" of recent years, but his goals for education (specifically, for the composition classroom) are similar to those of today's "critical" teacher: to demystify and thereby diminish the power of culture over the student and to help the student learn what is in her or his own best interest.

In the move from modern to postmodern conceptions of persuasion, configurations of rhetorical ethics change fundamentally—what is an ethical argument? what are the rules (if any) for ethical arguing? what is the relationship between arguers? what responsibilities must the arguer embrace? In the foundational conceptions of knowledge, arguers are responsible to the "truth" or the development of knowledge; as Aristotle told us, when two arguments are equally well represented, the one with truth on its side should win the day. But because postmodern ethics cannot rest on the same notions of truth and knowledge, we must look in different directions for understanding what responsible argumentation would be.

Marilyn Cooper has supplied an insightful definition of "responsibility" in argument: an arguer becomes responsible to the other in argumentation, to understanding the uniqueness of the other's viewpoint (see also Kastely). In addition, arguers must also assume a different kind of responsibility for their own positions, since they would acknowledge there exist neither unbiased positions nor universally applicable methods for arriving at justice or even consensus; so their interrogation of their own beliefs becomes an essential aspect in the activity of earning warrantable assent. We are "responsible" for the ideas we hold, and we are therefore responsible for understanding *why* we hold them and explaining those reasons to others. Among teachers and students, responsibility demands the ethical imperative to listen and listen again to students' ideas, no matter how distant from our own they are or how repugnant they are.

In this chapter and the following one, I argue that compared with modernist or liberal models of classroom persuasion (and we find such models in some surprising places), a postmodern sense of responsibility in the classroom is also more *effective* for bringing students to more democratic beliefs and attitudes about argument, knowledge, and self—the positions that theorists like Gere and Bruffee believed would follow when collaborative learning was practiced, and similar positions that theorists like James Berlin believed would follow from social-epistemic rhetoric.[2] That is, if we want our students to comprehend and embrace democratic forms of argument, we must ourselves practice democratic argument in the classroom. This is not only an ethical imperative; it is also perhaps more effective for long-term influence on our students.

Why do we even need to talk about "responsible" argumentation, either in the classroom or among ourselves as composition teachers? This is a question that is gaining more and more attention in composition studies. It arises, certainly, from a myriad of sources. It is probably a reaction to the charge of "political correctness." It also has much to do with recent changes in the classroom-society relationship, as many more composition teachers are coming to believe that they must do more than teach students how to attain critical distance from their society, but also to engage in public discourse. In my own case—and I gather that this is true for many others—this issue has arisen from my desire to make the writing classroom have a deeper and more permanent influence on my students. I have realized that overt political discussion (trying to bring my students to my side) simply does not work often enough to justify the practice, and even when such flash-in-the-plan conversion does occur, I doubt its longevity. Slow, piecemeal change, though more frustrating and less efficient, is in the long run more effective persuasion and more effective teaching practice.

Ideas of Argument and Responsibility in Academic and Popular Culture

Like Hill and Channing, many in composition studies today maintain that the citizenry and our students are inhabited by the rhetorical habits of their culture. As cultural analysts have noted, the very idea of "argument" is shaped largely by journalism and political argument, both of which are dominated by contentious models of winning and losing, with little sense that arguments might be enlightening or might lead to discovery, new knowledge, or consensus. Rather, the point is to be for or against one of the arguers. Argument in our culture is merely a spectacle—entertainment we can feel good about because in viewing we may think we meet the obligations of republican virtue: staying informed and "participating" in the public sphere. As John Trimbur writes, "That people rush to premature closure on complex issues, fail to consider alternatives, and ratify common sense should not be surprising. They've had little opportunity to participate meaningfully in public discourse or to be more than spectators when public discussion is framed as a spectacle of celebrities arguing for and against" ("Response" 249).

Like Hill and Channing, we recognize further that cultural models of public discussion also profoundly affect cultural understandings of self—how we communicate determines in large part who we are. As various composition and rhetoric scholars have noted, the model of argumentation and of self that predominates in America is similar to the one Channing criticized in his 1817 "Abuses of Political Discussion" and his 1819 "Inaugural Address": the point is to remain strong, impervious to the opposition's assaults; persons who allow themselves to be swayed or even influenced by the opposing side (the "losers" in the eristic model), are deemed, in various senses, weak, wishy-washy, unable to maintain "integrity." As Wanda Martin writes:

> College students, like their elders, suffer from an impoverished view of political argumentation. One source of this impoverishment is no doubt the transfer of most of our political processes to commercial mass media on which time is expensive, so that only the pithiest slogan, the most affecting image, will ever be seen.... When they think of politics, many undergraduates think of political parties, flags, and elections.... Politics is winning, having one's opinion prevail, maximizing one's own power and position. (39; see also Kroll)

Just as politicians' characters are impugned if they change their minds, our students often believe that they open themselves to harsh criticism when they change theirs. What might be called "openness" or "growth" is called "waffling" (it was termed an "effeminate" "lack of assertion" in the nineteenth century). John Trimbur explains the problem this way:

> The polarized, pro/con format of television programs such as *Firing Line*, *Crossfire*, and *Nightline* teaches, in the name of equal time and ostensible balance, that public discourse is always a matter of two (and only two) positions . . . and that the point is to be for one or the other. ("Response" 249)

To use the expression commonly used in alternative-news radio, decibels masquerade as diversity.

There seems to be a growing consensus that students come to our classrooms with models of argument and selfhood that are derived from the mass media. These models frustrate our efforts to get students to conduct the kinds of argumentation we tend to value. As Dennis Lynch, Diana George, and Marilyn M. Cooper write, "We don't blame our students" for the impoverished, unhealthful, unproductive models of argumentation they hold: "our students merely follow [the] models" of argumentation they see on television (61). From their experiences with media argumentation ranging from *Crossfire* to Rush Limbaugh to National Public Radio, "[s]tudents have learned to argue vigorously and even angrily, but not think about alternatives, or see complexities, or reconsider the position they began with, or even to make new connections across a range of possible disagreements" (61).

Just as Channing and Hill believed that the new nineteenth-century journalistic practices had impoverished their students' "habits of thinking," many composition-studies researchers have argued that televisual media have contributed to a new kind of student who is unable to envision or practice what we regard as healthy argument. Today's "new" journalism and styles of political argumentation teach students and citizens that "communicative responsibility," as we might call it, means maintaining one's integrity, maintaining one's distance from opposing views (getting only close enough to blast them), resisting the infection of enticing, alien ideas. Rarely have our students been exposed to communicative models in which a speaker or writer expresses or otherwise exhibits a responsibility to an audience that might share radically different views, or a responsibility to forwarding the process of inquiry. Rarely have they seen models in which arguers employ communication with an audience as a means for reaching beyond themselves and their ideas in order to develop alternative perspectives of their ideas. They have not seen communication function as a means for determining, for ourselves, individually and collectively, what is true and what is false, what is good and what is bad—a means of determining what we, individually and collectively, should believe and do.

"Responsibility" as a Keyword

Responsibility is becoming central in many scholarly discussions about the composition classroom. *Responsibility* was in the convention theme titles of the 1995 and the 1997 Conference on College Composition and Communication, and it appears with increasing frequency on the pages of rhetoric and composition journals. Composition has turned to the idea of responsibility in reaction, perhaps, to the difficulties that arose when, during the mid-1980s, social constructionism (or postmodern thought in general) was brought into the classroom, into the practical sphere of teaching, learning, and doing, where ideas' usefulness are put to the acid test. In the first-year writing classroom, unlike, say, a graduate class, teachers do not so much teach the subject of social constructionism, but many compositionists—Gere and Bruffee were among the first—have desired to help bring students to an awareness of the way that social constructionists believe that knowledge is made, shared, disputed, and disseminated. And they have desired that students gain such an awareness because they believed it would help them in many ways: to become better readers and writers as well as better citizens.

Teachers have found in the last decade that social constructionist theory—or "postmodern" or "critical" theory—needed some adjusting if it was to be a useful tool in the classroom. Specifically, the widespread movements of "critical thinking" and "critical pedagogy" seemed to be in stride with much of postmodern belief, but students do not always, or even often, respond to a theory the way their teachers do. Elizabeth's Ellsworth's "Why Doesn't This Feel Empowering?" (1989) has probably been the most influential and most cited article for questioning the efficacy and theoretical assumptions of the critical-thinking approach. Ellsworth pointed out how difficult it can be to get students to cooperate in a shared-responsibility classroom, how easily such a decentered classroom can devolve into cells of interest groups that will not, or feel they need not, converse with other groups. She clarified that while critical pedagogy depended on theories similar to social construction, it seemed in many practical ways to depend on modernist assumptions of knowledge, reason, and authority. In describing her graduate-level education course that was intended to explore racism on campus, Ellsworth was dismayed to see that her students, all of whom were committed to conquering racism, splintered into "affinity groups" (as Ellsworth calls them), separated by gender, class, race, sexual preference, and other dimensions. One group's "critical thinking" was another's "irrationalism," so that critical thinking became a substitute term of violence that could "otherize" discourse and discursants whose values did not square with one's own "community." Rather than challenging "oppressive social formations," Ellsworth's course reproduced them. The term "critical thinking" became a weapon for excluding others and rejecting difference (322).

At the heart of critical thinking lies the ability to *distance* oneself from one's world, to step back and critically (or ironically, even cynically) think about thinking, one's own thinking and one's community's thinking. However, as Ellsworth demonstrates, when real students with real histories are asked to work through real, complex problems, these students may use their critical-thinking skills mostly to distance themselves from those who hold beliefs different from their own. And when this happens, "critical thinking" can become little more than a synonym of "better thinking." Sometimes it seems to mean something like "scrutinize for error and then attack." Certainly, that is not the theory of "critical thinking" as explained by persons such as Freire, but when we bring these new ideas into the classroom, strange things happen. Perhaps the fundamental problem with "critical" is that it does not suggest to students any sort of relationship between the writer and the community with which the writer engages. The term itself does not help students, as S. P. Mohanty describes the process, "develop a sense of the profound *contextuality* of meanings in their play and their ideological effects" (171). Or another way to put this, the term does not encourage discursants to examine the discourse they create as a product of and *a producer of* the community for which the discourse is intended. "Critical thinking" as a heuristic does not help our students envision the relationship between themselves and their world, between their discourse and the community that is affected by that discourse, which, in hearing and responding to that discourse, would make their communication complete by taking action.

Lester Faigley's influential *Fragments of Rationality* expressed similar concerns and called for composition to turn its attention to the "ethics of rhetoric," where the purpose of writing and speaking lies in making choices about actions, striving to persuade others about the goodness of those choices, and making judgments in an always ad hoc, context-specific manner.

> Bringing ethics into rhetoric is not a matter of collapsing spectacular diversity into universal truth. Neither is ethics only a matter of radical questions of what aspires to be regarded as truth. Lyotard insists that ethics is also the obligation of rhetoric. It is accepting the responsibility of judgment. It is a pausing to reflect on the limits of understanding. It is respect for diversity and unassimilated otherness. It is finding the spaces to listen. (239)

But students do not always assume responsibility, nor do they always want it. Part of the problem, as many have argued, is that we treat our students as children or as individuals whose faults need correcting more than their voices and ideas need hearing. Composition classrooms are set up, in other words, in ways that encourage or reward students for considering themselves incapable, irresponsible citizens who cannot be trusted to engage in writing that really *does* something (besides fulfilling a writing-class requirement). As Susan Miller has written, rather than treating students as having something to say, "students in those freshman courses . . . are socially and politically imagined as children, whose Victorian innocence retains a tainted need for 'civilizing.' " They are never treated "as actual responsible 'authors' " (*Textual* 196). In a pleasantly bewildering mixture of praise and censure, Lynn Z. Bloom describes the rationale of the first-year writing course this way: "Like swimmers passing through the chlorine bath en route to plunging into the pool, students must first be disinfected in Freshman English" (656). Marilyn Cooper, in "Postmodern Ethics in the Writing Classroom," argues that writing teachers must work toward showing students that their writing *matters*; she makes a powerful argument that "teachers must . . . allow their students to make decisions about their writing and to take responsibility for the effects of those decisions if they are to help them be (not become) responsible writers and responsible citizens in the classroom."

I suggest that the deployment of *responsibility* as a keyword—in scholarly writing and in the classroom—is healthful, but we need to remember that the definition of "responsibility" as it is currently being worked out in composition studies scholarship (e.g., see Salvatori, "Conversations"; Fishman; Cooper, "Postmodern Ethics") probably does not match our students' definitions. Just as our students' notions of "self" and "argumentation" are highly influenced by the media, so are their definitions of "responsibility," which in turn have everything to do with their notions of "self" and of "argumentation."

Some Current Definitions of "Responsibility"

Today's students are already familiar with "responsibility"; in fact, they are most likely nauseatedly familiar with it.[3] In their homes and in the media, they hear it as a never-ending litany of moralizations aimed at them, warning them to shape up for the good of the nation. Therefore, by fundamentally challenging and altering their definitions of responsibility, we may fundamentally alter their ideas about communication, about community and conflict, and about the reasons for and the goals of writing and reading. Our students see and hear "responsibility" everywhere in the words of politicians and social and cultural spokespersons of all kinds. It has become a highly contested term in current popular discussion on culture and politics; the various factions in the cultural battles are fighting over what this term will *mean*.

Interestingly enough, in most popular writing on education and responsibility, students' lack of responsibility is portrayed as not *their* responsibility but the responsibility of their education and their culture. Often it is postmodernism and its antifoundational ideas about values and authority that are blamed directly. A "permissive" and "postmodern" system of education is everywhere invading the better sensibilities of Americans—especially its young people, the "GenXers." This is the point of the recent *Generation X Goes to College*, written by an ex-journalist (once nominated for a Pulitzer Prize) who has lived "in the trenches" of college English and whose pen name is Peter Sacks. It is a disheartening story (anyone who reads this, I think, would find it disheartening but for different reasons) of a "liberal"—who in fact drives an "old Volkswagen mini-bus" and even voted for "Carter, Mondale, and Jesse" (17)—who hears the higher calling to teaching, responds, and is thoroughly disillusioned by his students' expectations. They expect, among other things, that the teacher demonstrate the "relevance" of what they do in class. They feel "entitled" to their grades and entitled to an education that is "entertaining." Sacks writes that he approached his new role with passion, vigor, and hopes. He carefully examined numerous textbooks on writing, carefully chose one, then taught as he had been taught thirty years ago, only to find this new generation will not go along with it. (There is no suggestion that he ever consulted professional

literature on writing instruction or that his colleagues knew of such literature.)[4] For Sacks, the culprit in this mess is postmodernism and the
hyperconsumerism, relativism, and anti-authority spirit it commends. (It
may also be responsible for the militia movement's sympathy for the Okla-
homa City Bombing, courses in *Star Trek*, and the widespread belief in
angels [108–9]). Students do not see the value in arguing, he writes, since
our postmodern culture has taught them that "any idea is as good as another"; they have learned that a satisfactory reaction to opposing viewpoints
is "that's just your opinion, and you're entitled to it." It is postmodernism,
with its privileging of surface over substance, that makes them intolerant
of "messy thinking or expansion of their frames of reference beyond the
routine and predictable. . . . After all, how hard should a consumer have to
work at buying something?" (162). "Responsibility," as it is portrayed by
Sacks (to work hard, to account for one's actions), is opposed to postmodern
versions of academic work, which tell students merely that no idea is better
than any other, and then end the discussion there.

"Responsibility" is indeed a serviceable word for politicians and other
public pundits because it has that rough-hewn, commonsense feel to it. It
appeals to two strong currents in American thought, anti-intellectualism
(or "anti–political correctness") and to the liberal tradition. According to
my former local newspaper's editorial entitled "Responsibility 101," responsibility opposes intellectual gibberish and "psycho-babble silliness," which
"encourages adults to blame all their problems and ills on insensitive
parents[,] . . . a sad childhood," and on their mistreatment by society. This
particular editorial proposes "firm justice" as a way of ensuring responsibility, though others propose throwing out the welfare system, doing away
with insanity pleas, and so on.

According to these definitions of *responsibility*, the responsible citizen
fortifies himself or herself against being seduced into the rhetoric of victimization. The responsible person is not, victimlike, acted upon *by* the world,
but acts upon it. This is, for instance, the idea of responsibility forwarded
by several bestsellers on American culture, politics, education, and morality. Charles Sykes's *A Nation of Victims* (with the subtitle "The Decay of the
American Character") argues that American culture and politics has created
a citizenry of individuals who "compete not only for rights or economic
advantage but also for points on the 'sensitivity' index, where 'feelings'
rather than reason are what count." "Responsibility" means something like
not "exculpating one's self from blame": "the mantra of . . . victims is the
same: *I am not responsible; it's not my fault*" (11).

William Kilpatrick's *Why Johnny Can't Tell Right from Wrong* argues
that recent social horrors—such as "wilding" and "multiculturalism"—have
resulted in large measure from modern theories of teaching values. Values

Clarification pedagogy, he argues, mistakes student interest for intellectual and moral progress, and, worse, it "disorients" the student's sense of moral decision-making: "Like a roller-coaster ride, the [Values Clarification] dilemma approach can leave its passengers a bit breathless. . . . [But] it may also leave them a bit disoriented—or more than a bit" (84). What young students really need is straightforward lessons in what is moral and what is not, since there is "danger [in] focusing on [highly] problematic dilemmas. . . . [A] student may begin to think that all of morality is similarly problematic" (85). And when you take away a young person's certitudes, you leave her "adrift on a sea of relativism with no compass" (128). A similar sentiment is found in William J. Bennett's immensely popular collection of writings *The Book of Virtues*, which advocates the inculcation of what he calls "moral literacy" at an early age (13). For Bennett and other (mostly conservative, but see Sacks) spokespersons on culture and education, "responsibility" possesses an almost talismanic quality, or perhaps an inoculative quality. That is, the early inculcation of responsibility fortifies or inoculates one against future moral dangers, such as drug addiction, teen pregnancy, and even poverty.[5]

Possessing such "responsibility" empowers the individual with the capacity to resist pernicious social forces, that chaos of competing discourses, so that this individual is *secure* within her well-founded—and immovable—convictions. She is autonomous, objective, often alone; she is an agent, not a passive victim; she acts upon the world rather than being acted upon by it. The individual is portrayed as a "disinterested spectator" always above the fray of public debate. We can, of course, trace this idea back to the legacy of Lockean or Scottish Common Sense liberalism or, perhaps better, entrepreneurial capitalism (as Thomas Miller does), where the individual erects an identity that is independent and competitive. Just as the entrepreneur need not answer to others in the corporation, the responsible individual is wholly sufficient and answers only to herself. Identity is demarcated by barriers rather than bridges. In the tradition of Adam Smith and American liberalism, it is precisely by fulfilling the responsibility to themselves and their needs and beliefs that individuals fulfill their responsibilities to society.

In this popular sense of the word, "responsibility" opposes, sometimes explicitly, postmodern and social-constructionist concepts of knowledge-making and of the self. This definition of *responsibility* says the individual is *not* composed of various and sometimes conflicting subject positions; her knowledge does *not* come from her interaction with her social world. In these popular debates, we very often find responsibility proposed as the antidote for—the inoculation against—our society's creeping nihilism, rampant relativism, liberal humanism, or whatever. For instance, for Kilpatrick, relativism[6] is *the* root cause of much of the trouble that plagues American pre-adult culture, such as teen suicide, wilding, premarital pregnancy, guns in the schools, and so forth (14–15); for both Kilpatrick and Bennett, "moral literacy" (an acknowledged allusion to E. D. Hirsch's "cultural literacy") can be achieved by early inculcation of values and morality by providing young persons with stories that will instill a deep understanding of morality and virtue.

If we carry this sense of *responsibility* to rhetoric, such reasoning might be seen as the rationale for valuing eristic debate, in which the primary goal is *winning*—winning the argument in, as the public sphere is often referred to, "the marketplace of ideas." Here, there is no room for being influenced by one's counterpart, here configured as opponent. To *be* persuaded is to suffer loss—not only the loss of the competition, but a loss of self. Opposing ideas are like infections that must be warded off, with early education as the immunization.

In a writing course, this popular definition of responsibility might be translated into an idea of composing as a means of solidifying, rather than interrogating, a belief—of fortifying one's convictions rather than calling them into question. The goal of argument is to shore up the self, *not* to make oneself as arguer more permeable—more susceptible—to the ideas of others with incommensurable positions. At all costs, individuals should avoid risking their beliefs or "who they are."

Responsibility versus Cynical Egalitarianism

As much as I want to simply dismiss these arguments about "postmodern" philosophy and education, they are at least responding to and often exploiting a "legitimation crisis," to use Habermas's term, or a crisis of cynicism. In Sacks's criticisms of today's cynical and listless students, I recognize some of my own struggles, as would most teachers. But again, I would not blame the students, or at least I would try to get beyond such facile blaming. There are powerful cultural forces teaching our students to become cynical spectators. They witness in contemporary civic culture a place where everyone is portrayed as insincere: no one really takes a sincere stand on an issue; politicians are always merely posturing, playing the game of illusions rather than speaking substantively. And this is not limited to *Crossfire*-type journalism, where one side then the other dismantles the arguments and motivations of policymakers as well as those of their colleagues. As Jay Rosen writes in *Getting the Connections Right: Public Journalism and the Troubles in the Press*, even traditional journalists, in the name of objectivity, focus on dismantling public rhetoric, which leads to a widespread distrust of not only politics but also journalism and the efficacy of public discussion itself. In their misguided efforts to be "objective," "for" impartiality and fairness, journalism devolves into mere cynicism.

> What are journalists *for* . . . what do they stand for? . . . Often the answer seems to be a snarling and relentless cynicism—a categorical mistrust of all public figures. If the American press has a belief system, it tends toward the cultivation of a generalized disbelief. The journalist's characteristic way of seeing is to see through the phony facade, the arranged impression. If there's an identifiable tone, it is that of the zealous prosecutor, in search of the hidden motive or the telling lie. (24)[7]

In a sense, mainstream journalism is saying what some rhetoricians have been saying for twenty-five hundred years—that all public-speaking attitudes, even sincerity, authenticity, and clarity, are poses and can be analyzed, criticized, and even used against the opponent. This gleeful but lazy egalitarianism (in the name of objectivity) coupled with world-weary critique (in the name of analysis) is what people like Sacks believe is the inevitable outcome of postmodern thought, or for that matter any antifoundational thought.

Just as our students often come to us with the idea that conflict is a shallow but turbulent matter, they also often come to us well-primed to be skeptical (I would hesitate to use the word "critical") observers of their world and the positions and arguments of others. This is not to say that we no longer have anything to teach them in the way of analysis. I am suggesting only that they come to us believing that their primary responsibility lies in taking apart arguments, without a sense of responsibility to their fellow arguers, to the quality of the conversation, or to the project of coming to a shared public understanding.

In my own classrooms, I find that students are still hesitant to substantively criticize one another, a stance that may result from their experience in classrooms (where superficial criticism is the norm) and from their experiences with public conflict, where disagreement is tantamount to attack. I find that it is often difficult to bring my students to explore conflicts, in questioning the positions of the works we read or of their colleague writers. They sometimes feel that I am trying to goad them into a fight. During a recent small-group discussion, I asked one student, Gary, if he wanted to respond to an idea from the just-read draft of another student, Del. I addressed this to Gary because I remembered that Gary had criticized that very idea in his draft. (In responding to Neil Postman's "The Peek-a-Boo World," Del accepted his argument and applied it to MTV to see how it was changing its viewers for the worse; Gary had also focused on MTV but thought Postman had got the cart before the horse and found that, for him, MTV did not create or alter his worldview but helped him understand the one he already possessed. Together they articulated a key debate.) Gary was hesitant, so I tried reframing the question twice more, still with no success, and after about a minute or two moved on to other issues. Gary had said very little in class discussion, though he articulated strong positions in his papers, and I had been looking for an opening for him to break the ice. I did not think much of the incident until Gary wrote about it in his weekly email reading journal. His response, in my experience, is somewhat typical (even though such "private transcripts" [see Richard E. Miller] rarely enter into classroom discussion):

> I'm sorry about the Thursday discussion. . . . [but] why [do] you want us to argue with each other so much[?] Just because there wasn't agreement between [Del] and myself doesn't mean there needs to be a fight. He's entitled to his opinion. I didn't think it was worth getting all worked up about. . . . Can we be expected to solve problems when the government or the media can't even solve them[?] [The people in my group] like the class but would you mind telling us why we need to argue about every idea that comes up[?]

In his rich, commendable, and respectful response, Gary has voiced many of the problems I have identified with students' attitudes toward argument: (1) discussion about disagreement is tantamount to "fighting"; (2) difference of opinion is "just one of those things," not "worth getting all worked up about"; and (3) that the issue probably should not receive so much of the class's attention since we cannot solve it in our little classroom.[8]

One of the most damaging responses, I believe, would be to berate the student and his culture for believing such nonsense about argumentation. No matter how gently and tolerantly I expressed my beliefs about such matters, it would be perceived by my students as criticism, an assertion of my power. It would be a surefire method for ensuring that Gary would never again work up the cheek to dispute the way we do things. And even here, I will try to avoid the easiest approach: to blame the student, or to blame the television shows they watch and the strange brand of liberal ideology that inhabits them—the facile "those darned kids today!" position of Sacks, George F. Will, and countless others. Indeed, for the student it is *my* problem, *my* obsession with getting the students to "fight."

In *When Students Have Power*, Ira Shor rightly asserts that challenges like these can be signs of a healthy classroom negotiation of power. In fact, these questions must be addressed and even emphasized in a writing classroom. I do not mean we should explicitly focus on them in terms of analysis of argumentation in public discourse, although they could be (especially in a classroom writing about popular culture). Rather, the practices of everyday classroom life should help students in various ways consider these questions (practices I will discuss below and in the next chapter). As Susan Wells has written, such everyday classroom practices might "model . . . the public, or a concentrated version of the public" (338)—that is, might model what many of us would consider a healthy public.

Certainly, what might reasonably be called "postmodernism," in journalism, academia, and elsewhere, makes certain pedagogical problems more acute than they seemed to have been previously, but the answer does *not* lie in rejecting postmodernism, or blaming it and throwing up our hands. The problem, as writers such as Cooper, Faigley, and Barbara Herrnstein Smith suggest, lies in *not enough* "postmodernist" thought. Nonobjectivist ideas of argument and knowledge need not imply that "one idea is as good as another, so let's dispense with the emotional messiness of argument"— what Barbara Herrnstein Smith calls the "Egalitarian Fallacy," which asserts that if we believe there are no foundational values, then we must conclude that any idea is as good as any other and that we are therefore permanently disqualified from making an argument against or for anything. It only means that "responsibility" means something other than grounding our ideas in what is "demonstrably correct," or what all reasonable persons would agree to if they could see through the clouds of their ideologies. With a postmodernist-ethics approach, there are fewer hard-and-fast rules since we must account for the personal (historical and cultural) reasons for our beliefs. Things may become messier, more personal, and more difficult to resolve. The classroom may become more "expressivist" in its approach. The subject of the class need not become "postmodernism," but students benefit when they inhabit a classroom where postmodern ethics are practiced, where they can be tried and exercised, and where they can prove themselves as useful and important (see Lynch et al.; Cooper, "Postmodern Ethics"). I address what such a classroom might look like in the final chapter.

Responsibility and the Ethics of Earning Assent

Before I appear too enamored of my critique of popular public argument, I should recognize that I am in many ways duplicating an old response to an old problem. Although such discussions go back at least twenty-five hundred years, I point now to Wayne Booth, who in *Now Don't Try to Reason with Me* (1970) and *Modern Dogma and the Rhetoric of Assent* (1974) criticized public as well as academic argumentation for many of the same reasons I and others criticize it today.

Booth perhaps represents the thinking about argumentation and inquiry of the previous generation. Booth worried that his contemporaries were deeply suspicious about the possibility of rational persuasion, which has led to "the crisis in our rhetoric" (*Modern* 3–11). Booth locates many sources for this crisis, including the fact-value split and the rise of relativist thought, which undermines, he maintains, the very conditions necessary for warrantable assent. With Plato, Booth concurs that "reason, properly defined, is our most precious gift" (20), what makes a human being a human being. But the "motivist dogma," writes Booth, has undermined our faith in the power of "good reasons" to change the minds of others. Misguided philosophy from the last seventy-five years and the public discourse of politicians and the mass media have led his contemporaries to the motivist dogma, the belief that

> there are no good reasons for changing your mind. . . . Choices of ends and of worldviews and of political and religious norms are value choices, and since value judgments are not about matters of fact, there can be no final superiority, in arguing about them, of one line of reasoning over another. What we call reasons can always be seen though as rationalizations or superstructures or disguises or wishful thinking: our minds are really determined, in all of our values, either by nonrational conditioning in the past, or by present motives or drives, many of them lying so deep that we can never find them out. (24)

At times, Booth sounds much like Channing or like Godkin, as he makes a dire forecast for the future: "when any society loses its capacity to debate its ends and means rationally, it ceases to be a society of men at all and becomes instead a mob. . . . It would not really be surprising if fifty years from now no one in America would even know what I'm talking about tonight" (*Now Don't* 22–23). Booth wants to elevate the conception and practice of public rhetoric from "mere rhetoric" (a bag of tricks for fooling an audience) to a rhetoric of "good reasons" and of inquiry. Influenced by Burke and Perelman, he urges his readers to leave behind the conception of rhetoric as cajoling, fooling, and dominating and to create a space where individuals can work through their ideas and come to mutual understanding.[9]

But as more recent commentators have argued, Booth's efforts to redefine what constitutes a healthful model of rhetorical inquiry cannot square with many contemporary ideas about justice, knowledge, and power. Many would question Booth's insistence that relativist values inevitably undermine the possibility for "rational" inquiry or the possibility of arriving at decisions about what actions to take or what interpretations are valid; his insistence that reasonable appeals are always superior to ethical and emotional appeals; his alarmist tone; his belief that it is "natural" for human beings to want "meet minds" rather than just persuade. Perhaps most important, Booth's pluralistic community, with its assumption of an "essential humanity" and its master goal of "shared understanding," can too easily regulate out of existence the marginalized voices of a discussion. As Rooney and Kraemer convincingly argue, Booth, even with his often sophisticated discussion of selves as fields of selves, defines human beings as creatures who are capable of forming themselves without coercion, free from power struggles. In "open," "free" discussion, he assumes, one is free to make oneself as one desires (see Kraemer 379–80). For the purposes of a composition course, Booth's model of self and of cooperative inquiry focuses on ideas, on knowledge, and on essential, pluralized selves. It elides any sense of the inescapable and often unhealable differences among persons and among groups. In other words, the process of inquiry (the pursuit of knowledge) and "sustaining the life of the community" takes precedence over individual or group differences. "What is unthinkable" in Booth's model, writes Rooney, "is the determined outsider invoked by Audre Lorde, the oppositional critic who seeks to 'dismantle the master's house' " (11). In other words, Booth fails to question his underlying assumption about conflict and human beings, that there is a natural drive to resolve conflict in a definitively rational way. What is rational, or even legitimate, argument for one individual may not be so for others.

It might be fair to ask, then, is there anything left of Booth's project to embrace, considering that many writing teachers now strive to make the classroom a place where the drive for consensus does not overpower difference (e.g., see Trimbur, "Consensus"; Pratt; Jarratt)? The answer for me is, of course, yes. Booth wants to change the process of inquiry: he urges us (writing teachers, journalists, student protestors, politicians) to reject sterile eristic models and to establish and live by models of argumentation in which all voices are welcome. He also urges us to concentrate first on the process, and only then on our specific persuasive goals: the "process of inquiry . . . becomes more important than any possible conclusions, and whatever stultifies such fulfillment becomes demonstrably wrong" (*Modern* 137). By doing so, we might renew faith in the possibility that argument might get things done. Most important, Booth passionately insists that argumentation is an *ethical* project, that we must assume *responsibility* for our ideas, because ideas matter.

Consensus, Difference, and Change

Responsibility is not a keyword for Booth, but it is for John Gage, whose ideas were profoundly influenced by Booth's (see notes 41 and 42 for "Adequate" 283–84). Gage borrows the term "responsibility" from Josephine

Miles, who perhaps borrowed it from C. S. Peirce. Gage, very much in line with Freirean and poststructuralist epistemologies, insists that knowledge is not a *commodity*, not something "that can be packaged and traded and remain essentially stable in the interchange of minds"; knowledge is fundamentally an *activity*, "something that we *do* rather than something we *possess*" ("General" 164). Rhetoric for Gage involves the practice of dialogue, of reading and writing, and of constructing arguments. For the purposes of the classroom, Gage rejects *eristic*, rhetoric that concerns itself solely with persuasion, with winning arguments. In its place, Gage favors Aristotelian rhetoric, which he considers "philosophical rhetoric," a position that "view[s] rhetoric itself as a means of discovering and validating knowledge. . . . [It is the] purposeful use of language . . . [that] makes knowing possible" ("Adequate" 154, 153).

Knowledge for Gage is the activity that occurs when arguers—he emphasizes writing arguers—engage in "responsible" inquiry:

> Writing is a process of finding and structuring ideas. Having ideas is what creates the responsibility for searching for a way to express them. Writing is an occasion for making ideas matter, and without ideas to compel it, it is an empty exercise. Writing is the search, not only for the right words in the right order, but also for the right *reasons*. It is in this way that the serious attempt to compose one's thoughts in writing is what can lead one to the very important discovery not only of *what* to think, but *why*. ("Why Write?" 25)

Gage insists that having an idea implies a *responsibility* for that idea. Ideas are by definition generalizations and interpretations; they are products of meaning-making; "essays as units" are not merely "accumulations" of data, but "compositions" of ideas, perceptions of the world organized by a relatively consistent perspective. Ideas have origins—in our beliefs, feelings, prejudices, and so on. Having an idea—or a belief or attitude or prejudice—implies the responsibility to account for that idea; it requires the employment of reasoning to justify that idea, for oneself and for one's audience.

Writing in this sense, striving to understand and elucidate the reasons for one's beliefs, is fundamentally social, "because it externalizes, for an implied if not a real audience, what is otherwise private and inaccessible" ("Why Write?" 25), the process of writing and being read by an audience implies a kind of social responsibility for one's ideas. As Gage puts it, knowledge—the purpose underlying philosophical rhetoric—is an activity of *negotiation*, which occurs between the writer and his or her ideas, the audience, and the means of expressing those ideas (i.e., language). Unlike logic (in Aristotle's sense of the word), rhetoric does not—indeed cannot—begin "in premises known to be true, but in premises assumed to be shared" by one's audience; therefore, truth is conceived as a social agreement, what a community of readers and writers can agree on. What Gage calls "earning the reader's assent" means not earning "ultimate conviction" or "permanent answers" but finding grounds for agreement through negotiation.[10]

In their remarkable "Moments of Argument: Agonistic Inquiry and Confrontational Cooperation," Lynch, George, and Cooper find much that is useful in Gage's ideas, specifically his insistence that the process of writing-class argumentation must be established with care, that argumentation should focus on getting things done in the world, and that argumentation, properly conceived, poses fundamental risks to the arguer and her ideas. But they criticize Gage for some of the same reasons that Booth is often criticized. And while I do not find Gage's ideas *necessarily* to be as limiting as these authors do, I agree that the emphases they bring to the process of inquiry are crucial if a teacher wants to provide an atmosphere where students might be challenged at fundamental levels, so that the change is more than cosmetic, more than a fleeting change of mind, but an enduring change. They want students not only to risk their ideas but also "who they are."

For these authors, Gage's model for argumentation emphasizes the wrong thing. Gage, they argue, implies that the highest goal for argumentation is the "social production of knowledge." They criticize Gage's model, in other words, because it asks students to commit themselves to their ideas and knowledge, not to others or to understanding others' beliefs, why others' ideas are different from their own. In pursuing and negotiating knowledge, even in the social setting of a classroom, students might focus too much on ideas, thereby isolating themselves from their fellow discursants, in effect standing aside, alone with their ideas. When this happens, it becomes too easy to gloss over the inherent differences between one person (or group) and another. They will forget where ideas come from and forget that ideas and conversations are always constrained by configurations of power and by the subjectivities of the arguers themselves. Gage's "social inquiry," they argue, is not *social* enough, since production of knowledge itself is emphasized above the differences that separate us as individuals.

Therefore, Lynch et al. turn to Susan Jarratt's model of argumentation. In her model, beliefs, above all, are held by real individuals, with real histories; argumentation occurs within complex configurations of power that must be examined. Therefore, student-arguers must face issues of identity and power head on, which often leads to intense conflict, even agonistic conflict. Nonetheless, Jarratt finds conflict worthwhile, in fact necessary and productive. She envisions a writing course in which instructors help their students to locate personal experience in historical and social contexts—courses that lead students to see how differences emerging from their texts and discussions have more to do with those contexts that they do with an essential and unarguable individuality. (121)

But the authors note a problem with Jarratt's model too: when difference and conflict are central, the atmosphere of discussion may so daunt students that they will not take the kinds of responsibilities and risks that are necessary for engagement and change to occur.

For their model of argumentation, the authors deliberately choose a rough, imprecisely defined accommodation between the two positions. As in Gage's (and Booth's) model, they want students to believe in the efficacy of argument: argumentation is an activity in which individuals can and *should* (there is a moral duty here) consider and reformulate their positions as they interact with those holding conflicting positions. As in Jarratt's model, they want their students to see that "those positions are not just intellectual ones but positions of power and identity that come out of real histories"; students "must squarely face the differences among us" (Lynch et al. 68).

They strike this accommodation because they want to provide students with the opportunity to *change*. Again, they are interested not so much about particular changes in opinion (e.g., "Native American groups as team mascots may be a bad thing after all") but in fundamental changes in attitude about what argumentation is and what an arguing self is. They want to create a space where students might feel comfortable challenging and changing "who they are." As they point out, such change presents enormous *risk* that rarely occurs hastily or without significant emotional discomfort and struggle (see also the Fishman and McCarthy essays; Welch; and Spellmeyer "Culture and Agency"). Such risks must have rewards, or at least potential rewards, that would outweigh their habitual skeptical distance from the conflict or the comfort of maintaining already-held conceptions of who they are. As these authors put it, "the risk in argument is not that you may lose but rather that you may change" (80). If we want students to take *responsibility* for their arguments, we must provide a space in which these immense risks are worth it, where the risk would matter.

Students are rarely disposed to take the responsibility for such risks: why should they, when it is much easier and more familiar to hide behind cynicism or to conceive oneself as the liberal individual erecting an impermeable barrier between the self and world? If we want to facilitate responsibility-taking, then, students' arguments must matter: what they say must be taken seriously, not merely treated as another opinion to be critiqued and fed into the interpretation machine, then used as fodder for moving everyone to the position that the teacher (or anyone) had in mind from the beginning. The issues they explore must matter: the consequences of holding one position over another must be seen as significant for the immediate community, for the world, and for each individual. Their individual positions (why they believe what they believe) must matter: each of us brings to the discussion our unique perspectives that result from complex, personal, and historically induced experiences; to leave them out or, worse, deride them suggests that they really do not matter after all. Only when we treat students as if their ideas and their histories mattered, as responsible members of the classroom, might they themselves assume responsibility for the beliefs, as well as the disposition to change themselves and their ideas if and when the argument calls for such change. And this responsibility—the responsibility to change when change is warranted—may be the most difficult of all.

A Working Definition of Responsibility Pedagogy

So what would the term "responsible pedagogy" mean? It is very much like the "dialogic education" Freire advanced so many years ago:

> The *raison d'être* of libertarian [or liberatory, or critical] education . . . lies in its drive towards reconciliation. Education must begin with the solution of the teacher-student contradiction, by reconciling the poles of the contradiction so that both are simultaneously teachers *and* students. (*Pedagogy of the Oppressed* 59)

In any pedagogical situation, the teacher is responsible for participating not only in the interpretation of the word and the world, but also in the interpretation of her students and their perspectives. For a teacher to take for granted that her students suffer from a standard ideology is, in Booth's and Gage's terms, to accept assumptions that have not been explored and earned. It ignores the world as students understand it, and then we have returned to monologic teaching. Responsible teaching, then, requires an active learner-teacher, who respects the positions of her students, and responsibly strives to integrate their ideas, their resistances, and their objections into the classroom dialogue. Furthermore, the definitions of "responsible pedagogy" and the kinds of actions that would constitute such a concept are incessantly negotiated among the class. This would not be an "un-centered" classroom; such a practice is extremely difficult to implement and filled with difficulties.[11] But a teacher guides, influences, sometimes persuades and is sometimes persuaded by, but rarely (if ever) commands or dominates, a community of learners. And, once again, this does not mean that the teacher must strive to be politically- or value-neutral, and it does not mean that a teacher, or anyone else, should be prohibited from trying to persuade others—including students—toward her political beliefs. It only means that such persuasion is carried out through dialogue, rather than through imposing systems of belief. What students bring to the class (their personalities, histories, attitudes, as well as their texts) becomes central and in this way important to the community of discussion—something worth taking responsibility for.[12]

The classroom then becomes not a clearing house for distributing particular methods for organizing their beliefs but a public space where students and teacher alike develop their own, often unique, methods for organizing and understanding what has become public knowledge in the classroom. As Marilyn Cooper writes in "Postmodern Ethics":

> I would argue that courses grounded in critical pedagogy imagine students in the same way [as incapable of having or sharing responsibility] when they require students to see particular systems as dominant and oppressive in particular ways, when they forbid students from making arguments that are deemed to be racist, sexist, or otherwise offensive, and when they turn genuine social conflicts that have effects on those in the classroom into academic subjects to be analyzed. Such practices do not allow students to participate as responsible, capable human beings; they intervene in students' response to and for one another; they do not open a field of reactions and responses by recognizing the freedom of students to act.

Of course, it should be noted that imposing this model of argument and change upon students is just that, an imposition of our values. And in this sense, Cooper's efforts duplicate what academics have always tried to do— move students to positions or habits that we deem better. But Cooper is right, the classroom should be a place of dialectical change, where no party strives to dominate the other. If we fail to do this, we risk undercutting our efforts in trying to persuade students that rhetoric in general matters, and that public discussion might be something more than a bag of tricks of merely one immovable opinion bumping up against another.

Respecting Students, Changing Students

To be clear, here I am not agreeing with the cultural right, which sees "political correctness" running rampant and which thinks the infusion of politics into culture studies has enfeebled our educational system and our society. On this issue I disagree profoundly, for instance, with Maxine Hairston. In an article that rejects both the reactionary right and the radical left and that embraces "liberal" values, Hairston contends that "authoritarian methods" are becoming the dominant mode of teaching, and that teachers everywhere—especially young, poorly trained composition teachers—are becoming classroom authoritarians:

> The opportunity to make freshman English a vehicle for such social crusades is particularly rich: in many universities, graduate students in English teach virtually all of the sections, graduate students who are already steeped in post-structuralism and deconstruction theory, in the works of Foucault, Raymond Williams, Terry Eagleton, and Stanley Fish, and in feminist theory. (185)

Hairston unfairly oversimplifies the complex process of teaching writing when she further insists that composition teachers should stick to "what they know," as if a teacher might be a skilled teacher of writing but understand nothing else. I disagree further with her contention that the rejection of foundational versions of ethics and value will lead us down the slippery slope of relativism to a point at which we have no justification for opposing fascism, racial superiority, or any issue at all. Hairston's thinking seems confined to a pre–social constructionist view of knowledge, of the university, and of the classroom. It seems to me unwise and *impossible* to tidily cordon off the disciplines from one another, as if the infusion of knowledge from foreign disciplines might somehow result in the mongrelization of composition studies.

Nonetheless, my experience bears out that she has a point about how easy it can be to forget the needs of first-year composition students. As everyone in the field knows, composition pedagogy imposes tremendous demands upon the teacher; it is time-consuming, energy-draining, and often thoroughly frustrating. Furthermore, the composition course itself continues to be misconceived (even by many who teach it) as a service course that should have been taken care of in secondary school. All this makes it dangerously easy to forget to respect our students, their backgrounds, and their perspectives on the world. Like Hairston, I too have overheard composition-teacher conversations that shock and disappoint me with their contempt for the worldviews of their students. (For me, the disrespect voiced toward eighteen-year-olds because they have adopted the conventional values and habits of their environments is every bit as contemptible as the disrespect for working-class students shown by our forebear PhDs during the days of 1970s open-admissions policies, or as the disrespect Hill showed for his students' positions.) Students' conservative, quietist, uncritical views pose problems that require attention, yes, but not grounds for contempt or resignation. With Donald Lazere, I share the concern that

> some leftist teachers and theorists [tend] to assume that all students . . . agree—or *should* agree—with their views, rather than formulating their approach in a manner that takes respectful account of opposing views. ("Teaching" 195)

To use Freirean terminology, teaching by the banking model is quite simply *easier* than doing otherwise; it is less frustrating and there are more tangible signs of change—"now they understand semi-colons and how mass culture oppresses them." I am concerned that "radical pedagogy" can too easily slip into "banking models," and slip into them as perniciously and deeply as liberal and conservative models.[13]

Efficient versus Effective Change

It could be argued that a "pedagogy of responsibility" is simply a different version of "pedagogy as persuasion," this one somewhat better because it persuades better—in a way that is invisible to students and thus more powerful.[14] But I do not find it hypocritical or contradictory to discuss changes in social consciousness in the same argument in which I advocate respect for student views. A pedagogy of responsibility is, as I have defined it, a pedagogy of respect for students, of listening to the other; it is, in my opinion, also a more effective—and more *permanently persuasive*—pedagogical strategy. It encourages change more effectively not because it is ethically or morally superior, but because it has a better chance of engaging the student's subjectivity more completely.[15]

A radical banking pedagogy is more efficient, certainly, but such pedagogy tends to persuade only ephemerally. In fact, it can often work against the long-term changes in attitudes we are striving to bring about. When we address specific political issues and merely exhort our students to embrace our beliefs because we believe they are better, we are engaging in the kind of superficial kind of rhetoric I discussed in chapter 1, where it is assumed that information can act as an inoculation against subsequent pernicious rhetoric. I fear that such pedagogies may not only fail to bring about changes in our students' attitudes; they may also entrench their attitudes more deeply. To use the parlance of the social psychologists and communications researchers, whose work I examined in chapter 1, a *weak counterattitudinal effort may be in the long run worse than no counterattitudinal effort at all.*

I fear that informational rhetoric will result in the "boomerang effect," where, at the end of the semester, students will have fortified their "resistance" to the very beliefs we have tried to persuade them to. We may be *inoculating* our students against the very attitudes we want them to embrace. Socially responsible teachers need to remember that persuasion is a lifelong process and that they need to consider students' attitudes over the long run, not just from now until the end of the semester.

To be explicit, whereas Hill and Channing (and some forms of critical-thinking proponents) wanted immunization to occur, I *fear that it may occur*. Hill recognized that when his students left the insular confines of Harvard Yard, they would be exposed and susceptible to dangerous habits of discourse. Therefore, he *wanted* something similar to immunization to occur, so that student-citizens could avoid being taken over by these dangerous habits. But I fear that our flash-in-the-pan persuasion will ultimately "boomerang," so that our "small dose" of countercultural persuasion actually enables our students—after they leave us—to later "resist" the very kinds of questions we hope to raise in the classroom. Teachers should make the effort to attempt to engage as much of the student as possible, by taking the time, living with the frustration, and expending the energy to engage in dialogue with their students.

Teaching in more complex ways, more rhetorically responsible ways, and more respectful ways does in fact *tend* to move students away from the conventional cultural beliefs that our society instills in them. But of course there are never any guarantees. Neither radical course content nor radical methods can ensure radical visions of the world. Radical banking pedagogy may bring students to say and write more radical things in more radical ways, but it will not instantly bring about the kinds of changes that we (as teachers and citizens) desire. A pedagogy of responsibility is less predictable and more demanding than banking pedagogy, and its results are often invisible. As Freire cautions, we should not expect to change the world overnight through teaching; we must content ourselves with the "little transformations," neither changing persons in great leaps nor changing entire groups of persons (Shor and Freire, *A Pedagogy* 34). Fishman and McCarthy rightly argue that even when our students do not display "dramatic transformations" (in the classroom, or in their end-of-semester evaluations), teachers may still be doing social work, though they and their students may find it more difficult to recognize change: "the changes we report . . . are piecemeal and episodic, with students often contradicting themselves and denying any modification of their original views" ("Teaching for Change" 364). Such modest changes, rather than scorned as ineffectual, should be recognized as significant cultural and pedagogical work. This is not to say that composition teachers should cease their efforts to discover ways to forge connections between public discussion and composition. But it is doubtful that schooling alone will radically change the subjective experience of an individual in the space of a single course or even over four years of undergraduate study; individual and social change is more complex and subtle.[16]

Most teachers I know entered the profession, in large part, because, as my friend Lee Grove put it, "teachers matter." Teachers do not quixotically suppose they will bring about grand and quick changes, but they do deeply care about teaching as social action, as a way to "illuminate reality"[17] for their students. They want to help students reason in ways that encourage them to examine their assumptions, generate ideas, then take the responsibility to argue for their ideas. Such teachers do persuade. Sometimes the persuasion involves a specific political matter and at others encouraging students to think about their thinking, about their subject positions, in a way that may lead, ultimately, to changes. It is a slow, subtle, inevitably frustrating, but often rewarding process.

Critical pedagogies that place theories of cultural domination at the center of instruction (before students' experience of culture) may be doing less persuasive work than they sometimes appear to be doing, and they may be providing students with a limited and inflexible set of rules for examining the cultural texts they encounter. It can lead to what Jasper Neel calls a kind of "anti-writing," where students are asked to demonstrate mastery over a certain subject, text, or reading strategy but are asked also to keep their personal voice out of the fray. What matters for "anti-writing" is to master a form of reading, to produce as tidy a reading as possible. To use Hill's metaphors about "hack writers," it asks them to run their observations through the mill of such and such an interpretation. (I will be more specific about these matters in the next chapter.)

Perhaps my description of responsibility in writing and pedagogy comes down to a rather old idea justified by some newer reasoning: teachers need to take their students, their viewpoints, and their ideas seriously. To use Freire's very un-postmodern word, they need to "love" their students, that is, need to respect and engage with them no matter how repugnant they find their beliefs, no matter how conservative, no matter how colonized their consciousness, no matter how upper-, middle-, or lower-class-dominated are their attitudes. And again, this does not imply that we must accept racist, sexist, or homophobic discourse, only that effective, truly persuasive pedagogy is unlikely to occur when either the teacher or the student scorns the other. We may for good reasons scorn students who perplex us with their uncritical demand that we "cut the revolution crap and teach me how to make it in the world." This fear of students' unenlightened demands is nothing new. The "mob" of the 1810s scared the daylights out of Channing, and in an effort to see that the mob reigned in its worst instincts, he called for journalists ("teachers of the public," he called them) to reign in their newly acquired habits of writing about what today we call "news." For Hill, the "new students" from the late nineteenth century were already too much the product of their culture, and the university (in the short time it had with them), needed to inculcate the students so deeply with linguistic and mental soundness that they would be impervious to the dangerous world awaiting them. The "new students" from the 1970s open-admissions era seemed to many to be so far lacking in cultural knowledge to deserve our attention. And today, to many, students seem so steeped in and brainwashed by the agenda of their culture that there is little to do but rail against their conformity and exhort them to change. The poor slobs seem utterly incapable of understanding that the dominant order is oppressive and that their brains have turned to mush, colonized by mass culture, which they ignorantly refuse to regard as anything but simple entertainment. They are unworthy of our efforts and we can learn nothing from them. Dialogue is unnecessary because the information-transformation is one-way, the teacher bestowing the gift of knowledge upon the student (who often remains too dense to appreciate it). Of course, I am painting a stark caricature of some teachers, but I do fear it is too accurate of too many whose view on social action is noble, but whose attitudes toward their students are intolerant, and—in several senses of the word, including the one I explore here—irresponsible.

7

Conflict, Change, and "Flexibility" in the Composition and Cultural Studies Classroom

[W]e shall chant over to ourselves as we listen [to poetry] the reasons that we have given as a countercharm to [poetry's] spell, to preserve us from slipping back into the childish loves of the multitude.... [H]e who lends an ear to it must be on his guard fearing for the polity in his soul and must believe what we have said about poetry.

—Plato

[I]t is necessary to trust in the oppressed and in their ability to reason. Whoever lacks this trust will fail to initiate (or will abandon) dialogue, reflection, and communication, and will fall into using slogans, communiqués, monologues, and instructions. Superficial conversions to the cause of liberation carry this danger.

—Paulo Freire

[I]f we hope to get students to rethink (rather than merely repress) what strike us as disturbing positions—if we want, that is, to work with students who voice beliefs that are not so much "oppositional" as they are simply opposed to our own—then we need first to find ways of keeping them an active part of the conversation of the class.

—Joseph Harris

For years in the course of this ripening process, I used for myself to collect my ideas under the designation *fallibilism*; and indeed the first step toward *finding out* is to acknowledge you do not satisfactorily know already; so that no blight can so surely arrest all intellectual growth as the blight

cocksuredeness; and ninety-nine out of every hundred good heads are reduced to impotence by that malady—of whose inroads they are most strangely
unaware!

Indeed, out of a contrite fallibilism, combined with a high faith in the
reality of knowledge, and an intense desire to find things out, all my philosophy has always seemed to me to grow.

—C. S. Peirce[1]

Chapters 2 through 5 argued that nineteenth-century "intellectual" discourse was not "dominant" discourse, that in fact intellectuals tried to
countervail what they saw as the culturally dominant discourse, much as
intellectuals have always done and do today. The intellectual theories and
practices of rhetoric during the nineteenth century (Hill's rhetoric or
university-culture rhetoric) "dominated" only the very limited world of
academia and "gentleman culture." Adams Sherman Hill perceived himself
to be, and probably was, as alienated from "dominant" society as today's
"radical" pedagogues and academic critics of public discourse. Hill too
conceived himself as opposing a society (the capitalists, the media moguls)
that dominated a system of mass communications that enfeebled the critical powers of the citizenry. If indeed, then, much composition history is
correct in asserting that Hill's and others' composition pedagogy was designed to secure new members for managerial capitalism (Berlin, Ohmann,
Douglas), then we must surely rethink the "lessons" we learn from that
history. Specifically, that nineteenth-century compositionists saw themselves
not as participants but as culturally oppositional figures suggests a lesson
more like this: we never know how our classroom rhetorical theory will
play in the world outside the classroom; we cannot know exactly how our
students will use what we have taught them there.

But what does *this* imply? Perhaps, it is just another reminder that
teachers ought to rein in their hubris about changing the world and, in
fact, about changing their students. Perhaps it reminds us also how important it is to listen closely to our students, to strive as best we can to discern
what is happening in the dynamic relationship between our classroom and
the students' world. Perhaps it even means that we need to monitor what
happens when the semester ends and beyond. We do not know, really, what
happens to our students when they leave a "critical" classroom. Do they
remain "critical" or "radical"? Alan Kennedy tells the anecdote of two pro-
fessional-writing students who claimed their work in cultural studies better
allowed them to "make it" in the capitalist sphere of business, the world
that their cultural studies teachers believed they were dissuading them

from joining. As Kennedy remarks, "So, far from being an inoculation against success in late capitalist America, classes founded on resisting the dominant ideology might well be keys to success in it" (25). In the same volume of essays on cultural studies and composition pedagogy, *Left Margins*, Richard Ohmann asks more bluntly, "But what next, for those students—for the ones who say they will never see the world the same way again? Are they to live on as sad sophisticates, pessimists, smartasses, cynics?" ("Afterword" 329). To use the metaphors I have been stringing throughout this book, do our attempts to inoculate students against their culture result merely in stronger resistance to our own radical or postmodern ideas?

Another "lesson" has to do with rhetoricians' perception of the public and the nature of argument. Specifically, one of the main currents in the Western rhetorical tradition is the tendency to wax nostalgic for the public's capacity for responsible argumentation. The "decay of argument" argument has become one of the clichés of intellectual culture. Here is Ann Berthoff, who knows as much as anyone about the epistemological uses of argument:

> [W]here do students [today] hear argument? Mine do not have the faintest idea of the conventions of an editorial—and when have they ever heard an authentic, dialectical exchange on television information shows? . . . *Argument was the air you breathed, a hundred years ago.* I am not, of course, claiming authenticity or moral superiority for those who can argue. I mean only that the capacity to manage disputation is a *culture-bound skill.* (*Sense* 25, my emphases)

Berthoff is not wrong: argument in America, generally speaking, and the argumentative capacities of our students probably have deteriorated in the past hundred years, just as they had probably deteriorated in the hundred years prior to Hill's tenure as Boylston Professor as well as the hundred years prior to Channing's. Channing, Hill, and Berthoff, and many other commentators on contemporary argumentation concur that "disputation is a culture-bound skill"—or at least they concur that a culture whose civic debate has deteriorated will produce citizens and students with impoverished ideas about what constitutes good argument and how one might practice it. Since its inception in America, the composition course has been considered an academic institution where this culturewide problem of argumentation should be and could be redressed. This is not to suggest that because the "decay of argument" argument is an old one, it is unimportant or unsolvable or somehow quaint, but only that the power of culture to dominate our students' sense of argument has been recognized for some time.

We need to remember, further, that an impoverished conception of argumentation is *deeply* embedded both in our culture and in our students. This suggests the necessity of delving deep into students' consciousness (as far as we can, anyway, in our limited time with them) if we wish to make any significant change in their structures of feeling about argumentation or in the way they view their world and themselves. "Responsible argumentation" is, and has been for a long time, a countercultural concept, *alien* to our students. Our students' ideas about argumentation are deeply embedded, and we can hardly hope to countervail the widespread models of argument they understand by "giving" them—banking style—information about what the nature of argument and of an arguing self ought to be. Rather, they must *live* such argument. To use Berthoff's metaphor, such argument must become the air they breathe.

Our students have been taught that one begins, proceeds, and ends with positions of security and certitude. From their culture and often from their previous writing instructors, they have learned that one need not and probably *should* not address in any meaningful fashion the fundamental difficulties of an issue, because one does not want to muss up the argument. One does not want to portray the self behind the pen as less than autonomous, integrated, and mechanically and otherwise "sound" and "whole." Our students have learned that the art of any public discourse demands that they hide these complexities and ambiguities; they are embarrassing.

Even with all the fine work that has been done on initiating students into the writing and thinking styles of academic discourse, we academics still tend to forget that we have been trained to value and exploit ambiguity and difficulty. They are the tools we use to investigate, to move forward, and to create new ideas. But we need to keep in mind that such an attitude toward difficulty, ambiguity, and conflict is an attitude that runs counter to almost everything our students have experienced. Getting students to embrace *our* notions of argumentation and of difficulty requires a process of re-enculturation. As the various educational slogans go, "telling is not teaching," "depositing" information into student consciousness rarely causes real change, and, as Berthoff reminds us, a "pedagogy of exhortation" is a poor substitute for a "pedagogy of knowing" (*Sense* 12).

When it comes to cultural studies, certainly there is much to offer teachers of writing; the goals commonly associated with cultural-studies pedagogy, indeed, are among my own teacherly goals. However, many of the published descriptions of "composition and cultural studies" classrooms are strangely and unhelpfully *rationalist* in approach. In fact, many of these classrooms suffer from a structural contradiction between their theorization of the postmodern subject and their actual *treatment* of the subjects whom they teach in the classroom: many teachers seem to want their students to adopt a postmodern understanding of subjectivity, but these teachers themselves expect their students to react to their teaching in humanist, rationalist ways. They fail, that is, to take into account the complexity of any person's subjectivity. To use the "inoculation and resistance" metaphor, they seem to believe that merely *exposing* their students to postmodern theories of culture and of the self will bring about a change in subjectivity, so that students will be able to successfully *resist* those aspects of culture that we teachers deem particularly dangerous. But if we truly desire change in our students, neither mere conflict nor mere exposure is enough.

The Recent Tradition of Composition and Cultural Studies: Exposure, Inoculation, and Resistance Once More

Like critical thinking, composition and cultural studies (hereafter "C&CS") could be said to have perhaps a dozen direct ancestors, which have resided both within and beyond composition studies. Within composition studies, among the first (perhaps *the* first) to explicitly theorize the union of cultural studies and composition studies was John Trimbur, whose remarkably prescient "Cultural Studies and Teaching Writing" of 1988 specified the principal assumptions that have defined the C&CS movement up to the present day. Trimbur's article, with its theoretical bent and its emphases, has also proved to be remarkably representative of the movement. To provide context for his predictions, Trimbur noted the 1980s foregrounding of the politics of literacy and a growing sentiment that writing teachers were justified in "push[ing] our research and teaching—our sense of ourselves really—in frankly political directions" (5). Trimbur noted the growing political and cultural dissatisfaction among academics and the public alike. The infusion of cultural studies, he argued, could provide the means for transforming this mere sentiment into a cultural force; cultural studies could lead both students and teachers toward producing what Richard Johnson called "useful knowledge," that is, knowledge that links academic and political activities. Furthermore, argued Trimbur, cultural studies provided a way out of the Foucauldian morass of complete domination and a way toward reconceiving agency. It seems, in fact, to have become obligatory for C&CS essayists to remind us that cultural studies assumes domination is never complete and takes as its fundamental goal discovering opportunities for agency. It strives to create, as Trimbur puts it, "autonomous areas of public and private life where human agency can mediate between the material conditions of the dominant order and the lived experience and aspirations of the popular masses" (9). In other words, cultural studies, as Trimbur conceives it, is always searching for the means to *resistance*.

And to the question "what does one resist?" Trimbur answers, not only overt political oppression but also "the imposition and reproduction of dominant forms of thought, structures of feeling, and patterns of behavior" (9). In other words, cultural studies helps individuals resist the "subject positions" (a newer term then) imposed upon them. And before a student can do this, she must realize that indeed she inhabits a subject position, that her identity does not reside in some central, unified, autonomous self but is a product of history. Cultural studies, drawing on the lessons of postmodernism, theorizes a "radical de-centering of the self" (8).

This has been the central focus (the primary mission, if you will) of C&CS—to move students toward understanding postmodern versions of subjectivity, and to transform students from passive victims of culture to active agents who resist culture. It was James Berlin who most successfully thrust this emphasis into composition studies and who deserves the lion's share of credit for politicizing subjectivity in the composition classroom. In 1988, in one of the most influential and controversial articles of the decade, Berlin argued that we need to help students recognize that

> the subject is itself a social construct that emerges through the linguistically-circumscribed interaction of the individual, the community, and the material world. There is no universal, eternal, and authentic self that beneath all appearances is at one with all other selves. The self is always a creation of a particular historical and cultural moment. ("Rhetoric and Ideology" 489)

Within a very short time, this essay's three-part taxonomy of composition studies—"cognitive," "expressive," "social-epistemic"—became the subject of disciplinary dispute. Although many disagreed with Berlin's categories or with the impulse to divide and name the field (e.g., Flower; Schilb, "Comment"; Roskelly and Ronald), one the principal debates would soon focus on his demarcation between "expressive" and "social-epistemic" rhetoric. Both rhetorics interrogated the idea of a self, but expressive rhetoric, argued Berlin, ended there, sanctioning a moral holiday for students to bathe in the glory of mere self-understanding. The "social turn" had become dominant in composition studies, and, very quickly, "expressivism," much like "current-traditional rhetoric," became a term of opprobrium.

The problem with expressivism, explained Berlin, was its lack of social vision: for expressivists, "power is consistently defined in personal terms" (485). Berlin understood that the impulse behind expressionism was the radical politics of the 1960s, but such anti-establishment stances were merely romantic or vitalist. But it seems that what most bothered Berlin was not just the issue of escapism but the power of expressivism to undermine the goals of truly radical, anticapitalist, pedagogy.

In the first place expressionistic rhetoric is inherently and debilitatingly divisive of political protest, suggesting that effective resistance can only be offered by individuals, each acting alone. . . . Beyond this, expressionistic rhetoric is easily co-opted by the very capitalist forces it opposes. . . . It is indeed not too much to say that the ruling elites in business, industry, and government are those most likely to nod in assent to the ideology inscribed in expressionistic rhetoric. (487)

This fear of creeping expressivism continues. Indeed, Berlin remained, as Alcorn has noted, "uneasy with the emphasis [given] to personal experience" (344). In this more recent letter to Theresa Enos (written to her in her capacity as editor of *Rhetoric Review*), Berlin once again emphasized the danger of expressivism:

This disagreement is important since the wrong take on it can lead the expressivists in the audience to once again abandon the political and public in favor of the libidinal and private. This has already appeared in certain commentators on poststructuralist theory who call upon the challenge to foundations and the split subject to argue for a revival of Peter Elbow and the celebration of the personal. (Letter)

It is possible to support many of Berlin's goals for composition pedagogy but still maintain that the discipline-wide phobia of expressivism is unnecessary and unhelpful. How can a pedagogy that neglects the personal (for ideological reasons, perhaps) possibly hope to persuade students to *any* position, let alone a radical position—a position radically different from the one the student held at the beginning of the semester? Such fear of expressionism may lead to a refusal to acknowledge the importance of personal experience and personal beliefs for students, and thus fail ever to engage them except superficially. And when teachers fail to do this, it is doubtful whether they ever truly persuade anyone.

The categorical rejection of expressivism can lead to a failure to ever engage students meaningfully. This problem appears clearly in the collection of essays *Left Margins: Cultural Studies and Composition Pedagogy*. These essays, most of which were written by teachers of writing, were contributed in response to a proposal soliciting "exciting, 'nuts-and-bolts' strategies for teaching students to write critically about contemporary cultural media, thus developing awareness of their own ideological subjectivity" (x). There are many valuable and insightful essays in the collection. Henry Giroux's lead essay, for example, documents his discovery that merely reading cultural theory is not enough: students need to be given opportunities "to theorize their own experiences rather than articulate the meaning of other peoples' theories" (11). His writing assignments were intended to allow students to position themselves "as cultural producers and [enable] them to rewrite their own experiences and perceptions . . . , to create a borderland where new hybridized identities might emerge, . . . to appropriate knowledge as part of a broader effort at self-definition and ethical responsibility" (16).

But many of the essays in *Left Margins* tacitly approve of a pedagogy that seeks to show students that (to expose them to the argument that) their identity conforms to a 1990s standardized identity. By recognizing this, they will somehow be put on the permanent *qui vive* toward their culture—and thus they will effectively resist their culture. The most extreme such example is Mas'ud Zavarzadeh' s essay ("The Pedagogy of Pleasure 2: The Me-in-Crisis"), which takes the form of a letter written in response to a student essay in which the student had naively foregrounded her own experiences, her own "local narratives" by "spinning anecdotes, narratives, and tales of self-affirmation" (220, 222). He takes the student to task for "indulg[ing] in the pseudo-explanations (blame games), anecdotes, autobiographical meditations—that are a luxury of the leisured classes—etc., etc." (228) "The reason for being unable to write the paper," he explains to her,

> is a rather simple social (non)practice of yours: you do not *read* . . . you have not read the books which were the focus of our discussions and critique during the semester. You, in other words, have not labored to acquire the knowledges which are necessary for writing the paper—knowledges which are the enabling conditions for praxis.

The author expresses certainty of the student's motivations, all of which are "typical" of (white upper-middle-class) students:

> Why have you not read the books? Because the social practice of reading, the intellectual labor involved in producing concepts . . . is disruptive of the pleasures of "talking." Reading/writing/thinking require discipline—the *other* of pleasure . . . *pleasure* is the last privilege that the white middle class person would give up; it is the mark of autonomy; the *excessive* (i.e., the crisis-y). . . . By the way, why is it that all the letters I receive on the crisis of subjectivity are from white (upper-)middle-class students? I have never encountered a person of color who allowed herself/himself the luxury of being *in crisis*. (228, ellipses and emphases in original)

Perhaps there is a layer of irony that I am missing, but this is the rhetoric of ridicule and exhortation, not of engagement or responsibility. It is typical, as James T. Zebroski has pointed out, of pedagogies that masquerade as "radical pedagogy" but are really nothing more than what Freire had called "banking pedagogy" (92). That is, they masquerade as pedagogies that attempt to help students find problems and work out solutions, but they really tell students *what* the problems are and how they must solve them.[2]

Some More Modest and Realistic Goals for Student Change

Such C&CS pedagogy has three fundamental problems. The first, as *Left Margins* respondent Gary Tate explains, is its lack of understanding about what *writing instruction* is for and what it can do. Zavarzadeh's and others' essays typify the "tendency for writing teachers to teach something other than writing" (269). Rather than *teaching writing*, these teachers seem to be *using writing* to teach something else, which, again, typifies that belief among some teachers of composition that "the composition course is an empty pedagogical space that needs to be filled with 'content.' "[3] Whether some like it or not, we are expected to help our students improve their writing and their arguing abilities. Tate documents and objects to the way that the *Left Margins* contributors seem to want to sidestep that responsibility.

Another problem is the ethical one. Gerald Graff, another respondent to the volume, expresses his opposition to the pedagogical ethical stance in which "oppositional teachers [feel] licensed to counteract the official forms of indoctrination with their own counterindoctrination" ("Dilemma" 276). As Graff is well aware, postmodern ethics would call into question Graff's ethical argument; after all, is anyone capable of "rational choice"? is it possible to construct a student-teacher relationship without domination? These are obviously difficult issues, but teachers are left with the dilemma between accepting liberal pluralism or dauntlessly insisting that students accede to their positions, in which case teachers would find themselves, as Graff puts it, treating a student's opposing "view as an error to be corrected from a position of superior political insight" (279).

The third problem concerns *effectiveness*. All disciplinary and ethical issues aside, we should ask ourselves: *Can* a pedagogy of counterindoctrination, such a rhetorical strategy, possibly do what we expect of it— change our students? Can it really transform students from passive victims who merely consume culture into active agents who resist culture?

So, speaking of "spinning anecdotes," here are a few—some from former National Endowment for the Humanities chair Lynne V. Cheney and some of my own—that illustrate several difficulties in effectively and authentically changing our students. Cheney's book *Telling the Truth* argues that "political correctness" is "alive and entrenched" in American universities, responsible for everything from grade inflation to Nazi Holocaust apologists. It is also responsible, she writes, for reinforcing the cynicism of students, since the pressures of political correctness in the classroom force students into unauthentic poses. For instance, she quotes many students from several universities who have learned, Cheney says, "simply . . . to cope with what they find going on in the classrooms":

> [One student] "quickly discovered that the way to get A's [in a feminist anthropology course] was to write papers full of guilt and angst about how I'd bought into society's definition of womanhood and now I'm enlightened and free." . . . [Another student] told me . . . "If you write about misogyny, you'll do great." . . . One male instructs another on how to succeed in a feminist classroom. "Pretend to be a male chauvinist, then have a conversion. You're bound to get an A." (81)

And Cheney goes on with several more similar quotations from students who have sought her out. We might easily dismiss these anecdotes as merely those of a few, rare students who have sought out the high-profile conservative, but these passages troubled me because I hear students saying these kinds of things *frequently*. In fact, I wrote the first draft of this chapter before I had read Cheney, and in it I had included a conversation overheard that was remarkably like those told to Cheney. Overhearing two male students waiting to buy their food in the student union, I heard one, like Cheney's faux feminist, tell the other that to succeed in first-year composition, you have to fake a conversion if you want an "A."

These are common, now even tired, stories. Probably all of us have heard (or told) such stories, but their typicality should make us take notice, not reject them merely as banal and tired. Such stories are almost amusing at first, perhaps mildly disturbing. If they are more than braggadocio, they are probably the isolated cases of fairly isolated sociopaths. But I wrote down the conversation I overheard because I wanted to offer it to my undergraduates since we had been discussing the ethics of writing and taking responsibility for one's ideas. My students' responses surprised me. I realize now how naïve I was, but I thought my students would be outraged—or at least pretend to be outraged. To the contrary, almost everyone thought this was "business as usual." As one of my students wrote in her response journal, "Come on, everyone knows you have to play the game. Even if you don't mean to do it, in the end you do play the game. This student is just being honest." None said they approved of the faux feminist's gimmick, but none expressed surprise. The typical response came down to something like this: "Of course, *I* would never do such a thing, but I'm sure others do it all the time, and who can blame them?"

And such fraudulence is often not even consciously done. That is, students may not even recognize that the ethics of such posing might be questionable. Another of my anecdotes illustrates this. One young man, whom I have known for several years, now twenty-one years old, was recently taking his first semester of first-year writing at the university where I teach. When I asked how things were going, he said something like: "Not bad. Everything we write about has to be on feminist topics, but that's okay, I guess. It's kind of nice, really, because you never have to worry about what stand to take in your papers." In other words, there is only one stand any sane person *would* take—the stand of the teacher. This student, a bright student who gets good grades and enjoys school, had no sense that his automatically adopting the teacher's political stances was ethically questionable.

I do not suggest that other teachers are stupid, that somehow I am seeing through the unauthentic poses that others cannot. I am quite sure that I too am "duped" all the time. Indeed, cynicism itself spreads like a contagion, and teachers too are dubious of such political conversion. When I talk with my colleagues or graduate students about C&CS, they say they find many of the articles describing mass conversion, at best, improbable. These are teachers who are not politically neutral; for the most part, they are committed and serious, and they do wish (to varying degrees) to engage and alter their students' political views. But they, like me, suspect that the writers of these articles either (1) are being fooled by their students or (2) possess an extraordinary amount of persuasive charisma. My point is this: no matter how democratic one makes a classroom, for a majority of students, resisting the teacher's political (or any other) agenda is far more difficult—and I suspect far more rare—than going along with the flow.

As Richard Miller has suggested, teachers (especially composition teachers whose professional identities depend so much on the quality of their teaching) may fail to question the authenticity of student conversion and may expect to see radical transformations occurring right before their eyes because of the power of "pedagogy's master narrative." We see this story everywhere, not only in the usual spots in popular culture but also in our own scholarly writing in teaching. Pedagogy's master narrative is a "happy story," where "the violence of the educational process is always already understood to ultimately have been for the good of the student"; it assures us that radical transformation is indeed possible—it happens all the time, even in the short time we have with students. While in the rising action of this plot, there arises a conflict (usually between teacher and student), in the denouement a "love of learning emerges[, a] form of excellence is achieved," and our students, in the end, become just like us ("Making"). As Miller argues, we must recognize the power of this master narrative, and recognize how it may blind us or make us believe change has occurred when it may not have.

Of course, I am not suggesting that we become merely cynical about the authenticity of student change, but I do suggest we become more modest about what we expect to happen in the brief period we have with students. As Graff and others have argued for some time and in various places, students (in fact, most nonacademics) find it tremendously difficult to sort out the various positions within the culture wars. Therefore, merely providing students with postmodern, radical arguments about subjectivity and culture leaves them not only confused but also unmoved (though perhaps moved enough to conform, for the time being, to what they think the teacher expects). If we fail to bring our students *into* the argument, then we are not teaching *the* argument nor are we teaching the *practice* of argument. Instead, we are merely *exposing* them to *an* argument. And again, the largely unexamined logic behind such a pedagogy assumes that rational argument will bring our students to our alien understandings of self and culture. It assumes, in fact, the very liberal (or liberal-conservative) idea that once persons have acceded to the correctness of certain values, they can and will "live" such values. Subjects can will themselves, assumes this logic, into protecting themselves from the dangerous values that culture strives to inscribe within them. Student subjects can inoculate themselves with logic. Here, such pedagogues seem in agreement with Plato's Socrates (and with Hill and Channing, for that matter), who argued (see the chapter epigraph) that a rational argument—if "chant[ed] over [and over] to ourselves"—could act as a "countercharm" against the seductive rhetoric of culture.

Note how this rhetoric asks the students to make a rational choice— the "choice" to change themselves by, as Joseph Harris puts it, "adopt[ing] an adversarial stance toward their own culture, [and] to side somehow with the university and against the media" ("Other Reader" 233). Harris has described the model teacher-critic, whom students might not only imitate but become, this way:

> [she] presents a figure of the critic who can read (and often even enjoy) popular works without being injured or seduced by them. Yet each doubts that others can do the same, and so ends up arguing for a kind of censorship, or at least for a better world where the pleasures such texts offer are no longer needed.... A deep anti-democratic impulse, a kind of fear of the mob, runs through such writings. Those other readers can't be trusted. Their

> responses need to be trained, domesticated, disciplined. And in the
> meantime, they need to be guarded against the influences of popu-
> lar and thus suspect texts. (228)

And of course, per pedagogy's master narrative, the teaching goal here is to make the student just like us—above the fray, unaffected, immune. I agree with Harris. Students are asked, by a sheer effort of the will to adopt a habit, a way of seeing, their culture. They are asked to change "who they are." Furthermore, it is assumed that students can, by this choice, make themselves immune to getting duped by their culture: they can enter it, even enjoy it, and then emerge unscathed, immune to the appeals of popu-lar culture.

This should not suggest (per the "egalitarian fallacy") that postmodernist thinkers are permanently disqualified from making rational arguments. It suggests only that we should recognize the limits of such rational argu-ment when it comes to an issue as difficult, complex, and emotional as identity. As Marshall Alcorn argues, politically assertive teachers of compo-sition want their students to adopt a postmodern understanding of subjec-tivity, but, ironically, these teachers themselves seem to have very humanist, rationalist expectations of their students, as if rational argument by itself would bring about significant changes in subjectivity. "The human subject," he writes, "is more complex than Berlin and others theorize" (331). Changes in political commitment do not come easy, and yet politically active teach-ers rarely ask "how does the subject as one ideological composition, be-come another ideological composition?" (333) No one would deny that rational arguments *can* sometimes bring about such transformations, but to place all the pedagogical eggs in this one basket is an act of irrational faith, which ironically mirrors the cultural logic of capitalism such teachers want their students to resist.

> The effortless transformation of the poststructuralist subject from
> one that is a *victim* to a postmodernist subject that can be an
> *agent*, this easy theoretical flip from a theory that explains the
> subject's *incapacity* for political insight to a theory that facilitates
> the subject's *capacity* for political resistance is, like the claims of
> many television ads, an appeal to our fantasies for power and suc-
> cess. (337)

This power to convert students, as C. Jan Swearingen has noted, has become the benchmark of "good," "committed" teaching: "it has now become obliga-tory to mark one's seriousness, and loyalty as a compositionist by the peda-gogical equivalent of a conversion narrative, a testimony demonstrating" one has facilitated students' transformations into negotiating, resisting subjects ("Composing"). In short, teachers need to be more realistic about who they are, who their students are, and the nature of the profession. As Alcorn cautions, "Let us more carefully consider the transformation in which we are encouraged to put our faith" (337).

There is a danger, in other words, that C&CS may be encouraging teachers to focus on the materials of their course (the cultural-theory essays, etc.) and to lose sight of their students. It would be unfair to say that the contributors to *Left Margins are* doing this, but they primarily speak of their students as a *class* (in whatever sense of the word), very rarely discussing how individual students grapple with the difficult, complex, and discomforting issues presented to them. Students are discussed *en masse*, and when a course is described by its teacher as successful, it is evaluated in very general terms, through student evaluations (e.g., Berlin, "Composition and Cultural"), or the writer/instructor simply tells us something like "By the end of the semester, most of my students had come to a much broader understanding of . . ." (Caulfield 170). Such essays tell us very little about how students as individuals actually do negotiate their change, how they succeed or fail in becoming committed to different political beliefs.

Fear of Expressivism, Faith in Conflict

In addition to the power of "pedagogy's master narrative," there may be two other reasons for C&CS teacher-essayists' willingness to accept such superficiality. The first has to do with their unreasonable fear of expressivism and of the expressivist tradition in composition studies. The second involves the recent tradition in composition that views "conflict" as a good in and of itself.

C&CS has too readily dismissed anything that suggests the primary goal of the writing course is sounding the depths of the student's self, discovering who one is and can be, discovering one's "voices." Since Berlin's 1988 criticism, C&CS has seen expressivism and cultural critique as antagonists, as if the "pleasures of expressivism" were examples of what Herbert Marcuse called "affirmative culture" or "repressive desublimation." (It has become the "E-word," as one of our graduate students put it.) But I see little reason for so stark a demarcation between cultural studies and expressivism. The work of William E. Coles Jr., for instance, could be important for C&CS pedagogy. Although Berlin puts Coles in the "expressivist" category, Coles does not encourage his students to discover that single, unified self behind the pen—the self that Hill wanted his students to possess in order to make the self inviolable to cultural virulence. As is suggested by the *plural* in *The Plural I*, Coles (and the tradition furthered by such works as *Facts, Artifacts, Counterfacts*) wants students to "try on" multiple selves and to understand how the self is partly made by ideas that the individual does not consciously choose. That model of pedagogy, in my view, can do far more to undermine the students' notions of a stable unified self than a semester's worth of articles on cultural theory. Coles pushes his students toward rejecting the romantic ideal of a single core self. Such pedagogies are called by Coles "Let's just be Human Beans" approaches ("An Unpetty Place" 378). He recognizes, as do C&CS critics, that "formal education . . . has everything to do with the personhood of those who are involved with it." He explains that while all his writing assignments have to do with the relationship between the self and the world,

> the self I am speaking of here, the one with which I am concerned in the classroom, is not a mock or false self, but a literary self, a self construable from the way words fall on a page. The other self, the identity of the student, is something with which I as a teacher can have nothing to do. . . . This relation [between these selves] is the center of both the course as a course and the course as more than that . . . [but it is something] that only an individual writer or thinker has the right to work out, and it can hardly become the province of any public intellectual discourse without a teacher's ceasing to be a teacher, a student's ceasing to be a student. (379–80)

There is no reason why Coles's pedagogy would *necessarily* lead students to bourgeois notions of subjectivity. When he writes, for instance, that he wants students to learn that using language is "the primary means by which all of us run orders through chaos thereby giving ourselves the identities we have" (*Plural I* 285), he means something like, pragmatically making and remaking such selves through writing is the means by which we create meaning and enable ourselves to do meaningful things in the world. Rather than disengaging the student from her world, Coles's pedagogy can move the student into an extended and rigorous examination of the relationship between the self and culture. In short, Coles's pedagogy strives to bring about, as Trimbur put it, "a radical decentering of the self."[4]

Another reason for this superficial aspect of C&CS may stem from the superficial way that composition studies in general has been treating the idea of "conflict." A few years ago "community" dominated discussion about writing classrooms, but that metaphor was abandoned when it was realized that "community" provided little room for the important idea of "conflict." "Contact zone," Mary Louise Pratt's term for the place of intersection between competing languages and worldviews, became the new metaphor.[5] The contact-zone metaphor highlighted conflict and made the idea of conflict central to student writing. No longer were compromise and negotiation (which tend to silence less powerful voices) the goal, but conflict itself, the pointing up of conflict. However, as Joseph Harris has written, promoters of this appealing idea are too vague about what happens during and after the point of conflict in the contact zone. They are silent to questions, "What is the relationship between conflict and student subjectivities?" and "How do students change?"

> Pratt is vague . . . about how one might actually go about making sure such dissenting voices get their say. What she seems to be doing is *importing* difference into her classroom through assigning her students a number of readings from diverse cultures. Students are thus brought "in contact" with writings from diverse cultures. ("Negotiating" 32)

Again, it is assumed that *exposure* to a conflict, the mere meeting of two different arguments, will somehow *change* students. Pratt and others do not explain, says Harris, "how she tries to get students to articulate or negotiate the differences they perceive among themselves" (32). Furthermore, "The very metaphor of *contact*" suggests a kind of superficiality: "The image is one of cultures banging or sliding off each other" (33). (We might call this the "fusion theory of conflicting ideas," the idea that somehow "truth" or "negotiated settlements" or "changes in opinion" alchemically appear when conflicting arguments collide with one another.)[6] Harris points out that Pratt offers her students "safe houses," places of short-term refuge from the conflict, but she neglects to show why students would want to ever venture out of these safe houses and into struggle (38–39). Neglected is an explanation, to C&CS readers or to students, *why* students should change their positions, rather than merely defend them tooth and nail. Such take-it-or-leave-it conflict mirrors, ironically, the culturally dominant modes of argumentation (such as *Nightline* argumentation), of which our students are already too well aware.

Once again, change is presumed to happen, though too few have paid much attention to *how* change happens. Harris describes in detail "some of the best work being done in composition," which shows an "interest in how differences get negotiated (or not) in varying situations by particular teachers and students" (37–39). To his list I would add the C&CS studies that, sometimes ethnographically, monitor the progress of individuals through a semester or several semesters—the work, for instance, of Fleisher, George and Shoos, Robison, Robinson and Stock, and Schriner. Such studies are working toward what Gary Cronkhite called for over twenty years ago, the study of "psychoepistemology," or "how people come to believe what they believe." Such studies could perhaps transform this pedagogy of exposure to a pedagogy of knowing.

Contrite Conflictualism

Again, it is very difficult and very rare to significantly alter students' identities by exposing them to information. With apologies to William Coles, we cannot alter students' structures of feeling in such a way that they will intuit that subjectivity is radically decentered, and we cannot with consistent success implore them to become committed to political change, but we can put them in a position to learn these things for themselves.[7] The best way to do this, I think, is to follow some of the so-called expressivist practices that were begun by William E. Coles and extended by Bartholomae and Petrosky, Harris, and others. By allowing students to focus on the conflicts within themselves, which get expressed by them through their writing, we can get them, as Coles put it, to challenge "the bullet-proof consonance of character and situation" (*Plural* 79).

As Harris has argued, we need not "import" cultural conflict into the classroom ("Negotiating" 32; "Symposium"); our students come to us packed full of cultural conflict. Composition studies is unique in its capacity for engaging student response, for addressing students as individuals, and for helping them wrestle with the conflicts *they* bring with them to the classroom (see also Bartholmae, "Tidy"). The study of culture as it manifests itself within our students can be our unique contribution to cultural studies (Harris, "Students"). Embracing this kind of conflict—conflict that does not fit between the covers of a textbook—leads inevitably to messiness and very often to writerly selves that "fall apart" both mechanically and ethically. Focusing on this sort of conflict may not always "inoculate" students against the dangerous strains of discourse within their culture, but it can do much, I think, toward bringing them to a healthful understanding of the complexity and confusion of their culture as well the complexity and confusion of their role in that culture.

For me, this suggests that we need to put "difficulty" at the center of our pedagogy. This is, of course, a familiar strategy in composition studies,[8] but anyone who has tried this approach understands that using "difficulty" in the classroom is itself difficult. It is different from the way most of us and most of our students have been educated. Furthermore, when difficulty is at the center of composition pedagogy, the self behind the essay may fall apart in many aspects: ethically (that is, the ethos may seem to flutter and fade, come apart), grammatically, and structurally. If students are permitted to "wonder out loud" and rewarded for doing so in their essays, and if they are encouraged to incorporate ambiguous or conflicting viewpoints, then the stable, mechanically sound writerly self that we value so much may vanish into chaotic, fragmentary, and perhaps even ungrammatical confusion. This is not to suggest we encourage confusion for the sake of confusion, but that we ask for and figure out how to reward what William A. Covino calls "thoughtful uncertainty":

> I am suggesting that [students] trade certainty for ambiguity, trade preservative writing for investigative writing, trade conclusions for "counterinduction." ... Thoughtful uncertainty ... provokes the investigation of possibilities beyond one's stock response. (*Art* 130)

Channing, Hill, and other nineteenth-century intellectuals despaired about students' and citizens' inability to get beyond stock responses and about their desire "to have all the great questions of the time disposed of in at most half a column" (Godkin, "Newspapers Here" 165). I fear that writing teachers may be duplicating an old mistake when they ask students to trade stock responses for what students perceive to be our stock responses. As Covino argues, we need to make the lost "art of wondering" worth their while.

The discomfort we composition teachers feel about fragmentary student texts or texts that wonder out loud comes from innumerable and invisible sources, including the culturewide discomfort with argumentative insecurity. But another source, I would suggest, is Harvard's general legacy to higher education: that education should help students acquire and maintain a "manly independence" from a world that everywhere conspires against the individual. By sheer acts of will and by assiduous practice, one might acquire the habit of resistance. For Hill, such habit could in part be acquired by students putting their autonomous "real selves behind the pen, and keep[ing] them there." Healthy writers and persons are "whole," their individual health reflected by the soundness of their compositions. For Hill, such a presentation of self was culturally significant: by attending to one's own individual health, the public health of civic discussion might be improved. And such a presentation of self *countered* what Hill perceived to be the conception of self produced by nineteenth-century mass culture. In Hill's thinking, encouraging such a stable writerly self was a healthful and countercultural pedagogical maneuver. But our thinking has changed, so that Hill's stable, autonomous writerly self now seems to be the problem.

As far as the "politics and composition" controversy, while the teaching of composition is ineluctably political, we should question whether foregrounding political and cultural controversy—"importing" it into the classroom—is the wisest way to spend the limited time we have with our students. In our anxiety over ensuring that our students remain interested, it is all too easy to believe that we are doing something socially useful so long as we expose our students to politically difficult issues and then engage in some sort of dialogue about those questions. But our students are real human beings, with real beliefs, attitudes, and real differences among them. Is there not, among the students themselves, sufficient capacity for conversation and conflict? If we want our students, for instance, to recognize the diversity of our culture, rather than asking them to read specimens from various areas of our culture, we can ask them to explore the differences among their own responses to an essay or some cultural experience.

Perhaps *one* of the goals of the composition course should be dismantling the security and certitude of the writerly, arguing self. We can compose writing assignments and revision assignments that help students interrogate themselves and their writing.[9] Perhaps the worst of assignments would be one that provides trivial and easy-to-manage tasks that merely provide students with the opportunity to present that mechanically flawless and autonomous human being behind the pen, organizing information to be consumed by his or her readers. So, rather than providing the student with the occasion to shore up the self, to create the "bulletproof argument," we need to employ reading, writing, and revising activities that point up ambiguity and conflict. Reading and writing assignments should challenge writing and thinking to the point of failure, so that habitual forms of writing "break down," demanding that the student discover different and more sophisticated forms for thinking and writing. Such revision not only puts students in the position to interrogate their writing proficiency, but to interrogate also the writerly selves they present in their writing. It is in this sense that wondering out loud and the diffusion of self are potentially healthful signs of development in a writer.

And of course having our students "live" in conflict means that their responses must make an impact on the character and direction of conflict in the "culture" of the classroom. This means, as I have suggested, that teachers take students, their work, and their ideas seriously. This also means putting student response at *the* center of the classroom. Students, ideally, come to see the classroom as a community or contact zone where responsible argumentation is *enacted*, not just talked about. We should not have them simply read about postmodernist versions of knowledge and of subjectivity; students benefit from *living* a situation where the socially constructed nature of knowledge and of themselves is experienced and made central to the process of inquiry. In this way, as Lynch, George, and Cooper suggest, students might be led to the habit of listening to and valuing the positions of others, where there is a healthy tension between responsibility for one's ideas and arguing them and the responsibility to listen to the ideas of others. It might lead also to the belief that one can change one's ideas, change oneself, when such change is warranted. Perhaps practicing the kind of teaching that "aims more to keep the conversation going than to lead it toward a certain end" (Harris, *A Teaching* 116) will not change the world. But it has a much better chance, I think, of changing students, changing their habits of argument, and changing who they might conceive themselves to be in the public world. This is still "trickle-down" change, perhaps, but I am not sure what else we have.[10]

But this conflict must be deliberate, and even "deliberative." That is, conflict should always keep in mind the goal of negotiation and even the goal of deciding upon a course of action. In this way, students learn not only that conflict is everywhere in their world—they have already learned this from their culture, from *Crossfire*, from talk-radio, and from the other prominent models of argumentation. They might learn also that the inevitability of conflict does not imply throwing up one's hands in despair and becoming merely a spectator to the arena of culture and politics. Similar to what C. S. Peirce said of "contrite fallibilism," "contrite conflictualism," combined with an understanding that negotiation and change can occur, challenges students to move forward and, we hope, garner an intense desire to find things out about themselves and their culture, allowing them to continue to grow as participants in important argumentation.

Postscript: Immunity, Flexibility, and Business

This conception of the arguing self, who is willing to take the risk of foraying into unknown, alien discourses, willing to recognize that the outside always gets inside, and that there is no permanently good distinction between self and nonself, the arguing self who is willing to *risk* who she is—this mirrors, as Emily Martin explains in *Flexible Bodies*, emerging ideas about the body's immune system and emerging ideas of the "ideal and fit person." What I am calling "contrite conflictualism," or a willingness to live in conflict and irresolution and respond to the immediacy of the situation and the actual human being we converse with—this is in many ways similar to the "flexibility" of mind and body that is, according to Martin, emerging as the new standard of mental, moral, and physical health. Immunity is coming to be conceived less as a force that fortifies the self and identifies and attacks what is "not us," and more as a complex system that constantly adapts itself to an ever-changing environment, where the distinction between self and nonself is both impractical and undesirable. The continuous shifting of various material and ideological forces, including the continued focus on auto-immune diseases such as AIDS, has moved us into new conceptions of health, new conceptions of what defines a healthy individual. In the nineteenth century, the ideal and fit person was conceived (by people like William James and, as I argued, Hill) as having "mental resistance," which was acquired by sheer acts of will. However, since it was impossible to keep the will "on guard" at all moments, the habit of mental resistance had to be instilled by practice and routine. In the contemporary paradigm, the healthy individual, like the healthy immune system, must acquire the ability to be flexible. If an individual is to thrive in contemporary American culture, says this model, she must be able to adapt to a world where risk is everywhere. She must acquire the habit of risk-toleration.

In what sense, if any, would helping students acquire such a habit be countercultural? In what sense might such a habit allow students to continue resisting the dominant ideology? Perhaps, as Alan Kennedy says, it does just the opposite: this model of "resisting the dominant ideology might well be keys to success in" corporate America (25). And indeed, as Martin notes, corporate America has insisted on such flexibility and risk-toleration for some time, not only for the way a business is run (e.g., "just in time" inventory flows, "Total Quality Management" or "TQM") but also for its workers. The "cutting edge" of corporate training now includes learning to place the body at risk, which, supposedly, will lead to a willingness to take other kinds of risk as well, including a willingness to put *what one knows* and *how one thinks* at risk. Martin describes her experience in the "high ropes course," a training program for white-collar workers at innovative corporations (and even at universities, including mine), where the body is placed in risky and unpredictable situations, thus "teaching people to tolerate life-threatening risk" (221):

> Many exercises involved walking across a high wire. Not only did I experience the fear of no visible support at a great height, but, on those wobbly poles, wires, or platforms, the fear of being unmoored in space was almost intolerable. . . . I was literally moving from one position of instability to another and experienced the necessity for great flexibility. (213)

The risk is mitigated somewhat by reliance on others. For instance, the trainees jumping from platforms depend on their colleagues (or teammates) to belay them. But the main emphasis is risk, and the willingness to live, somewhat comfortably, in risk. As Martin explains:

> The experience [of the high ropes course] models physically the nature of the new workers that corporations desire: individuals— men and women—able to risk the unknown and tolerate fear, willing to explore unknown territories, but simultaneously able to accept their dependence on the help and support of their coworkers. In a word *flexibility*. (214)

The new, innovative worker, in short, is ideally the one who (reflecting new ideas of the ideal, sound immune system) can respond intelligently and effectively to a "continuously changing environment while constantly communicating with other such [flexible and innovative] bodies" (215).

Again, this sounds a great deal like the student I am saying we should try to create in our writing classes. So, I suppose that I, like E. T. Channing and A. S. Hill, am responding to my ideas of what the sound and healthy individual is, and at the same time I am acquiescing to the dominant ideology's (even corporate America's) demands for fit workers. Just as managerial capitalism in the late-nineteenth century needed managers who could distance themselves from their culture and from mainstream consciousness, to become the captains of industry, perhaps today we need managers who can engage in teamwork and listen to their subordinates and colleagues (not just give orders). Industry needs workers who are comfortable taking risk, because the workplace now requires flexibility, not just an authoritative and perhaps elitist critical distance to size up a situation on their own. In both cases, in the nineteenth century and now, our composition pedagogy has almost ideally fashioned the student to the desires of American business. (Talk of paranoid fantasies!) So this, perhaps, is why we keep hearing from corporate America that a liberal education is once again at a premium. No wonder Alan Kennedy's students believed it was their radical, rhetorical education that best prepared them for the workforce. It may certainly be the case that compositions studies' new pedagogical strategies (those I have described and advocated) are, as much as anything, accommodations to the latest manifestations of capitalism.

So, what are we to do? Should we teach some other way, since it seems that this version of the ideal and fit student now corresponds precisely (uncomfortably so) to corporate America's ideal and fit worker? Should we (per the recommendations of Peter Sacks and the neoconservative cultural critics I described in the previous chapter) stop teaching postmodern ethics because it sanctions and reinforces what is most damaging to American consciousness—not only does it inculcate cynicism, but the flexibility it teaches is precisely what corporate America wants (which we must not want)? And if these concerns motivate us, then what would allow us and our students to "resist" that oppressive subjectivity? Should I therefore return to a banking pedagogy, which would render my students (as if we had such power) more passive, less the servant of business interests? Should I examine explicitly the rhetoric of "TQM" in my writing courses, to inform my students that this kind of flexibility is part of emergent American ideology and that they should be on the *qui vive* for it, so they will not be so taken in by it?

But it is a perversion, I believe, to cease engaging in a certain teaching practice *merely* because it mirrors an emerging ideology, or *merely* because it provides business with the flexible workers it needs. As Richard

Lanham observes, this humanistic reflex to automatically reject what society finds important and useful is a recent perversion, having pervaded the humanities for about the last hundred years:

> But the "humanities crisis" that has been our routine cry for a century and more is one we have manufactured ourselves by distancing ourselves from the world. Claim to be above the struggle, specialize in "values" that others have to embody, and then wonder why the world sets you aside. Implicit in the revolution in the liberal arts I have tried to describe is a return to a systemic and systematic involvement in the social purposes of our time. (*Electronic Word* 117, and passim)

It is as wrongheaded as the goal of critical distance for the sake of critical distance, which is an old mistake that dates back to English studies in the British cultural provinces (Thomas Miller), to Channing, to Hill, to Leavis, to Allan Bloom, and, as I have argued, to some contemporary radical pedagogy. It makes little difference whether I rationalize my actions in "disinterestedness" or enlightened political interestedness; in either case, I define myself and my goals in *ideal* terms (*for* beauty and truth or *against* the values of corporate America), and in doing this, as Lanham has noted, I have purified my actions, tried to make them—and my students—immune to the contagion of mainstream, oppressive, dangerous thinking. This may free us and our students somewhat from the domination of cultural systems and values, but we ought to ask: Does it make us or our students better citizens?

While I do not pretend to have the answers, I would suggest that merely turning one's back on society, or positioning oneself and one's students against society, is so purified (so idealized) an action that it can do very limited good in the messy world of real public discourse. It would be far more valuable to allow our students to, as Lanham puts it, "mix motives," oscillating between the critical distance of the intellectual and the "getting things done" motive—or even the profit motive—of the everyday world; between our views of the media and culture and their lived experience with the media and in culture. Surely, many students will use this training as their key to success in the corporate world, and for many of us this means we have failed in our pedagogical and social mission. But almost as surely, many of our students will learn that the forms of argument and analysis practiced in that classroom have a place in the world outside the university. Our writing, then, rather than acting as a one-time inoculation against an ever-changing dominant ideology, might bring our students toward more healthy attitudes about argument and public participation. It is a small change, but a worthy one.

Notes

Chapter 1. The Idea of Discourse Immunity

1. Silverstein 387; Kennedy's words come from a Senate hearing and are quoted by R. L. Berke (1); Golub is quoted in Haraway (203); Chase was a medical student when interviewed by Emily Martin (*Flexible Bodies* 126, all ellipses and bracketed words in original); Corbetts's words come from *Classical Rhetoric for the Modern Student* 30.

2. Kastely writes: "What I am calling the classical thread of rhetorical skepticism should not be confused with the philosophical skepticism of antiquity that began in Plato's Academy in the third century BCE. Such philosophical skepticism is rooted in a concern with the reliability of sense perception as a guide to reality, but a rhetorical skepticism arises from a concern for the ways in which language as both a formal system and as a historically developed mode of action promotes injustice" (259).

3. Quoted by Wayne Booth, *The Vocation of a Teacher* 34 (originally: R, "Column," *Encounter* 45 [November 1975]: 44).

4. In passing, I will note that *inoculation*'s etymology connects the word itself to the idea of surveillance, though this connection is thoroughly specious (an invalid line of argument that plays on the "illogical, fortuitous similarity of words" [Lanham, *Handlist* 168]). Nonetheless, it is an interesting accident. *Inoculation* comes ultimately from the Latin for the horticultural process of engrafting an *eye* (i.e., a bud, like a potato eye), onto/into another organism; this "eye," in later senses, prevents disease from overcoming the individual: "*inoculāre* to engraft, implant, f. *in-* + *oculus* eye, bud." All senses were horticultural until the eighteenth century, when the sense of engrafting a disease within a human being to render them resistant to disease or poison was in use: "To engraft or implant (a disease, or the germ or virus) upon an individual, by a process of INOCULATION (q.v.) to introduce (cells or organisms to be cultured) *into* a culture medium or its container" (*Oxford English Dictionary* [OED], 2nd ed.).

Chapter 2. The Uses of Composition History

1. Burke, *Attitudes toward History* 159; McKeon 44.

2. For models that contemporary composition can use, see Stewart's work on Fred Newton Scott (especially "A Model for Our Time"). Robert J. Connors as well, in his recent *Composition-Rhetoric*, argues that our knee-jerk rejection and condemnation of current-traditional rhetoric needs rethinking.

3. *Rhetoric in American Colleges, 1850–1900* (Dallas: Southern Methodist UP, 1990). To clarify, it is only within the last fifteen years or so that Kitzhaber's history has become "influential" within composition studies. Before this it was, as John Gage has written in the introduction to the published work, an "underground" classic with a "grass-roots circulation," available only through University Microfilms International (vii).

4. This desire might also be traced also to the period during which the "renaissance" in composition history occurred. During the late 1970s and the 1980s many disciplines had become very critical of their origins and their historiographic traditions. Later in this chapter, I discuss the historiography of literary studies and of education and literacy studies.

5. This is Susan Miller's argument in *Textual Carnivals*—that we should rethink our "good story" about the provenance of composition. Rather than striving to make the connection with the 2,500-year classical tradition, she argues, we should be writing about the *politics* of composition's formation, specifically, how composition was figured as the necessary despised other of literary studies. Miller is certainly right that there is little reason to suspect that simply arguing, from a historical perspective, that our discipline has intellectual, academic, and social merit would cause these colleagues to believe they *should* accept us and our arguments, changing their attitudes and helping to change our working conditions, especially when these colleagues were simultaneously questioning the beliefs and practices of *their* forebears. This kind of belief, argues the leading New Historicist Stephen Greenblatt, was merely the "academic left's current dream" that "history will somehow save one from the complacencies of humanism": "But why should we believe any of this? . . . Why should we imagine that if we grasp more firmly the 'historical' roots of conflict we will then choose the morally preferable alternative?" (119) We were asking Greenblatt and other academics to consider our arguments, to consider choosing the "morally preferable alternative," but not enough resulted from those efforts. While we were addressing ourselves and other academics, the New Historicists were addressing (or thought they were) the public at large, both missions having, at best, questionable results.

Miller contends that in order to change composition's status we must radically reconsider the role of composition and the role of the composition student. She concludes that composition studies must reconsider the subjectivity of its professionals by reconsidering its students' subjectivities. Specifically, composition histories should examine how students became figured as "children" in need of "civilizing," who were incapable of assuming the responsibility to write meaningful (rather than "intransitive") essays. In this sense, this book attempts to further a small part of the project Miller calls for.

6. "Current-traditional rhetoric" was coined by Daniel Fogarty (in *Roots for a New Rhetoric* 1959), from whom Richard E. Young borrowed it ("Paradigms and Problems" [1978] 29). James Berlin first used the term in print in 1980 ("Richard Whately and Current-Traditional Rhetoric"), followed by scores of others within the next few years. By 1986, its usage had become standardized enough that Sharon Crowley could write "The Current-Traditional Theory of Style: An Informal History" without once defining the term or mentioning the work of Fogarty, Young, or Berlin. The most complete treatment of the current-traditional history (at least in terms of its intellectual foundations and definitions) is Crowley's *Methodical Memory*.

7. Historians have focused on different dimensions of hegemony. Some concentrate on its origins in the changing ideologies of late-nineteenth-century corporate capitalism (Berlin, *Rhetoric*, *Writing*, "Rhetorics and Poetics," "Transformation"; Thomas Miller; Douglas; Ohmann); others focus on the pressures exerted by the emerging textbook industry (Connors, "Textbooks," "Personal," "Rhetoric of Mechanical" 47–50, "Thirty Years"); others argue that current-traditional rhetoric emerged via the institutional pressure of overworked composition instructors and the privileging of literary communication over the more prosaic type taught in composition courses (Connors, "Rhetoric of Mechanical," "Textbooks"; Kitzhaber; Parker; R. Reid; Ried, "First and Fifth," "Francis J. Child"; Stewart, "Status," "Nineteenth Century," "Two Model Teachers," "Which Is Your Job"); others trace its rhetorical/philosophical lineage (see especially Crowley, *Methodical*), finding blame not only in the Common Sense school of rhetoric, but also in thinkers as diverse as Locke, Ramus (Dickson), Whately, and Edward T. Channing (Berlin, *Writing*, "Transformation"; Crowley, "Current"; Dickson; Douglas; Kitzhaber); and others place most of the blame with the first architects of America's composition courses, most notably with Adams Sherman Hill (Kitzhaber; Ried, "First and Fifth").

8. Ironically, Berlin's isomorphic relationship between rhetorical training and society-wide ideology seems similar to George Campbell's eighteenth-century assertion of an isomorphic relationship between *the* human mind (human nature, the operations that are universal in *all* human minds) and rhetoric. Campbell argues that rhetoric helps us understand how the human mind works: "It is [my] purpose in this Work . . . to exhibit, he does not say, a correct map, but a tolerable sketch of the human mind; and, aided by the lights which the Poet and the Orator so amply furnish, to disclose its secret movements, tracing its principle channels of perception and action, as near as possible, to their source" (lxvii). Similarly, Berlin proposes that by examining rhetorical training, we can better understand its "source"— not (as with Campbell) the operations of the human mind but the operations of the social mind.

9. I have in mind here Adorno's concept of the "standardized personality," which asserts that modern culture strips citizens of individuality by imposing a

"standardized personality" (128–61). Similarly, in chapters 6 and 7, I will criticize leftist pedagogies that encourage teachers to envision their students as falling into standardized categories. The analogy between historical composition theorist and actual-student-we'll-face-this-Monday may seem a bit strained, but one of the fundamental themes of my work here is resisting the urge to assume the possibility of standardization, whether the standard comes from the political left or the right, from the premodern or postmodern, from the student or the teacher.

10. I make this analogy with ambivalence. Since Kitzhaber's Chair's Address at the 1963 Conference on College Composition and Communication (CCCC), followed by Maxine Hairston's of 1985, a persistent theme in composition studies has been that rhetoric and composition needs to escape the stifling control of literary studies. And here I am using literary scholarship from the last decade to "correct" some historiographic trends in composition studies. Nevertheless, I do make the analogy because, as I hope will become evident, the analogy is apposite and illuminating.

11. As Nietzsche argues, the historian and the reader of history must never become "a strolling spectator . . . [having] arrived at a condition in which even great wars and revolutions are able to influence him for hardly more than a moment. . . . And what a school of decorum is such a way of contemplating history! To take everything objectively, to grow angry at nothing, to love nothing, to understand everything, [*sic*] how soft and pliable that makes one" (83, 105).

12. There are all sorts of difficulties, I realize, with the "high-low" depiction of culture, and this is particularly true with the figures I discuss, since they thought themselves members of "high" culture but decidedly not of the dominant culture (see especially chapters 4 and 5). That is, like so many of today's composition instructors, they at least *perceived* themselves as adversaries of the dominant order—the underdogs.

Chapter 3. To "Fortify the Immunities of a Free People"

1. Channing's quotation is from "On Models of Literature" 205, Aronowitz and Giroux's from *Education under Siege* 51, Emerson's from "The Conservative" (*Complete Works*, 1:320).

2. For an enlightening discussion about how Channing and other Whig-Federalist Harvardians aligned themselves with this mission, see Broaddus's chapter 1.

3. These are the words of the first editor of the magazine, William Tudor (*North American Review* 4 [March 1817]: 432). For further discussion of the magazine's policies, see William Charvat 174–75.

4. *The Flowering of New England* 43. Charvat concurs that his influence was "immense" (185).

5. See Richard Beale Davis's "Edward Tyrrel Channing's 'American Scholar' of 1818." For a rich discussion of the complex relationship between Channing's ideas

and their manifestations in the young and mature Emerson, see Broaddus (chapters 1 and 2).

6. According to Van Wyck Brooks and more recently Sacvan Bercovitch ("Emerson" and "The Problem of Ideology"), American letters—even and perhaps especially within the canonical tradition—has had at its center questions of how society conspires against the individual and how the individual engages in dissent. In this sense, Channing reflected (and probably helped create) a larger cultural attitude.

7. See, for instance, Wallace Douglas and James Berlin ("Richard Whately").

8. See S. Michael Halloran's "Rhetoric and the English Department" and Wallace Douglas.

9. See, for instance, William Riley Parker, and Donald Stewart ("Some History Lessons" and "The Nineteenth Century").

10. Clark and Halloran also describe this change in some detail. For an excellent "sociocultural analysis" (which nicely summarizes a great deal of the scholarship in this area), see David S. Kaufer and Kathleen M. Carley.

11. Plato's ideal republic, for instance, could "grow so long as in its growth it consents to remain a unity, but no further. . . . [T]he city shall not be too small, nor great only in seeming, but . . . it shall be a sufficient city and one" (665). For a recounting of early republic debates about geographical size and democracy, see Robert A. Dahl's *Size and Democracy*; for a recounting of the role of communications in this debate, in particular the post-Revolutionary debate in America, see James W. Carey's Communication as Culture, 3–9.

12. For a discussion of the differences between Greek democratic ideals and actual Greek political practice, see Robert A. Dahl's *Democracy and Its Critics* 13–23, and I. F. Stone's *The Trial of Socrates*.

13. See, for instance, Frank Luther Mott, *American Journalism* 160–61, 193–94; Richard A. Schwarzlose 4–6; and Allan R. Pred 78–103.

14. As James Carey points out, before the advent of the telegraph there was literally no distinction (semantic or otherwise) between *communication* and *transportation*, since communication without transportation was an impossibility (*Communication as Culture* 14–18).

15. Backers of the Erie Canal had argued that better transportation was necessary if Americans were to enjoy a national market. These backers, after unsuccessfully petitioning the federal government for financial support, received the help they needed from the New York State government. Begun in 1817 and completed in 1825, the Erie Canal was not only financially successfully, but "generated a transportation revolution" (Sellers 40–43).

16. Quoted by Sellers, 78 (*Annals of Congress* 14th Congress, 2nd Session, 851–58).

17. As Sellers writes, "the revenue/general-welfare clause . . . empowered Congress to 'collect taxes . . . to pay the debts and provide for the common defence and general welfare.' . . . Monroe professed to believe . . . that state sovereignty was less liable to invasion under a broad power of appropriation than under a broad construction of the enumerated powers. In any event he discovered and propounded a Republican reading of 'general welfare' that would serve . . . to sanction a virtually unlimited federal role in the political economy of a market-organized society. . . . [Monroe] made the decision that placed the federal government fully at the service of the republic's capitalist destiny" (150–51).

18. [*Alumnus*], *Independent Chronicle & Boston Patriot*, September 25, 1819, 1, emphasis in original; quoted in Ronald F. Reid, "The Boylston Professorship" (245).

19. *Records of Overseers* IV, May 1, 1804, cited in Warren Guthrie, "The Development . . . 1635–1850" 101.

20. See Anderson and Braden xxx. For a more general discussion of the idea of "progress" in Scottish Common Sense rationalism, see Louis Schneider's introduction to *The Scottish Moralists on Human Nature and Society*.

21. *Fighting for Life* 43–4. Rhetoric involved the rhetor's mental *and* physical capacities. In passing, I would note that much of American culture still adheres to this idea of debate, and this (as I explore the idea in chapter 6) continues to profoundly affect our students' ideas about the nature of public discussion and working out ideas. For a fascinating discussion of contemporary political debate in terms of the public ritual of mortal combat, see Carolyn Marvin's "Fresh Blood, Public Meat: Rituals of Totem Regeneration in the 1992 Presidential Race." For a contrasting (but not necessarily conflicting) view, see Jamieson's chapter 5 ("The 'Effeminate' Style") in *Eloquence in an Electronic Age*. For a discussion more specific to composition history see Robert J. Connor's chapter 1 of *Composition-Rhetoric* as well as his "Teaching and Learning as a Man," which looks even more directly at the contemporary implications of a "feminized" rhetorical training.

22. Havelock, *Preface to Plato* passim; Ong, *The Presence* 53–76 and *Orality and Literacy* 79–116.

23. The term "unchecked democracy" was clearly a term of opprobrium for Channing and for others in his class. See Broaddus (chapter 1) for a detailed analysis of Channing's attitudes (and those held by others in his social group) about what was emerging to become "popular democracy." See also McGerr for discussion of later (the latter third of the nineteenth century) patrician intellectuals' reactions to "popular politics."

24. Channing's reservations about adopting Greek oratory wholesale into American public discourse were widespread in America. As James P. Young notes: "The starting point for the discussion [about the nature of American democratic debate] was the inspirational value of the ancient republics, combined with the deeply troubling perception that these republics had been highly unstable. . . . More

specifically, the dominant belief was that these ancient regimes had perished owing to decay from within, that they had fallen victim to the twin evils of 'corruption' and 'faction' " (47).

25. Campbell continues, "Besides, this study [of rhetoric], properly conducted, leads directly to an acquaintance with ourselves; it not only traces the operations of the intellect and imagination, but discloses the lurking springs of action in the heart. In this view it is perhaps the surest and the shortest, as well as the pleasantest way of arriving at the science of the human mind" (lxxiv). As Nan Johnson has shown, this epistemological rationale for the study of rhetoric (that it helped discern the nature of human nature and human thought) dominated North American rhetorics throughout the nineteenth century (65–110).

26. Although this chart does some violence to the complexity and subtleties of Campbell's rhetorical and psychological systems, it may help for the present purpose.

Faculty	End (Purpose)	Form/Characteristic
Understanding	Instruction	Perspicuity
Understanding	Conviction	Argument
Imagination	Pleasure	Beauty
Passion	Sympathy/Indignance	Pathos
Will	Persuasion	Vehemence

27. Campbell 336, emphasis added. It may be more accurate to say that Campbell was unsure of the distinction between speech and writing, or that he was unconcerned or unaware of the need to make the distinction. As Sharon Crowley has shown, Campbell, in step with eighteenth-century linguistic theory, described the nature of style with "images and figures [such as 'perspicacity' and 'obscurity'] which heighten the visual aspect of language" ("The Current-Traditional Rhetoric"). Crowley does not note that the default medium for Campbell is oral, with writing representing a special case.

28. Or, more accurately, Channing is very much unlike the Socrates in *Phaedrus* and *Gorgias*, that is, the Socrates who castigates those proposing written rhetorics (for an excellent commentary on this aspect of Plato, see Susan Miller's chapter "Philosophy Confronts Writing: Plato's *Gorgias* and *Phaedrus*," in *Rescuing the Subject*). On the other hand, Channing's insistence on discovering Platonic truths is very much like the Socrates of *The Republic* and *Laws*, for which, see Havelock, *Preface* passim and especially 254–75. For a brief synopsis of both aspects of Plato and Socrates, see Ong, *Orality and Literacy* 24–28 and 79–81.

29. As Richard Hofstadter writes, "Since the days of Jefferson there had been no major turnover in the staff of officeholders, whose members were becoming encrusted in their posts. . . . However, the people, the propertyless masses, were beginning, at first quietly and almost unobtrusively, to enter politics. Between 1812 and 1821 six western states entered the Union with constitutions providing for

universal white manhood suffrage or a close approximation, and between 1810 and 1821 four of the older states substantially dropped property qualifications for voters" (*The American Political Tradition and the Men Who Made It* 62–63).

30. The decay of the American listening/reading audience has been a perennial activity. Frederick Antczak's *Thought and Character* addresses nineteenth-century efforts at reforming American audiences. He shows how the decay of the character of American audiences was bemoaned throughout the century, with Tocqueville (6–7) commenting on it and Emerson worrying about the decreasing attention span of American hearers (5). He shows further how much of American educational thought can be seen as a direct reaction to these anxieties.

31. Since Douglas Hofstadter first proposed the "liberal consensus" argument in *The American Political Tradition* (1948), historians of American political thought have commonly argued that liberalism has unhelpfully dominated *all* American political thought so that it is difficult to hold a public conversation in which the individual might be portrayed as something other than a Lockean liberal self or in which the relationship between individual rights and the common good might be considered differently. James P. Young (in *Reconsidering American Liberalism*) provides a helpful and exquisitely detailed summary of the debate over the prominence of Lockean liberalism in American thought; he also insists that historians must note the exceedingly complex relationship between the liberal idea and the republican ideal (an insistence I try to heed here).

32. As James P. Young states, "one of the most persistent themes of liberal thought and action . . . [is] the idea that government exists to maintain the conditions necessary for private individuals to purse their own privately defined sense of the good. . . . [I]t is a theory of the primacy of individual rights over the good of the community" (37).

33. While my separation of these words and phrases from their contexts makes it appear that Channing's argument stridently opposes speaking to writing, Channing actually successfully mutes the forcefulness of his opposition. My guess is that Channing felt such subtlety was necessary, since the place of oratory in the republic was a much-debated issue.

34. "In quiet seasons, when the state seems an invisible trifle to be *talked about only* and men's consciences can sleep under their duties, they are very willing to listen to a fine orator as they would to the players; they are *entertained* by his frolicks, and give in to all his illusions as they would to the fairy work of a dream" (380, my emphasis).

35. Channing 380. Channing probably has in mind the ancient "imperfect hearer" justification of rhetoric. In the words of Aristotle, "[W]e ought in fairness to fight our case with no help beyond the bare facts: nothing, therefore, should matter except the proof of those facts. Still, as has been already said, other things affect the result considerably, *owing to the defects of our hearers*. The arts of language cannot help having a small but real importance . . . : the way in which a

thing is said does affect its intelligibility" (*The Rhetoric, The Rhetoric and Poetics of Aristotle*, trans. W. Rhys Roberts [New York: Modern Library, 1984] 165 [Immanuel Becker's 1403b], my emphasis).

36. "His long habit of popular declamation led him, in preparing his book, to adopt the same mode he had practised on the Rostrum, of moving the affections, and neglecting the judgment" (404–5).

37. Daniel J. Czitrom describes how the telegraph altered the ways Americans conceived of information. In passing, I will remark that Channing's tenure as Boylston Professor spanned an era that saw the nature of information gathering and transmission fundamentally transformed. As I noted earlier, James Carey points out that before the advent of the railroad and telegraph, there was no distinction between "transportation" and "communication." By the end of Channing's tenure, canals, steamboats, turnpikes, and railroads linked America, and the telegraph was already changing the cultural conception of "information" and of "knowledge"; see James Carey, Michael Schudson (*Discovering the News*), and Richard A. Schwarzlose (vol. 1).

38. As historian of literacy Harvey J. Graff describes the era in which Channing was writing, "Early-nineteenth-century North America witnessed an explosion of print. Competing religious sects, political parties, educational interests, and cultural promoters plumbed the market, seeking sales and influence. . . . [P]eriodicals, especially newspapers and tract and pamphlet literature, were the largest categories of print" (*Legacies of Literacy* 352).

39. The first penny paper, *The Sun* (New York), began in 1833, but as Mott and Schwarzlose point out, the content of papers and the audience to which they were targeted were changing even during the Constitutional crisis and the newspaper wars between Jefferson and the Federalists.

40. See Tebbel (*Media* 71–90), Mott (*American Journalism* 113–34, 143–62), and Nord.

41. *Origins* 42; the embedded quote is from Kames's *Art of Thinking* 176, chapter 25.

Chapter 4. A. S. Hill (i): Nineteenth-Century Journalism

1. H. D. Thoreau, *The Illustrated "A Week on the Concord and Merrimack Rivers"* 197–98; Henry George's words are quoted by Bledstein 226 (Charles Albro Barker, *Henry George* [New York: Oxford UP, 1955] 330); E. L. Godkin, *The Gilded Age Letters* 371; Hill's words comprise the entire body of letters written May 6, 1886 to Mr. E[dwin].M. Bacon, newly appointed editor of the *Boston Post*; it resides in his general folder in the Harvard University Archives.

2. Marshall Kremers, for instance, compares himself to Hill in order, it seems, to chastise himself and his pedagogical foibles. David Jolliffe calls Hill "the man

most responsible for developing English A, true progenitor of freshman composition" (166).

3. Throughout this chapter, I will be concentrating on what Richard Hofstadter calls "intellectual" culture (*Anti-Intellectualism in American Life*). Following Hofstadter and Trachtenberg, I will also refer to the persons in this culture as "elite" and "patrician intellectuals." I want to employ these terms neither disparagingly nor honorifically. I use these terms to signify the group in America that was characterized by high levels of education, privilege, intellectualism, and very often academic capacity or profession. I do *not* want "elite" to imply "influential" and especially not "dominant": as Richard Hofstadter has shown, this group, especially during the period I am examining, has historically been characterized by its lack of and desire *for* public influence.

4. For a broad-scope inquiry into the creation of a professional, "middle" class, see Burton J. Bledstein, *The Culture of Professionalism*; for a discussion of the creation of a professional class in the context of oratorical and public culture, see Clark and Halloran 3–8. Some superb accounts of the changes in academic/intellectual epistemology, purpose, and methods are in the essays within Oleson and Voss's *The Organization of Knowledge in Modern America, 1860–1920*, especially those by Veysey, Higham, and Hawkins. An analysis of the causes and effects surrounding the change from a rural to an urban nation is provided by Robert H. Wiebe's *The Search for Order*. On the changing relationship between Americans and American society, see Alan Trachtenberg's *The Incorporation of America*, who uses the metaphor of "incorporation" to described a "general process of change, the reorganization of perception as well as of enterprise and institutions, . . . not only the expansion of an industrial capitalist system across the continent, . . . but also, and even predominantly, the remaking of cultural perceptions this process entailed" (3).

5. Nell Irvin Painter's *Standing at Armageddon* provides an excellent overview of the historical research as well as the various cultural, material, and political forces creating this anxiety. T. Jackson Lears, in *No Place of Grace*, describes how "crises in cultural authority" created for educated Americans "spiritual and psychological turmoil" (xi), a crisis over the definition of the "self."

6. The term "communications revolution" was first used by Robert G. Albion in 1932, who employed it to distinguish the influences of canals, new forms of transportation, postal networks, and printing and electronic-communications technologies from the influences of the Industrial Revolution in America.

7. Daniel J. Czitrom's *Media and the American Mind* provides a fascinating discussion of the technology of America's first telegraphs as well as the cultural repercussions caused by them. Postman's is a similar discussion, but is far more critical of the kind of public discourse he maintains resulted from these electronic forms of communication.

8. See Harold Innis, *The Bias of Communication*, passim, esp. 159–60, 25–26, and David Kaufer and Kathleen Carley (27).

9. Kaufer and Carley provide an excellent rehearsal and discussion of the impact of all these technologies on communications.

10. Richard Boyd has provided an interesting account of how the "ritual" of the composition classroom provides some measure of security against these imposing cultural uncertainties and changes.

11. This diary was purchased by Harvard in 1975; officials at Harvard Archives would not reveal the source of the diary.

12. Hill realized that his physical infirmities matched those which men like Sylvester Graham were claiming resulted from "onanism": he was terribly nearsighted, often suffered from skin problems, had a weak voice, was nervous, and in general was quite frail. Personally, I found Hill's intense anxiety about his sixteen-year-old hormonal yearnings moving. I do not want to seem to be engaging in some cute preterition, but someone bolder than I might analyze nineteenth-century composition theory in terms of the "spermatic economy," in which sperm needed to be saved, lest the "onanist" suffer from inanition (Ben Barker-Benfield, "The Spermatic Economy," *The Horrors of the Half-Known Life*). Hill, perhaps more than any of his contemporary composition theorists, advocated a plain style of brevity in which words are not wasted; as Hill defined it, rhetoric was the "art of efficient communication"; such "wasting" of words, such lack of concision, Hill called in various places "unmanly." Similarly, the "onanist" was typically deemed by health experts throughout the century as "lacking in will," having lost self-control and completely subjugated to determinist influences (see Fellman and Fellman 100–107). It is at least interesting to note that Hill believed that the benefits of composition training for the student (as I describe it in the next chapter) included a stronger, more inviolate sense of self, self-mastery, and resistance to external and determinist influences.

13. Another collection of Hill material, seventy-five letters received by Hill during his work at the New York *Tribune*, resides in the Duke University Archives (I have found no mention of these letters in any published writing except my own "Composition Course and Public Discourse"). About 350 letters from Hill to Sydney Howard Gay (editor of the New York *Tribune* from 1862 to 1866) reside in the Gay Papers in the Butler Library of Columbia University. Most of these letters recount the quotidian problems and questions of running a newspaper. Many are quoted in Louis M. Starr's *The Bohemian Brigade*. J. Cutler Andrew cites a letter from Hill to Darwin Ware, a "[m]iscellaneous MSS in the possession of Arthur Hill, Esq., Boston, Massachusetts" (656). "Arthur Hill" was A. S. Hill's only child, Arthur Dehon Hill (1869–1947, LL.B., Harvard 1894); my research has so far revealed no information on the current location of this letter.

14. Hill may have suffered from chronic, nonlethal tuberculosis. Such tuberculosis often manifested in iritis, inflammation of the irises that brought on temporary, periodic blindness.

15. Dana to Hill, April 24, 1860, Adams Sherman Hill Papers, Duke University Archives.

16. Letter from W[illiam] A[ugustus] Croffut, December 16, 1862, Duke University Archives.

17. Letter May 26, 1864, Adams Sherman Hill Papers, Duke University Archives. Just what Hill had submitted to *The Atlantic* I have not discovered.

18. Once again, I want to stress that I am not endorsing Hill's politics. To reiterate, the similarity between Hill's theory of culture and teaching writing and contemporary theories should make compositionists worry a little bit, and perhaps rethink their theories.

19. For example, John Clifford has criticized contemporary textbooks for propagating the illusion that the student writer is "the locus of significance, the originator of meaning, an autonomous being, aware of . . . authorial intentions and motivations." In particular, Clifford singles out Andrea Lunsford and Robert Connors's *St. Martin's Handbook* for furthering "the illusion that we can transcend ideology with three well-developed paragraphs of evidence, that we can somehow change the minds of others in a rhetorical vacuum freed from the pollutants of prior social alignments" ("The Subject in Discourse" 39, 44). But anyone familiar with Lunsford's or Connors's critical work on composition, rhetoric, and the pedagogy of teaching writing realizes that the philosophy named by Clifford does not match that of the authors. My point is that it has always been difficult to judge an author by her or his freshman rhetoric.

20. William Henry Smith 526. Although contemporary press historians may disagree over the details of when and why Americans acquired the habit of reading newspapers, during the late nineteenth century it was common for writers in elite periodicals to comment (usually with remorse and nostalgia) that the Civil War had led to the popular reception of journalism, placing the editor and the correspondent in the cultural place previously occupied by the teacher and preacher.

21. While the story of Hill's turning tale at Blackburn's Ford is included in several histories of Civil War journalism, the sole documentation is a letter written by Edmund Clarence Stedman: "Hill, [Edward H.] House's assistant, got there after the fight commenced, had one ball whiz by his ear, got frightened, galloped 22 miles to Washington and there reported five hundred killed . . . and the Press had fled the field. No one left but him. . . . My letters to the *World* tell the whole story" (1:231 [Stedman to Laura Stedman, July 20, 1861]).

22. Press historians usually count Bennett's *Herald* as the most influential newspaper, but the *Tribune* was a very close second.

23. All quoted in Starr, 123–26 (the letter from Gay resides in the Robert T. Lincoln Collection, Library of Congress, and the Lincoln quotation from Roy P. Basler, ed., *The Collected Works of Abraham Lincoln* 5:353).

24. Having read only the Hill-to-Gay letters in the collection (and the half-dozen Gay-to-Hill letters in the Duke University Archives), I certainly don't feel informed enough to concur or disagree with Starr's assessment about Hill's role in

the issuance of the Emancipation Proclamation (arguably the most revolutionary document since the Declaration of Independence). Nonetheless, the Hill-to-Gay letters make clear that throughout the summer and fall of 1862 Hill was assiduously finding out from senators, congressmen, generals, and cabinet members what would be the public, military, and political reaction to such a decree, and he was passing his impressions and judgments on to Gay.

25. As early as November 24, 1863, Hill was writing to Gay about preparing his replacement, and suggests that, in fact, he has already been fired "at Mr. Greeley's instance, peremptorily & with very short notice" (Hill to Gay, November 24, 1863).

26. It is also possible that Hill left on his own accord, either because one of the many offers he had described to Gay throughout 1863 had materialized (e.g., "I have received a handsome offer proposition to which an answer is desired by the close of the week" January 21, 1863), or because Hill was simply disgusted with Greeley or newspaper work.

27. His resignation letter suggests it was a letter to Secretary of War Edwin Stanton (n.d. [November or December 1863], Gay Collection, Columbia University Archives).

28. As Hill himself wrote to Gay, "As to [my ability for] getting to the news, I fear my friends and rivals have flattered me into an opinion of myself beyond my deserts. One thing is certain. If I am not fit for the place now, I never shall be. I believe that I am fit for something better than a newspaper hack's life: & rightly or wrongly I intend to believe so." He goes on to say that he intends to move ahead and up in the world of journalism and does not intend to "resume the 'back seat'" (n.d. [November or December 1863], Gay Collection, Columbia University Archives).

29. As Schwarzlose points out, this organization never possessed so official a status that it needed an official name. Press historians have dubbed this organization the "Independent News Room," with some historians using capitals and others not. (I will use capitals for the sake of clarity.) See Schwarzlose 331–32, note 67.

30. Thomas Reilly explains that the six subscribing newspapers "appear to have several points in common. They were all Republican (White, Hill, and Villard were strongly Republican and pro-Union); they had prospered during the war and were expanding; they were not particularly satisfied [an understatement on Reilly's part] with the coverage supplied to them by the New York Associated Press, and the editors of four of the six were among the best outside the New York metropolitan area—Murat Halstead of the *Cincinnati Commercial*, Joseph Medill of the *Chicago [Daily] Tribune*, Samuel Bowles of the *Springfield Republican* and Benjamin Gratz Brown of the *Missouri Democrat*." The other two papers were the *Boston Advertiser* and the *Rochester Democrat* (234).

31. Schwarzlose writes, "For Craig, his associates, and New York's AP editors the new technologies of electricity and steam propelled them into a ruling stratum, which was arising around the new central role for news and information in an increasingly complex society. . . . Singularly and daily imposing itself upon the elites

and the smaller newspapers, Craig's news report was an ingredient in businessmen's and speculator's decisions, a guide to opportunities and misfortune.... [Various "treaties" among telegraph companies] abruptly consolidated telegraphy's growth and erected seemingly impenetrable common technological fortification that excluded the nation's editors and newsbrokers. That some telegraph leaders sought to assimilate newsbroking into the new consolidation made telegraphy even more dangerous to journalists, who after a decade were accustomed to controlling their own dispatches" (236).

32. Letter from Medill to Hill n.d. (c. March–August 1861) and September 14, 1861, Duke University Archives.

33. Quoted in Schwarzlose 191 (Associated Press, *Annual Report* [1896]: 156–57). See Schwarzlose for further accounts of the hatred felt by journalists toward Craig. Schwarzlose demonstrates that the general feeling toward Craig's news monopoly was marked by anger and fear for the public good; his numerous quotations by journalists, government officials, and others provide a convincing testimonial to the nationwide sense of outrage.

34. Quoted in Reilly 236 (Letter, Villard to Frank Garrison, April 5, 1864, Villard Papers).

35. As I argue later in this section, Hill's later writings suggest that he did indeed possess a marked sense of moral duty for the press and that the press in America was not living up to that duty.

36. The example of James Gordon Bennett and his *Herald* was well known to all journalists, demonstrating that patriotic fervor was essential if a newspaper was to survive, either financially or physically. Before the firing upon of Fort Sumter, Bennett was perceived as soft on the South (he had lived there briefly) and his paper was firmly antiwar; Bennett even maintained the South had the "right of revolution" and editorialized about the folly of opposing the South's secession. When word of Fort Sumter arrived in New York, there arrived at the *Herald*'s office a mob which threatened to burn the building down and demanded that Bennett "display an American flag.... [t]he paper executed the quickest about-face of its eccentric career, dropped its argument against coercion, and declared that the rebels must be crushed, and crushed immediately by guns and bayonets" (Mott, *American Journalism* 349; see also Stewart and Tebbel 50–52).

37. In 1864, "a meeting of New York journalists representing fifteen daily and weekly newspapers, under the chairmanship of Horace Greeley, passed a set of resolutions denying the right of the press to uphold treason or rebellion" (Mott, *American Journalism* 358).

38. Quoted in Reilly 252–53, 250 (*Chicago Tribune,* May 21, 1864, p. 1, Col 2); *Cincinnati Commercial,* May 21, 1964, rpt. by the *Chicago Tribune,* May 22, 1864, p.1, Col 2).

39. Reilly is mistaken in his statement that "Hill and White continued their small news bureau until the end of the war" (259). He documents this statement

with a biographical article "Horace White" from the 1936 *Dictionary of American Biography*, which says only that White continued in the operation, but says nothing about Hill. Schwarzlose (whose "discussion relies heavily on Reilly's penetrating research" [331–32]) concurs (258). Reilly's belief that the Independent News Room continued its operations, perhaps, comes from David Homer Bates (manager and cipher-operator of the War Department telegraph office, 1861–66), who had written that "although no apologies were made to [Villard, Hill, or White by Stanton], some choice scraps of news later found their way to the office of the syndicate, which supplied material for new 'scoops,' and had a soothing influence generally" (242). In sum, with the exception of Reilly's undocumented suggestion, there is no evidence that Hill continued with the Independent News Room after May of 1864.

40. Rantoul 139–40, my emphasis. This is by far the most detailed account of the Independent News Room's methods I have come across. None of the historians of the Civil War press that I know of impugn the integrity of the Independent News Room or its members, perhaps because historians tend to side with these underdogs, seeing the bureau mostly as opposition to Craig's much-hated monopoly, which threatened journalistic independence for the sake of company profits.

41. Editors were continuing to curtail Hill's freedoms even on the eve of the birth of the Independent News Room. Andrew Shurman, editor of the *Chicago Evening Journal* (which employed Hill as a special correspondent), wrote to Hill that he must not criticize the president, since his newspaper supported him "*unconditionally* so long as there is war in the land, and that which I will not allow myself to do editorially, I cannot permit correspondents to do in its columns" (January 5, 1864, Duke University Archives).

42. Letters from C[harles]. A. Dana, August 7, 1861;, from J[oseph]. Medill October 28, 1861.

43. Letter from S[idney] H. Gay, May 23, 1862.

44. See Frederick J. Antczak's *Thought and Character* for a lively (often humorous) description of this change and its impact on American rhetoric and the rationales for education.

45. *The Bias of Communication* 204. Ong and others have pushed this determinism even further, arguing that alterations in communications technologies (writing, print, etc.) actually transform consciousness and the nature of cognition so that the idea of objectivity, impossible to an oral mind, becomes possible (see *Orality and Literacy* 31–138). Schwarzlose looks more closely at the effects of the telegraph on journalism, examining the political battles between the large, monopolizing news brokerages (the various "Associated Press"es) and the editors of local papers to account for these changes.

46. *Discovering the News* 6, 57. See also Schudson's "Preparing the Minds of the People" for a discussion of the processes by which news "became an intimate part of citizenship and politics . . . and a collected and visible [public] good" (435).

47. This is James A. Berlin's argument in *Rhetoric and Reality*.

48. 87–88. The final quotation is from Frederic Hudson, *Journalism in the United States: From 1690–1872* (New York: Harper, 1872) xxvii.

49. Cited by Schiller 88–89 (Isaac Clar Pray, *Memoirs of James Gordon Bennett and His Times* [New York: String and Townsend, 1855] 472).

50. The full title is *The American Conflict: a History of the Great Rebellion in the United States of America, 1860–65. Its Causes, Incidents, and Results: intended to exhibit especially its Moral and Political Phases, with the Drift and Progress of American Opinion respecting Human Slavery from 1776 to the Close of the War for the Union*, 8 vols., (Hartford: O.D. Case & Co., 1866) [872 pages].

51. Orestes Brownson wrote, "Mentioning this 1840 [presidential campaign], we must say that it marks an epoch in *our* political and social doctrines. The famous election of that year wrought a much greater revolution in us than in the government. . . . We for our part frankly confect—and we care not who knows it—that what we saw during the presidential election of 1840 shook, nay, gave to the winds, all our remaining confidence in the popular democratic doctrines" (quoted by Antczak 12). Antczak argues that the poverty of intelligent debate during this campaign so outraged cultured Americans that they supported public education, in order to fortify Americans against such despicable, non-issue-oriented rhetoric. Horlick provides a rich discussion of the relationship between education and politics during the latter half of the nineteenth century; Horlick argues that patrician intellectuals (prominent in his discussions are E. L. Godkin and Charles Francis Adams Jr. [first author of the Harvard literacy reports]) looked to education to reform politics and to ensure that patrician values won the day. Jerome McGerr argues that Godkin and Adams were some of the most outspoken "reformers" of popular politics; they argued against universal suffrage and advocated education as the key to reform the citizenry: "The reformers' political style rested on an elitist dream of cultured and enlightened leaders educating a receptive electorate. This was a politics with the educated man once more at the center, his principles the yardstick of public life, his pamphlets the means of shaping the people to his will" (67).

52. Stewart and Tebbel write "The eminent men of his time, at least many of them, viewed [Greeley] with disdain. James Fenimore Cooper . . . thought Greeley a vulgarian. Edwin L. Godkin . . . was openly contemptuous of his more popular contemporary" (60; see also Emery 229–30). It should be noted, however, that the insults hurled at Greeley by intellectuals may have been unfair and misguided. Greeley may have been the best known and the most peculiar editor of the penny press, but he was hardly the worst of them; as Emery argues, Greeley was largely responsible for the penny press's moving away from sensationalism (230–37).

53. Quoted in Emery 229–30 (*Notes and Anecdotes of Many Years* [New York: Scribner's, 1925] 24).

54. The form of Hill's criticism reminds me of the formula used by writing teachers for commenting on student essays. He seems to give Greeley the grade "A

over a C-minus" (good style, poor substance). Or, per the writing teacher's formula, his review proceeds along these lines: "This is a well-written and well-organized essay. You have used your sources well. *However . . .* "

55. Hofstadter 176, 178. The embedded quotation is referenced by Hofstadter: "Adams to Gaskell, quoted in Ernest Samuels: *The Young Henry Adams* (Cambridge, Mass., 1948), p. 182." Hofstadter continues with this quotation from George Haven Putnam, whose optimism about the transformative power of education seems to closely resemble the modern Gramscian "war of position" hoped for by contemporary educators: "It was our hope that as the youngsters came out of college from year to year with the kind of knowledge of the history of economics that would be given to them by professors like William Graham Sumner of Yale, we should gradually secure a larger hold on public opinion, and through the influence on leaders bring the mass of the voters to an understanding of their own business interests" (*Memories of a Publisher* [New York, 1915] 42–43).

56. It is significant that Grimes was one of Hill's closest sources for congressional intelligence while Hill was "Washington man" for the *Tribune*. In dozens of his letters to Gay, Hill cited Grimes as the source for various pieces of intelligence. In fact, in one letter, Hill objects to Greeley's treatment of Grimes, complaining to Gay that "Mr. Greeley has alienated almost all the prominent men of party here from himself and *The Tribune*." After citing several instances, Hill objects profoundly to Greeley's latest contumely against Grimes, who "has been of more service to me & to the *Tribune* that any other man here. My relations with him have been most intimate, boarding at the same house, as I do. As a thoroughly brave and true man, he has not his equal in the Senate." He warns that Grimes "has one failing. He is not apt to be barged to forgive what he conceives an injury" (March 6, 1863). In these two articles, as in this letter, Greeley and Grimes oppose one another, Greeley representing the problem with public discussion, Grimes the kind of person who battles against such problems.

57. Hill makes the point that seems very modern: new media of political reporting lead to impoverished forms of communication and argumentation. While recent critics of the media blame television for creating the sound-bite and blame *USA Today* (with its large typeface and color plates) for creating "McNews," Hill's contemporaries also engaged in some rather unconstructive carping about the newspaper.

58. As is evident in the class notes of Hill's Harvard students, "manliness" was a key term for Hill in his discussion of writers and their styles. As one student wrote in his notes of Hill's lectures, "Daniel Webster . . . was a man of wonderful manliness and magnetism. He had a keen sense of humor but never let this run away with him" (Fred N. Robinson, Notes in English A, 1887–88 [Harvard University Archives]). In his lectures and in his rhetorics, Hill said that newspapers had a "fine" and "unmanly" style. It should be noted, however, that the equation of sophistry with daintiness and effeminacy was not invented by Hill or his contemporaries; we often see it in Hugh Blair's *Lectures*: e.g., "In the hands of [sophists, such as Gorgias] we

may easily believe that Oratory would degenerate from the masculine strain it had hitherto held, and become a trifling and sophistical art: and we may justly deem them the first corrupters of true Eloquence." By contrast, the style of Isocrates (for Blair, apparently, not a sophist) is "swelling and full" (2:16, 17). See Miriam Brody's *Manly Writing* for a broad discussion about the ideals of manliness and their impact on rhetorical training.

59. 192, 193 (the last two quotations come from a Grimes letter quoted by Hill).

60. Hill makes this point about Grimes in several places: he "despised twaddle" (186); "he had no patience with declamation or sentiment" (187); "he made few set speeches, but he often took part in debate" (190).

61. It might be argued that this transition had occurred earlier. Tocqueville's comments on the importance of newspapers for a democracy are well known, as he credits them with helping a vast nation cohere (489–91). But intellectuals held that newspapers had become far more influential and socially harmful; they argued, further, that there had been a fundamental shift from "criticism" to "intelligence." E. L. Godkin describes this transition in 1890: "It is now forty years since Tocqueville compared a newspaper to a man standing at an open window and bawling to passers-by in the street. Down to his time the newspaper press in all countries except Europe, and almost down to his time in America, was looked upon as simply, or mainly, an ill-informed and often malignant critic of the government. . . . The ideal editor of those days was a man who expected to be locked up on account of the boldness of his invectives against the government, but did not mind it. Although he also gathered news, his news-gathering was so subordinate to his criticism that he was hardly thought of as a news-gatherer at all. . . . Tocqueville's man bawling out of the window was not bawling out the latest intelligence. He was bawling about the blunders and corruption of the ministry, and showing them the way to manage the public business" (Newspapers Here and Abroad" 197).

62. "Preparing the Minds of the People" 438–39. Before the 1850s it was an unknown practice for newspaper correspondents or editors to speak with politicians or other public figures. Lincoln was the first president who strived to communicate with a broad spectrum of the news media, and not just those from friendly partisan journals. Indeed, Greeley's *Tribune* was by and large a Republican-inspired newspaper, but it often was very critical of Lincoln and other Republicans. The interview was an American invention: when in 1859 Horace Greeley spoke to and recorded the answers of Brigham Young, it "may have been the first time a newspaper interview was reported in direct question-and-answer form, instead of the formal, indirect manner used until that time" (Stewart and Tebbel, 59). As Schudson points out, "When the practice [of interviewing] began, it was not highly regarded. *The Nation* in 1869 attacked it as 'the joint product of some humbug of a hack politician and another humbug of a newspaper reporter'" (437 [*The Nation*, January 26, 1869]).

63. Norton to Godkin, November 3, 1871, cited in Hofstadter 174, who derives the quotation from Ari Hoogenboom, *Outlawing the Spoils* (Urbana, Ill., 1961), 99.

64. Alan Trachtenberg argues such passiveness of observation was more and more defining "experience": "The most common, if most subtle, implication of transformed human relations appeared in the steady emergence of new modes of *experience*. In technologies of communication, vicarious experience began to erode direct physical experience of the world. Viewing and looking at representations, words and images, city people found themselves addressed more often as passive spectators than as active participants, consumers of images and sensations produced by others. . . . [In viewing circuses and sporting events,] instead of interacting with performers, audiences were now 'passive prisoners of their own excitement and bewilderment' " (122–23; the embedded quotation is an unspecified passage from Neil Harris's *Humbug: The Art of P. T. Barnum* [Boston, 1973]). According to Trachtenberg the "[n]ew styles of journalism" were indistinguishable from these other new forms of entertainment (123–25).

65. Godkin 202. In making these and similar charges, Godkin was joined by a wide range of public intellectuals, university intellectuals, and journalists: see Marzolf, esp. 4–33.

Chapter 5. A. S. Hill (ii): Reforming the Public

1. E. L. Godkin, *The Gilded Age Letters* 470–71; A. S. Hill, *Beginnings of Composition* 3.

2. For instance, he claims to have helped bring about the transformation at Harvard from oral-based pedagogy to writing-based pedagogy, having administered the first written test at Harvard. "Finding the existing method of conducting oral examinations twice a year in the presence of visiting committees of the Board of Overseers very unsatisfactory as a test of the students' knowledge and capacity, we asked leave of the Faculty to conduct the mathematical examinations of the Freshmen and Sophomores in writing. After a good deal of hesitation the Faculty granted us leave to make the experiment; and these examinations were the first examinations in writing ever conducted for entire classes in Harvard College. The innovation was gradually adopted in other departments, and ultimately spread to the whole University" (98).

3. This is not to say that Harvard in effect succeeded. As Townsend shows, scholars such as William James, Henry Adams, and John Jay Chapman often pointed out how Harvard itself resembled the "passive" and "effeminate" new world of business, finance, and technology. They bemoaned the effect of higher education on its students, encouraging them not to "grapple with knowledge" but to conform. As Townsend portrays their criticism, the Harvard system of education did not train "men to *oppose*"; as Adams put it, the system "could lead only to inertia" (134; Adams quoted in Townsend 135). Nevertheless, the *ideal* at Harvard ("the manly ideal") emphasized independent thinking coupled with decisive action, the belief that "any time a man accommodates himself to the opinion of others, he necessarily diminishes his being" (Townsend 154).

4. And thus I disagree fundamentally with Paul E. Ried (and others), who writes that Hill's was a rhetoric of fitting into an established culture: "The country had definitely [!] entered upon its freedom and was settling its disordered household to suit its democratic taste. . . . This sense of nationhood culminated in the seventies, the years when Hill was writing his rhetoric, a period labeled by astute observers as the 'Gilded Age' . . . [and] the 'Chromo-Civilization' " ("First and Fifth Boylston Professors" 231). Ried seems not to realize that Godkin's term "Chromo-Civilization" is thoroughly and unquestionably one of disparagement, used by Godkin to signify how much has gone wrong in America, which was exemplified for Godkin in the color photographs of newspapers, "chromo-engravings" (see Godkin's "Chromo-Civilization" and "Newspaper Pictures" for Godkin's intense objection to newspaper pictures, which he feared was further degrading Americans' critical habits). Ried continues, "What Hill saw as important for students was not the construction of a culture, but rather the absolute necessity of adjusting to one already in the building, humming and sizzling with all sorts of technological advances" (231). Ried's argument, which goes on to explain that Hill was delighted at the democratizing effects of communications technologies, exemplifies how inaccuracies can occur when we assume that American intellectuals and compositionists were unquestioningly pro-society, pro-status quo, and pro-conformity with regard to the new order.

5. Godkin goes on to criticize this new class of readers for "valu[ing] above everything what is called 'intelligence,' that is, a very slight and imperfect acquaintance with a large number of things" (166). Godkin's fears resonate with contemporary fears. I would add that the shift from "criticism" to "intelligence" reflects a current concern in composition studies: as Van E. Hillard has noted, our students have difficulty understanding the difference between "knowledge" (creating knowledge through "opposition" and argument) and "information." (See also Roszak and Postman.) Furthermore, for both Godkin and Hillard, it is the rapidly changing "information technologies" that are bringing about these changes.

6. *Our English* 65. Hill's discussion of students and other writers of the late 1880s who seem content to be the carriers of their culture's ideas parallels in interesting ways Lester Faigley's commentary about the cynical student of the 1990s, whose "sense of self is set out exclusively in how she believes she is perceived by others," and who desires, in Baudrillard's words "to be taken profoundly as an object"(216, 215).

7. *Our English* 122. What is perhaps most distressing to Hill is the kind of "class jumping" that journalists attempt, affecting, all too transparently, a higher-class writing style by employing sophisticated words, or, in Hill's words, "the ambition to command language that moves in the highest circles[,] . . . the practice of using the longest and most high-sounding words and expressions" (128). (This seems similar to Pierre Bourdieu's description of upper-class scorn at "petite bourgeoisie pretention" [62, 294].) Similarly, Carolyn Marvin discusses late-nineteenth-century upper-class anxieties about class-boundary violations in terms of another new communications technology, the telephone (*When Old Technologies* 63–108),

and Pierre Bourdieu discusses such phenomena from a sociological perspective, using his terms "mastery," "habitus," and "cultural competence" (65–66).

8. This strategy of changing the press emerges as a popular one among intellectuals about ten years after Hill wrote this essay. See Marzolf, who argues that intellectual press criticism played an important role in the reformation of the American press after the turn of the century. Another much-discussed strategy was the creation of an endowed press.

9. For instance, "A style may be rapid without being slovenly, plain without being low, and racy without being provincial" (*Our English* 238).

10. In *Professional Correctness* Stanley Fish says it is *impossible* for academics to make an impact in the public arena and that such public rhetoric is best left to the people who are good at it—not academics, but lawyers, politicians, and public-relations personnel.

11. Larrabee, Fred Robinson, Segerblohm. Most of these notes were taken of lectures not delivered by Hill, but by his "lieutenants," including R. S. Hurlburt and Wendell. Robinson's notes indicate that by 1887–88, Hill had already delegated responsibilities for teaching grammar and propriety to his assistant Hurlburt, with Hill taking responsibility for the more philosophical or social aspects of writing. These notes also suggest that grammatical principles were dealt with in a hurried and sterile fashion, or at least these note takers wrote very little: e.g., "Easier to tell how not to offend than to tell how to please. Two ways to fail using not the proper number of words: too few, and too many. Omission of necessary words makes sentence ungrammatical (35–38 Rhet). Restrictive clauses are not set off by commas. Explanatory clauses are. Omitted prepositions make sentence obscure. Connectives" (Robinson December 5, 1893). During that year, apparently, Hill delivered only a single lecture (another breakdown?), but he devoted that lecture to the differences between Dryden and Pope, where Dryden is portrayed as a stalwart man of the public and Pope a withdrawn and "effeminate" writer (this echoes a similar discussion in *Our English*). "Dryden & Pope near to each other in time. D big stalwart Eng. P slim woman Frenchm [*sic*]. D a *man* letters P man *letters*.... [Pope was] limited. had a contest. feeble & weak. had many physical peculiarities. Pope wrote with his brains not his muscles. A country boy. sensitive to external influences. Here endeth A. S. Hill's Lectures" (January 9, 1894). Perhaps this was Hill's attempt to inculcate the manly standard of civic virtue, but such a message seems to have been surely lost on this student.

12. As Hill writes in *Beginnings of Rhetoric and Composition*, "Ease of expression in this its highest form few of us can expect to secure. It will come to us, if it come at all, not as the result of conscious effort (for in language, as in manners, apparent effort is fatal to ease), but as incidental result of a sincere purpose to express in the best English at our command *what we really think and feel*" (470). Being oneself is a matter, then, of largely "forgetting oneself" (as Hill puts it elsewhere). Allowing one's true self to emerge in writing is something only a few (the elect?) can "secure." (To turn once again to Bourdieu's social critique of taste, Hill's

valuing of linguistic ease seems a fine example of the importance of linguistic ease for distinguishing oneself as a member of the upper classes [Bourdieu 255–56].)

13. Consider Oswald Garrison Villard's account of Hill's typical response to students' essays he did not like: "Professor Hill sat silent for nearly five minutes, then gave us no moral lecture but so demolished the offender in two sentences that the class almost felt a glimmering of sympathy for him. Nothing could have been more perfect than those few words" (90). Talk about rhetoric as the art of "efficient communication"!

Chapter 6. Classroom Argument, Responsibility, and Change

1. The SCANS (U.S. Department of Labor Secretary's Commission on Achieving Necessary Skills) definition of responsibility is quoted by William A. Covino (*Magic* 111); Perelman and Olbrechts-Tyteca, *The New Rhetoric* 62.

2. Myron Tuman criticizes these theorists for believing that their teaching methods and theories will "inevitably" lead to more democratic conceptions and uses of knowledge (*Word Perfect* 91–105).

3. For instance, the first edition of John T. Gage's writing textbook *The Shape of Reason* (1987) made mention of the importance of "responsibility" in argumentation throughout the book, but in the second edition (1991), he removed the word entirely. Gage did so because many students felt the word "responsibility" made the book seem "preachy" (personal conversation). On the other hand, I regularly use the word "responsibility" in my discussions of the nature of writing and have found that my students' response to the term seems almost entirely positive. Of course, our definitions differ (see the discussion that follows here), and I expend a great deal of effort trying to get my students to embrace and see the value of my definition. The mainstream (e.g., Will, Edmundson) as well as the academic press (e.g., Zucker) portray young people ("Generation X") as irresponsible, uncaring, lazy, and just plain stupid. But my students seem eager to dispute these definitions of themselves, and I exploit this eagerness.

4. While this will surprise nobody who works in composition, we hear once again that writing instruction is so straightforward that any capable writer (and certainly a Pulitzer Prize nominee) *should* be able to teach it well—under reasonable circumstances teaching to reasonable students. When this obviously great writer cannot effectively teach writing, his reaction is identical to that of nineteenth-century outsiders (e.g., the writers of the Harvard literacy reports): blame the students, their educational upbringing, and (as I have argued in this book) their culture. Press historian Michael Schudson has written that "Journalism is an uninsulated profession," meaning that because newspapers "are directly dependent on market opinion" and "appeal to popular opinion," everybody feels qualified to criticize it as if they were experts; everyone feels expert enough to criticize what journalism is *really* about, "objectivity" (*Discovering the News* 9). If journalism is "uninsulated," then composition instruction is naked.

5. The first quotation on the back cover of Bennett's volume, under "Advance praise for *The Book of Virtues*," comes from Rush Limbaugh (which suggests that the book's publisher, at least, sees its market consisting significantly in conservative book buyers); he writes "*The Book of Virtues* is a superb collection, certain to *fortify* you and yours for a lifetime of morality, goodness, and right thinking" (my emphasis). Considering that so much conservative rhetoric stresses the position that "the dominant elite media" controls the consciousness of Americans, such responsibility (as inoculation against seductive discourse) becomes important.

6. Relativism, according to Kilpatrick, began with Nietzsche, was passed from Hitler to Mussolini, and was then gathered up by the feminists, especially Carol Gilligan. Kilpatrick engages in some preterition to insinuate the connections among relativism, Naziism, and feminism: "It is a big jump from Nazism to current feminist philosophies of education, and it is not a connection I intend [!] to make. But there is a connection with Nietzsche" (157).

7. Compare Rosen's position to John Fiske's in "Popularity and the Politics of Information," where he argues that popular attitudes are not skeptical enough and that tabloid journalism serves a valuable social function by moving popular sentiment away from its unquestioning credence in "official journalism" and its objectivity; tabloid journalism invites citizens to "read" rather than "decipher" the news. Whereas Rosen wants a "public journalism" that helps the citizenry to become more politically active, Fiske admires tabloid journalism for its ability to teach citizens how they might gain critical distance from their journalism. (Fiske does make one weak wave to popular involvement, however: "I see some evidence that this informed popular scepticism can be, if all too rarely, turned towards events in the public, political sphere, though I do not wish to overemphasize this" [61]).

8. Gary's education, by the way, was a "happy" story, one that fits tidily into Richard Miller's "master narrative of education": by the end of the semester, Gary had become just like me in the sense that he became an arguer who could live comfortably in conflict and who came to agree with me that these issues were worth arguing about, and in fact that our work on these issues was (somehow) important.

9. Booth works hard to earn our assent that we should believe in the possibility and importance of a rhetoric of inquiry, concluding this way: "The supreme purpose of persuasion in this view could not be to talk someone else into a preconceived view; rather it must be to engage in mutual inquiry or exploration. . . . It is good for men to attend to each other's reasons—and we all know that it is, because without such attending none of us could come to be and questions about value could not even be asked—it is also good to work for whatever conditions make such mutual inquiry possible" (*Modern Dogma* 137).

10. Mark Weinstein has written about similar ideas, but from a more traditional "philosophy of education" perspective.

11. Of course, the teacher always reserves the authority to criticize or even eject a student from the class, if that student seems not to be himself or herself engaging in responsible inquiry and dialogue in the class, if, for instance, he or she

refuses to participate or to take the views of others seriously. For accounts of such problems, see Ira Shor's comments (Shor and Freire, *A Pedagogy* 138–40) and Marilyn M. Cooper's account of the student she calls "Bartelby," who preferred not to ("Unhappy Consciousness in First-Year English" and "Why Are We Talking about Discourse Communities"). Again, for an inspiring experiment in sharing power, emphasizing difficulties as much as it emphasizes rewards, see Shor's *When Students Have Power*.

12. These ideas were much influenced by John Trimbur's "Consensus and Difference in Collaborative Learning," especially pp. 612–16.

13. Berthoff makes a similar point about the right, the left, and the poststructuralists, calling them the "old positivists" and the "new positivists" ("Rhetoric as Hermeneutic" 280).

14. Gage makes a similar point about "Rogerian persuasion" ("Adequate" 164). Indeed, such cooperative inquiry can very easily devolve into conscious unethical manipulation, as in Stephen R. Covey's *The Seven Habits of Highly Effective People*, where he advocates "reflective listening" in order to better understand others, but the goal of such listening and understanding is quite openly to "reply, to control, to manipulate" (240). Again, here is an example of how our classroom practices (here "cooperative inquiry" or "confrontational cooperation") might unintentionally play into the hands of the worst of corporate America by preparing students who are "highly effective," highly manipulative "reflective listeners" (see the "Postscript" to the work's chapter 7). Detractors of this idea of "responsible pedagogy" (say, those who would see this project as another instance of "political correctness") would state a valid objection in saying this project (changing students' conceptions of argument and of themselves) is merely a more powerful (trickier) rhetoric—a new virus of rhetoric against which nationalistic and other public discourses have not yet immunized the students. Of course, in a sense, they are right: there are no value-neutral principles of argumentation that will lead us, in all cases, to consensus, justice, or even illuminating dissensus. A "postmodern" responsibility itself implies that value-neutral principles do not exist. Indeed, while these principles of responsible argumentation are, I believe, *generally better* for fostering classrooms where students have the freedom to change, I can imagine some contexts, certainly, where I would find it necessary to (temporarily) rescind open discussion and tell a student s/he must stop what s/he's saying, or even eject the student from the class. But most often, as a guiding principle, I would avoid that because the principle of cooperative exchange does a certain kind of persuasive work that I find valuable and important for students. This is a position similar to Stanley Fish's on hate speech. Fish, who often stridently glories in the idea of denying certain persons their "free speech," has recently argued that it is sometimes more persuasive to let groups whose positions you despise have their say, since this may get the work done that you desire. On the question whether to impose speech codes, Fish writes "You can ask if in this situation, at this time and in this place, it would be reasonable to deploy [speech codes] in the service of your agenda. . . . The answer will often be no, and, in fact that is my usual answer; for in most cases speech codes will cause more

problems than they solve, and, all things considered, it will often be the better part of wisdom to tolerate the sound of hate. . . . At that moment you will be talking like a liberal, but there's nothing wrong with that as long as you don't take your liberalism too seriously and don't hew to it as a matter of principle" ("Boutique Multiculturalism" 394).

15. Using her research of women learning to write at Radcliffe, JoAnn Campbell makes a strong case that our pedagogy will probably be more effective when we begin by accepting our students' positions: "If critical thinking is our goal, aren't students more likely to question cherished beliefs and articulate the assumptions they live by when there is no expectation that they must change themselves to be acceptable?" (481).

16. See the final chapter. It is interesting that Frederic Jameson (not exactly a theorist of education, but an admired scholar of culture and subjectivity nonetheless) concurs that modest changes are the ones most likely to occur. As Jameson comments, "I myself do not particularly believe (as liberals generally do) in the power of rational persuasion, and in the accessibility of the conscious mind to deep political and ideological commitment. Commitments of that kind are basic existential ones: they are unconscious and generally flow from family and class experience of a more all-encompassing time, which largely predates the hours spent in the college classroom. This is why it is ludicrous to imagine that the most eloquent 'Marxist spokesperson' is capable of indoctrinating anybody. Our task is rather to make available an intellectual tradition, or what . . . might be called a Marxist or a 'Marxian' culture. . . . Our task is above all not to persuade or indoctrinate, but to interest the students, and show them that this tradition has theorized the problems and dilemmas, the most acute or urgent issues, of our own times" (9).

17. The phrase is Freire's (Shor and Freire, *A Pedagogy* 36).

Chapter 7. Conflict, Change, and "Flexibility"

1. Plato, *The Republic* (Book X) 833; Freire, *Pedagogy* 53; Harris, "Negotiating"; Peirce, *Philosophical Writings of Peirce* 4.

2. My criticism of the essays in this work is milder than that of Kurt Spellmeyer, who criticizes the contributors and editors for believing that "the point of doing cultural studies is not to learn anything new, but to apply an accepted paradigm over and over again, and also, more crucially, to induce other people to apply it in the same way" ("Out" 428). He singles Zavarzadeh and another contributor for their "resolute and doctrinaire hostility": their "contributions to this collection might be mistaken for a truly hilarious parody of 'oppositional pedagogy' were they not offered in deadly earnest" (428).

3. Tate 269. For a similar argument (but about composition pedagogy in general), see Phelps ("Constrained") or Reed Way Dasenbrock. Dasenbrock recognizes that in teaching writing, we inevitably teach something else, some other topic

or issue. He suggests, however, that that "something else" should not be the "central concern" of a writing course: "I don't think we as writing teachers should concern ourselves primarily with our students' sense of self, their 'inner' development, their identification with or alienation from society. . . . The central concern of a course in writing ought to be learning to write well" (30).

4. Joseph Harris makes a similar argument about the value of what many denigrate as expressivism in chapter 2 ("Voice") in *A Teaching Subject: Composition since 1967*. Like me, he does not believe that expressivism necessarily goes against the efforts of political or cultural critique. He concurs with my argument here that there is a very strong tradition of expressivism (he closely examines the line running through Theodore Baird at Amherst, to William E. Coles Jr., to David Bartholomae) that has always resembled a "postmodern" version of the decentered self, argument, and conventions, where the "key to finding your own voice . . . was more a question of working *against*" the constraints of academic writing (38). The process is not one of discovering "who am I and what is my real voice" but "who do I become when I adopt such and such a voice, such a way of expressing ideas?" Expressivism, Harris shows, as practiced by many, is not a procedure for locking out the ways of speaking and writing that come from culture and the discourses within it, but a way of understanding how those ways of speaking and writing inhabit *our* speaking and writing, and how we might resist or at least question them. As Harris concludes: "It is for me precisely in that tension—between the issue or argument at hand and the ways we have of arguing, between the voice of an individual and the demands of discourse of which she is part—that much of the interest of teaching writing lies" (45).

5. Pratt first published her ideas about contact zones in MLA's *Profession 91*, and it quickly became an important concept in composition (see Harris, "Negotiating" 31–33).

6. This is of course an ancient idea about argumentation, that even eristic rhetoric could bring us to the truth. It was a popular idea in the "rhetoric as epistemic" debates of the 1970s. For example, Richard Cherwitz wrote in 1977, "rhetoric can bring forth knowledge only when it involves the collision of the subjective experiences which undergird man's selective experiences and prejudices. . . . [I]n order for man to gain adherence, rhetoric must be viewed as an activity of correction, wherein the class of contradictory ideas exposes error and yields truth" (217).

7. William Coles's words are, "But do not expect to be given a formula with which to improve your writing. When it comes to a subject like writing, the best a teacher can do, a course can do, an education can do, is to put you in a position to improve yourself for yourself" (*Seeing* 10).

8. For contemporary commentary, see, for instance, Mariolina Salvatori's "Toward a Hermeneutics of Difficulty" and "Conversations with Texts," Hephzibah Roskelly's "The Dialogue of Chaos," and James Seitz's "Roland Barthes." For a historical description of the evolution of these ideas, see Robin Varnum's *Fencing with*

Words: A History of Writing Instruction at Amherst College during the Era of Theodore Baird, 1938–1966, which describes what may be the less-recent origins of these ideas by tracing the influence from Baird to William H. Pritchard, Richard Poirer, Ruben A. Brower, Walker Gibson, and William E. Coles Jr.

9. See David Bartholomae and Anthony Petrosky, "Facts"; Bartholomae, "Wanderings"; David Bartholomae proposes that compositionists take a dose of this same medicine, that they "radically revise" their own conceptions of who they are and what they do in "The Tidy House."

10. For a discussion that addresses the goals, strategies, and difficulties of engaging public writing in university writing courses, see Susan Wells's "Rogue Cops and Health Care: What Do We Want from Public Writing?"

Works Cited

Adams, Charles Francis, Jr. "A College Fetish." *Three Phi Beta Kappa Addresses*. Boston: Houghton, 1907. 3–46.

Adams, Charles Francis, Jr., E. L. Godkin, and George R Nutter. *Report of the Committee on Composition and Rhetoric*. Cambridge: Harvard University, 1897. Rptd. Brereton, *Origins* 101–27.

Adorno, T. W. *The Authoritarian Personality*. New York: Norton, 1982.

Albion, Robert G. "The 'Communications Revolution.' " *American Historical Review* 37 (July 1932): 718–20.

Alcorn, Marshall W., Jr. "Changing the Subject of Postmodernist Theory: Discourse, Ideology, and Therapy in the Classroom." *Rhetoric Review* 13 (1995): 331–49.

[*Alumnus*]. *Independent Chronicle & Boston Patriot,* September 25, 1819: 1.

Anderson, Dorothy I. "Edward T. Channing's Teaching of Rhetoric." *Speech Monographs* 16 (1949): 69–81.

Anderson, Dorothy I., and Waldo W. Braden. "Introduction." In Channing, *Lectures*.

Andrew, J. Cutler. *The North Reports the Civil War*. Pittsburgh: U of Pittsburgh P, 1955.

Antczak, Frederick J. *Thought and Character: The Rhetoric of Democratic Education*. Ames: Iowa State UP, 1985.

Aristotle. *Aristotle on Rhetoric: A Theory of Civic Discourse*. Trans. and ed. by George A. Kennedy. New York: Oxford UP, 1991.

———. *The Rhetoric and Poetics of Aristotle*. Trans. W. Rhys Roberts. New York: Modern Library, 1984.

Aronowitz, Stanley, and Henry Giroux. *Education under Siege: The Conservative, Liberal, and Radical Debate over Schooling*. South Hadley, MA: Bergin & Garvey, 1985.

———. *Postmodern Education: Politics, Culture, and Social Criticism.* Minneapolis: U of Minnesota P, 1991.

Barker-Benfield, Ben. *The Horrors of the Half-Known Life.* New York: Harper & Row,

Bartholomae, David. "Inventing the University." *When a Writer Can't Write: Studies in Writer's Block and Other Composing Process Problems.* Ed. Mike Rose. New York: Guilford, 1985 134–75.

———. "The Tidy House: Basic Writing in the American Curriculum." *Journal of Basic Writing* 12 (1993): 4–21.

———. "Wanderings, Misreadings, Miswritings, Misunderstandings." In Newkirk, 89–118.

Bartholomae, David, and Anthony R. Petrosky. "Facts, Artifacts, and Counterfacts: A Basic Reading and Writing Course for the College Curriculum." *Facts, Artifacts, Counterfacts.* Portsmouth, NH: Boynton/Cook, 1986.

Bartholomae, David, and Anthony Petrosky, eds. *The Teaching of Writing.* Chicago: U of Chicago P, 1986.

Bates, David Homer. *Lincoln in the Telegraph Office.* New York: Century, 1907.

Bennett, William J. *The Book of Virtues: A Treasury of Great Moral Stories.* Simon & Schuster, 1993.

Bercovitch, Sacvan. "Emerson, Individualism, and the Ambiguities of Dissent." *South Atlantic Quarterly* 89 (1990): 623–62.

———. "The Problem of Ideology in American Literary History." *Critical Inquiry* 12 (1986): 631–53.

Berke, R. L. "Bennett Asserts Drug Education Isn't Key." *The New York Times.* February 3, 1990: 1.

Berlin, James. "Composition Studies and Cultural Studies: Collapsing Boundaries." *Into the Field: Sites of Composition Studies.* Ed. Anne Ruggles Gere. New York: MLA, 1993. 99–116.

———. "Composition and Cultural Studies." In Hurlbert and Blitz, 47–55.

———. Letter to Theresa Enos. January 18, 1994. Quoted in Alcorn, 344–45.

———. "Postmodernism, Politics, and Histories of Rhetoric." *Pre/Text* 11 (1990): 169–87.

———. "Revisionary History: The Dialectical Method." *Pre/Text* 8 (1987): 47–61.

———. "Rhetoric and Ideology in the Classroom." *College English* 50 (1988): 477–94.

———. "Rhetoric and Poetics in the English Department: Our Nineteenth-Century Inheritance." *College English* 47 (1985): 521–33.

———. *Rhetoric and Reality: Writing Instruction in American Colleges, 1900–1985*. Carbondale and Edwardsville: Southern Illinois UP, 1987.

———. "Richard Whately and Current-Traditional Rhetoric." *College English* 42 (1980): 10–17.

———. "The Transformation of Invention in Nineteenth-Century American Rhetoric." *Southern Speech Communication Journal* 46 (1981): 292–304.

———. *Writing Instruction in Nineteenth-Century American Colleges*. Carbondale and Edwardsville: Southern Illinois UP, 1984.

Berlin, James A. and Michael J. Vivion, eds. *Cultural Studies in the English Classroom*. Portsmouth, NH: Boynton/Cook-Heinemann, 1992.

Berthoff, Ann E. *The Making of Meaning: Metaphors, Models, and Maxims for Writing Teachers*. Upper Montclair, N.J.: Boynton/Cook, 1981.

———. "Rhetoric as Hermeneutic." *College Composition and Communication* 42 (1991): 279–87.

———. *The Sense of Learning*. Portsmouth, NH: Boynton/Cook, 1990.

Blair, Hugh. *Lectures on Rhetoric and Belles Lettres*. 2 vols. Carbondale and Edwardsville: Southern Illinois UP, 1965.

Bledstein, Burton J. *The Culture of Professionalism: The Middle Class and the Development of Higher Education in America*. New York: Norton, 1976.

Bloom, Lynn Z. "Freshman Composition as a Middle-Class Enterprise." *College English* 58 (October 1996): 654–75.

Booth. Wayne C. *Modern Dogma and the Rhetoric of Assent*. Notre Dame and London: U of Notre Dame P, 1974.

———. *Now Don't Try to Reason with Me*. Chicago: U of Chicago P, 1970.

———. *The Vocation of a Teacher*. Chicago: U of Chicago P, 1988.

Bourdieu, Pierre. *Distinction: A Social Critique of the Judgement of Taste*. Trans. Richard Nice. Cambridge: Harvard UP, 1984.

Boyd, Richard. "Mechanical Correctness and Ritual in the Late Nineteenth-Century Composition Classroom." *Rhetoric Review* 2 (1993): 436–55.

Braun, John E. "The Philosophical Roots of the Nineteenth-Century 'Repose' in Rhetoric, with Emphasis on the Idea of Communication in the Thought of Josiah Royce." Ph.D. Dissertation, University of Michigan, 1977.

Brereton, John C. "Business Writing, Charles Francis Adams, and the Harvard Reports." Paper presented at Conference on College Composition and Communication, Milwaukee, March 28, 1996.

———. *The Origins of Composition Studies in American College, 1875–1925*. Pittsburgh: U of Pittsburgh P, 1995.

Briggs, LeBaron R. *To College Teachers of English Composition*. Boston: Houghton, 1928.

Broaddus, Dottie. *Genteel Rhetoric: Writing High Culture in Nineteenth-Century Boston*. Columbia: U of South Carolina P, 1998.

Brock, Timothy C., and Arnold H. Buss. "Dissonance, Aggression and Evaluation of Pain." *Journal of Abnormal and Social Psychology* 65 (1962): 192–202.

Brody, Miriam. *Manly Writing: Gender, Rhetoric, and the Rise of Composition*. Carbondale and Edwardsville: Southern Illinois UP, 1993

Brooks, Van Wyck. *The Flowering of New England*. New York: E. P. Dutton, 1936.

Bruffee, Kenneth A. "Social Construction, Language, and the Authority of Knowledge." *College English* 48 (1986): 773–90.

Bryce, James. *The American Commonwealth*. Vol. 2. 3rd ed. New York: Macmillan, 1906.

Bryson, Gladys. *Man and Society: The Scottish Inquiry of the Eighteenth Century*. Princeton: Princeton UP, 1945.

Buell, Lawrence. *New England Literary Culture: From Revolution through Renaissance*. Cambridge: Harvard UP, 1986.

Bullock, Richard and John Trimbur, eds. *The Politics of Writing Instruction: Postsecondary*. Portsmouth, NH: Boynton/Cook, 1991.

Burke, Kenneth. *Attitudes toward History*. Berkeley: U of California P, 1984.

———. *Language as Symbolic Action*. Berkeley: U of California P, 1966.

Burgoon, Michael, Michael Pfau, and Thomas S. Birk. "An Inoculation Theory Explanation for the Effects of Corporate Issue/Advocacy Advertising Campaigns." *Communication Research* 22 (1995): 485–505.

Campbell, George. *The Philosophy of Rhetoric*. Carbondale and Edwardsville: Southern Illinois UP, 1963.

Campbell, JoAnn. "Controlling Voices: The Legacy of English at Radcliffe College 1883–1917." *College Composition and Communication* 43 (December 1992): 472–85.

Cappella, Joseph N., and Kathleen Hall Jamieson. "Broadcast Adwatch Effects: A Field Experiment." *Communication Research* 21 (June 1994): 432–65.

Carey, James W. *Communication as Culture*. Boston: Unwin Hyman, 1988.

———. "The Communications Revolution and the Professional Communicator." *Sociology of Mass Media Communicators*. Ed. Paul Halmos. Keele: University of Keele (UK), 1969: 23–38.

Carr, Jean Ferguson. "Rereading the Academy as Worldly Text, " *College Composition and Communication* 45.1 (1994): 93–97.

Caulfield, Peter J. "Teaching Rhetoric as a Way of Knowing." In Fitts and France, 157–172.

Cayton, Mary Kupiec. "The Making of an American Prophet: Emerson, His Audiences, and the Rise of the Culture Industry in Nineteenth-Century America." *American Historical Review* 92 (1987): 597–620.

Channing, Edward T. "The Abuses of Political Discussion." *North American Review* 4 (January 1817): 193–201.

———. *Lectures Read to the Seniors in Harvard College*. Boston: Ticknor and Fields, 1856. Facsimile edition: Carbondale and Edwardsville: Southern Illinois UP, 1968.

———. "Ogilvie's Philosophical Essays." *North American Review* 4 (March 1817): 378–408.

———. "On Models of Literature." *North American Review* 3 (July 1816): 202–9.

Charvat, William. *The Origins of American Critical Thought, 1810–1835*. Philadelphia: U of Pennsylvania P, 1936.

Cheney, Lynne V. *Telling the Truth: Why Our Culture and Our Country Have Stopped Making Sense—and What We Can Do about It*. New York: Simon & Schuster, 1995.

Cherwitz, Richard. "Rhetoric as 'A Way of Knowing': An Attenuation of the Epistemological Claims of the 'New Rhetoric.'" *The Southern Speech Communication Journal* 42 (1977): 207–19.

Cicero. *Of Oratory*. Trans. E. W. Sutton and H. Rackham. In *The Rhetorical Tradition*. Ed. Patricia Bizzell and Bruce Herzberg. Boston: St. Martin's P, 1990. 200–50.

Clark, Gregory. *Dialogue, Dialectic, and Conversation: A Social Perspective on the Function of Writing*. Carbondale and Edwardsville: Southern Illinois University P, 1990.

———. "Rescuing the Discourse of Community." *College Composition and Communication* 45 (1994): 61–74.

Clark, Gregory, and S. Michael Halloran. "Introduction: Transformations of Public Discourse in Nineteenth-Century America." In *Oratorical Culture in Nineteenth-Century America*. Ed. Gregory Clark and Michael Halloran. Carbondale and Edwardsville: Southern Illinois UP, 1993. 1–26.

Clifford, John. "The Subject in Discourse." In Harkin and Schilb, 38–51.

Clifford, John, and John Schilb, eds. *Writing Theory and Critical Theory*. New York: MLA, 1994.

Coles, William E., Jr. *The Plural I—and After*. Portsmouth, NH: Boynton/Cook-Heinemann, 1988.

———. *Seeing through Writing*. New York: Harper, 1988.

———. "An Unpetty Place." *College Composition and Communication* 23 (1972): 378–82.

Connors, Robert J. "Academic History/Agonistic History." Paper presented Conference on College Composition and Communication, Phoenix, AZ, March 13, 1997.

———. *Composition-Rhetoric: Backgrounds, Theory, and Pedagogy*. Pittsburgh: U of Pittsburgh P, 1997.

———. "Current-Traditional Rhetoric: Thirty Years of *Writing with a Purpose*." *Rhetoric Society Quarterly* 11 (1981): 208–21.

———. "Foreword." *Dialogue, Dialectic, and Conversation: A Social Perspective on the Function of Writing*, by Gregory Clark. Carbondale and Edwardsville: Southern Illinois UP, 1990.

———. "Personal Writing Assignments." *College Composition and Communication* 38 (1987): 166–83.

———. "Rhetoric in the Modern University: The Creation of an Underclass." In Bullock and Trimbur, 55–84.

———. "The Rhetoric of Mechanical Correctness." In Newkirk, 27–58.

———. "Teaching and Learning as a Man." *College English* 58 (1996): 137–57.

———. "Textbooks and the Evolution of the Discipline." *College Composition and Communication* 37 (1986): 178–94.

———. "Writing the History of Our Discipline." In Lindemann and Tate, 49–71.

Cooper, Marilyn M. "Postmodern Ethics in the Writing Classroom." Available: http://www.hum.mut.edu/cccc/97/cooper.html.

———. "Unhappy Consciousness in First-Year English: How to Figure Things Out for Yourself." In Cooper and Holzman, 28–60.

———. "Why Are We Talking about Discourse Communities? Or, Foundationalism Rears Its Ugly Head Once More." In Cooper and Holzman, 202–20.

Cooper, Marilyn M., and Michael Holzman, eds. *Writing as Social Action*. Portsmouth, NH: Boynton/Cook, 1989.

Corbett, Edward P. J. *Classical Rhetoric for the Modern Student*. 3rd ed. New York: Oxford UP, 1990.

Covey, Stephen R. *The Seven Habits of Highly Effective People: Restoring the Character Ethic*. New York: Simon & Schuster, 1989.

Covino, William A. *The Art of Wondering: A Revisionist Return to the History of Rhetoric*. Portsmouth (NH): Boynton/Cook, 1988.

———. *Magic, Rhetoric, and Literacy: An Eccentric History of the Composing Imagination*. Albany: State U of New York P, 1994.

Croffut, W[illiam] A[ugustus]. Letter to A. S. Hill. December 16, 1862. Adams Sherman Hill Papers. Duke University Archives.

Cronkhite, Gary. "Rhetoric, Communication, and Psychoepistemology." In *Rhetoric: A Tradition in Transition*. Ed. Walter R Fisher. East Lansing: Michigan State UP, 1974. 261–78.

Crowley, Sharon. "The Current-Traditional Rhetoric: An Informal History." *Rhetoric Society Quarterly* 16 (1986): 233–50.

―――. *The Methodical Memory: Invention in Current-Traditional Rhetoric*. Carbondale and Edwardsville: Southern Illinois UP, 1990.

―――. "Response to Robert J. Connors, 'The Rise and Fall of the Modes of Discourse.' " *College Composition and Communication* 35 (1984): 88–91.

Czitrom, Daniel J. *Media and the American Mind*. Chapel Hill: U of North Carolina P, 1982.

Dahl, Robert A. *Democracy and Its Critics*. New Haven: Yale UP, 1989.

―――. *Size and Democracy*. Palo Alto: Stanford UP, 1973.

Dana, C[harles]. A[nderson]. Letters to Adams Sherman Hill. April 24, 1860 and August 7, 1861. Adams Sherman Hill Papers. Duke University Archives.

Dasenbrock, Reed Way. "The Myths of the Subjective and of the Subject in Composition Studies." *Journal of Advanced Composition* 13.1 (1993): 21–32.

Davidson, Cathy N. *Revolution and the Word: The Rise of the Novel in America*. New York: Oxford UP, 1986.

Davis, Richard Beale. "Edward Tyrrel Channing's 'American Scholar' of 1818." *The Key Reporter* 25 (Spring 1961): 1–2.

Dickson, Richard E. "Ramism and the Rhetorical Tradition." Ph.D. dissertation, Duke University, 1992.

Douglas, Wallace. "Rhetoric for the Meritocracy: The Creation of Composition at Harvard." In *English in America: A Radical View of the Profession*. Ed. Richard Ohmann. New York: Oxford UP, 1976. 97–132.

Edmundson, Mark. "On the Uses of a Liberal Education: As Lite Entertainment for Bored College Students." *Harpers* September 1997: 39–59.

Eliot, Charles W. "Charles William Eliot." In Harvard University, 95–118.

Ellsworth, Elizabeth H. "Why Doesn't This Feel Empowering? Working through the Repressive Myths of Critical Pedagogy." *Harvard Educational Review* 59 (1989): 297–324.

Emery, Edwin. *The Press and America: An Interpretive History of Journalism*. Englewood Cliffs, NJ: Prentice Hall, 1962.

Enos, Theresa. " 'A Brand New World': Using Our Professional and Personal Histories of Rhetoric." In Enos, ed., 3–14.

Enos, Theresa, ed. *Learning from the Histories of Rhetoric: Essays in Honor of Winifred Bryan Horner*. Carbondale and Edwardsville: Southern Illinois UP, 1993.

Faigley, Lester. *Fragments of Rationality: Postmodernity and the Subject of Composition*. Pittsburgh: U of Pittsburgh P, 1992.

Fallows, James. *Breaking the News: How the Media Undermine American Democracy*. New York: Pantheon, 1996.

Fellman, Anita Clair, and Michael Fellman. *Making Sense of Self: Medical Advice Literature in Late Nineteenth-Century America*. Philadelphia: U of Pennsylvania P, 1981.

Felton, Cornelius Conway. Review of *Lectures Read to the Seniors in Harvard College*, by Edward Tyrrel Channing. *North American Review* 84 (January 1857): 34–48.

Fish, Stanley. "Boutique Multiculturalism, or Why Liberals Are Incapable of Thinking about Hate Speech." *Critical Inquiry* 23 (1997): 378–95.

———. *Doing What Comes Naturally: Change, Rhetoric, and the Practice of Theory in Literary and Legal Studies*. Durham: Duke UP, 1989. 471–502.

———. *Professional Correctness: Literary Studies and Political Change*. Oxford and New York: Oxford UP, 1995.

Fishman, Stephen M., and Lucille Parkinson McCarthy. "Community in the Expressivist Classroom." *College English* 57 (Jan 1995): 62–81.

———. "Teaching for Student Change: A Deweyan Alternative to Radical Pedagogy." *College Composition and Communication* 47 (1996): 342–66.

Fiske, John. "Popularity and the Politics of Information." *Journalism and Popular Culture*. Ed. Peter Dahlgren and Colin Sparks. London: Sage, 1992. 45–63.

Fitts, Karen and Alan W. France, eds. *Left Margins: Cultural Studies and Composition Pedagogy*. Albany: State U of New York P, 1995.

Fleischer, Cathy. "Forming an Interactive Literacy in the Writing Classroom." In Berlin and Vivion, 182–99.

Flower, Linda. "Comment [on 'Rhetoric and Ideology in the Writing Class' and 'Problem Solving Reconsidered']." *College English* 51 (1989) 765–69.

Fogarty, Daniel Fogarty, S.J. *Roots for a New Rhetoric*. New York: Teachers College P, 1959.

"The Foundations of Rhetoric." [Book review.] *The Dial* 15 (November 1895): 293–94.

France, Alan W. "Theory Cop: Kurt Spellmeyer and the Boundaries of Composition." *College Composition and Communication* 48 (May 1997): 284–88.

Freire, Paulo. *Education for Critical Consciousness*. New York: Continuum, 1973.

———. *Pedagogy of the Oppressed*. Trans. Myra Bergman Ramos. New York: Seabury P, 1973.

———. *The Politics of Education: Culture, Power, and Liberation*. South Hadley, MA: Bergin & Garvey, 1985.

Gage, John. "An Adequate Epistemology for Composition Studies: Classical and Modern Perspectives." *Essays on Classical Rhetoric and Modern Discourse*. Ed. Robert Connors, Lisa S. Ede, and Andrea A. Lunsford. Carbondale and Edwardsville: Southern Illinois UP, 1984. 152–69.

———. "Doing the History of Nineteenth-Century Rhetoric." Paper presented Conference on College Composition and Communication, Washington, DC, March 25, 1995.

———. "A General Theory of the Enthymeme for Advanced Composition." *Teaching Advanced Composition*. Ed. Katherine H. Adams and John L. Adams. Portsmouth, NH: Boynton/Cook-Heinemann, 1991. 161–78.

———. "Introduction." *Rhetoric in American Colleges: 1850–1900*, by Albert R. Kitzhaber. Dallas: Southern Methodist UP, 1990.

———. "On 'Rhetoric' and 'Composition.' " In Lindemann and Tate, 15–32.

———. *The Shape of Reason*. New York: Macmillan, 1987.

———. "Why Write?" *The Teaching of Writing*, Part 2. Ed. Anthony P. Petrosky and David Bartholomae. Chicago: U of Chicago P, 1986. 8–29.

Gardiner, J. H. "Adams Sherman Hill." *Harvard Graduates Magazine* 19 (1911): 377–80.

Gay, S[idney] H. Letter to Adams Sherman Hill. May 23, 1862. Adams Sherman Hill Papers. Duke University Archives.

George, Diana, and Diana Shoos. "Issues of Subjectivity and Resistance: Cultural Studies in the Composition Classroom." In Berlin and Vivion, 200–210.

Gere, Anne Ruggles. "Teaching Writing: The Major Theories." In Petrosky and Bartholomae, 30–48.

Giroux, Henry. "Who Writes in a Cultural Studies Class?, or, Where Is the Pedagogy? In Fitts and France, 3–16.

Godkin, E. L. "Cheap Newspapers." *The Nation* 37 (1881): 346.

———. "Chromo-Civilization." *Reflections and Comments, 1865–1895*. New York: Scribner's, 1895. 192–205.

———. *The Gilded Age Letters of E. L. Godkin*. Ed. William M. Armstrong. Albany: State U of New York P, 1974.

———. "The 'Libertine Press.' " *The Nation* 10 (May 5, 1870): 285–86.

————. "The Mystery of the Newspaper." *The Nation* 21 (August 12, 1875): 104–05.

————. "The Newspaper and the Reader." *The Nation* 1 (1865): 165–66.

————. "Newspaper Pictures." *The Nation* 56 (April 27, 1893): 306–07.

————. "Newspapers Here and Abroad." *North American Review* 150 (February 1890): 197–204.

————. "Opinion-Moulding." *The Nation* 9 (August 12, 1869): 126–27.

————. "The Profession of Journalism." *The Nation* 17 (July 17, 1873): 37–38.

Godzich, Wlad. *The Culture of Literacy*. Cambridge: Harvard UP, 1994.

Graff, Gerald. "The Dilemma of Oppositional Pedagogy: A Response." In Fitts and France, 275–86.

————. *Professing Literature: An Institutional History*. Chicago: U of Chicago P, 1987.

————. "Teach the Conflicts." *South Atlantic Quarterly* 89 (1990): 51–68.

Graff, Harvey J. *Legacies of Literacy*. Bloomington: Indiana UP, 1991.

Guthrie, Warren. "The Development of Rhetorical Theory in America, 1635–1850." *Speech Monographs* 13 (1946): 14–22; 14 (1947): 38–54; 15 (1948): 61–71; 16 (1949): 98–113; 18 (1951): 17–30.

Hairston, Maxine. "Diversity, Ideology, and Teaching Writing." *College Composition and Communication* 43 (1992): 179–93.

Halberstam, David. *The Fifties*. New York: Villard, 1993.

Halloran, S. Michael. "From Rhetoric to Composition: The Teaching of Writing in America to 1900." *A Short History of Writing Instruction*. Ed. James J. Murphy. Davis, CA: Hermagoras P, 1990. 151–82.

————. "Rhetoric and the English Department." *Rhetoric Society Quarterly* 17 (1982): 3–10.

————. "Rhetoric in the American College Curriculum: The Decline of Public Discourse." *Pre/Text* 3 (1982): 245–69.

Haraway, Donna J. "The Politics of Postmodern Bodies: Constitutions of Self in Immune System Discourse." In *Simians, Cyborgs, and Women*. New York: Routledge, 1991.

Harkin, Patricia, and John Schilb, eds. *Contending with Words: Composition and Rhetoric in a Postmodern Age*. New York: MLA, 1991.

Harris, Joseph. "The Idea of Community in the Study of Writing." *College Composition and Communication* 40 (1989): 11–22.

————. "Negotiating the Contact Zone." *Journal of Basic Writing* 14 (1995): 27–42.

———. "The Other Reader." In Olson and Dobrin, 225–35.

———. "The Rhetoric of Theory." In Clifford and Schilb, 141–47.

———. "Students as Intellectuals." Paper presented at Conference on College Composition and Communication, Washington, DC, March 23, 1995.

———. "Symposium on 'After Dartmouth: Growth and Conflict.' " *College English* 54 (1992): 705–14.

———. *A Teaching Subject: Composition since 1966.* Upper Saddle River, NJ: Prentice Hall, 1997.

Hart, Albert Bushnell. "Ten Years of Harvard," *Harvard Graduates Magazine* 11 (1902): 64.

Harvard University. *Report of the Harvard Class of 1853, 1849–1913, Issued on the Sixtieth Anniversary for the Use of the Class and Its Friends.* Cambridge: The University P, 1913.

Havelock, Eric A. *Preface to Plato.* Cambridge: Harvard UP, 1963.

Hawkins, Hugh. "University Identity: The Teaching and Research Functions." In Oleson and Voss, 285–312.

Hench, John B., ed. *Three Hundred Years of American Newspaper.* Worcester, MA: American Antiquarian Society, 1991.

Higham, John. "The Matrix of Specialization." In Oleson and Voss, 3–18.

Hill, Adams Sherman. *Beginnings of Rhetoric and Composition.* New York: American Book Co., 1902.

———. "Causes of the Commune." *North American Review* 116 (January 1873): 90–109.

———. "The Chicago Convention." *North American Review* 107 (July 1868): 167–86.

———. *Foundations of Rhetoric.* New York: Harper, 1893.

———. "Greeley's American Conflict." *North American Review* 104 (January 1867): 238–47.

———. "The Influence of Emerson." *Studies and Notes in Philology and Literature* 5 (1896): 23–39.

———. Letter to Dr. [James] Walker. June 5, 1856. Columbia University Archives.

———. Letter to E[dwin] M. Bacon. May 6, 1886. Adams Sherman Hill General Folder. Harvard University Archives.

———. Letters to Sidney Howard Gay. 1860–63. Sidney Howard Gay Collection. Columbia University Archives.

———. *Our English.* New York: American Book Company, 1888.

———. Papers, 1859–64. Duke University Archives.

———. [Personal Diary.] Harvard University Archives.

———. *The Principles of Rhetoric and their Application*. New York: Harper, 1887.

———. "Salter's Life of Grimes." *North American Review* 123 (July 1876): 186–93.

———. "Sub-Freshman English." *Educational Review* 9 (December 1899): 468–95.

Hill, A. S., L. B. R. Briggs, and B. S. Hurlbut. *Twenty Years of School and College English*. Cambridge: Harvard UP, 1896.

Hillard, Van E. "Boredom and the Rhetoric of Responsibility." Unpublished manuscript.

———. "Raiders and the Lost Art: The Erosion of Knowledge Making in the Information Age." Paper presented Conference on College Composition and Communication, San Diego, April 1, 1993.

Hofstadter, Richard. *The American Political Tradition and the Men Who Made It*. New York: Vintage, 1973.

———. *Anti-Intellectualism in American Life*. New York: Vintage, 1963.

Hofstadter, Richard, and Walter P. Metzger. *The Development of Academic Freedom in the United States*. New York: Columbia UP, 1955.

Horlick, Allan S. *Patricians, Professors, and Public Schools: The Origins of Modern Educational Thought in America*. New York: E. J. Brill, 1994.

Horner, Winifred Bryan, ed. *The Present State of Historical and Contemporary Rhetoric*. 2nd ed. Columbia: U of Missouri P, 1990.

Hudson, Frederic. *Journalism in the United States: From 1690–1872*. New York: Harper, 1872.

Hurlbert, C. Mark and Michael Blitz, eds. *Composition and Resistance*. Portsmouth, NH: Boynton/Cook-Heinemann, 1991.

Innis, Harold A. *The Bias of Communication*. Toronto: U of Toronto P, 1951.

———. *Empire & Communication*. Toronto: U of Toronto P, 1950.

Isocrates. *Aeropagiticus*. In *A Synoptic History of Classical Rhetoric*. 2nd ed. Ed. James J. Murphy and Richard Katula. Davis, CA: Hermagoras P, 1994.

———. *Against the Sophists*. In *The Rhetorical Tradition*. Ed. Patricia Bizzell and Bruce Herzberg. Boston: St. Martin's P, 1990. 46–49.

Jameson, Frederic. "Frederic Jameson, Program in Literature" [Interview]. *Missing Link* [Duke University] March 1992: 5, 9.

Jamieson, Kathleen Hall. *Eloquence in an Electronic Age: The Transformation of Political Speechmaking*. New York: Oxford UP, 1988.

Jarratt, Susan C. "Feminism and Composition: The Case for Conflict." In Harkin and Schilb, 105–23.

Johnson, Haynes, and David S. Broder. *The System: The American Way of Politics at the Breaking Point*. Boston: Little, Brown, 1996.

Johnson, Nan. *Nineteenth-Century Rhetoric in North America*. Carbondale and Edwardsville: Southern Illinois UP, 1991.

Johnson, Richard. "What Is Cultural Studies Anyway?" *Social Text* 16 (Winter 1986/87): 38–80.

Jolliffe, David A. "The Moral Subject in College Composition: A Conceptual Framework and the Case of Harvard, 1865–1900." *College English* 52 (1989): 163–73.

Kaestle, Carl F. "Literacy and Diversity: Themes from a Social History of the American Reading Public." *History of Education Quarterly* 28 (1988): 523–49.

Kaestle, Carl F., Helen Damon-Moore, Lawrence C. Stedman, Katherine Tinsley, and William Vance Trollinger Jr. *Literacy in the United States: Readers and Reading since 1880*. New Haven: Yale UP, 1991.

Kastely, James L. *Rethinking the Rhetorical Tradition: From Plato to Postmodernism*. New Haven: Yale UP, 1997.

Kaufer, David S., and Kathleen M. Carley. *Communications at a Distance: The Influence of Print on Sociocultural Organization and Change*. Hillsdale, NJ: Lawrence Erlbaum, 1993.

Kennedy, Alan. "Politics, Writing Instruction, Public Space, and the English Language." In Fitts and France, 17–38.

Kilpatrick, William. *Why Johnny Can't Tell Right from Wrong*. New York: Simon & Schuster, 1992.

Kirkland, Edward Chase. *Charles Francis Adams, Jr., 1835–1915: The Patrician at Bay*. Cambridge: Harvard UP, 1965.

Kitzhaber, Albert R. *Rhetoric in American Colleges, 1850–1900*. Dallas: Southern Methodist UP, 1990.

Kraemer, Don. "Achieving the High Intention? Wayne Booth's Pluralist Equivalence and Postmodern Difference." *College English* 52 (April 1990): 377–84.

Kremers, Marshall. "Adams Sherman Hill Meets ENFI: An Inquiry and a Retrospective." *Computers and Composition* 5 (1988): 69–77.

Kroll, Barry. "Arguing about Public Issues: What Can We Learn from Practical Ethics?" *Rhetoric Review* 16 (1997): 105–19.

Kurtz, Howard. *Air: All Talk, All the Time*. New York: Times Books, 1996.

Lanham, Richard A. *The Electronic Word: Democracy, Technology, and the Arts*. Chicago: U of Chicago P, 1993.

———. *A Handlist of Rhetorical Terms*. 2nd ed. Berkeley: U of California P, 1991.

———. *Revising Prose*. New York: Scribner's, 1979.

Larrabee, R. C. "Notes in English A, '93." Harvard University Archives.

Larsen, Elizabeth. "The Progress of Literacy: Edward Tyrrel Channing and the Separation of the Student Writer from the World." *Rhetoric Review* 11 (1992): 159–71.

Larson, Charles U. *Persuasion: Reception and Responsibility*. Belmont, CA: Wadsworth, 1989.

Lazere, Donald. "Spellmeyer's Naive Populism." *College Composition and Communication* 48 (May 1997): 288–92.

———. "Teaching the Political Conflicts: A Rhetorical Schema," *College Composition and Communication* 43 (1992): 194–213.

Lears, T. Jackson. *No Place of Grace: Antimodernism and the Transformation of Culture, 1880–1920*. New York: Pantheon, 1981.

Lentricchia, Frank. *Ariel and the Police: Michel Foucault, William James, Wallace Stevens*. Madison: U of Wisconsin P, 1988.

Lincoln, William. *History of Worcester*. Worcester, MA: Charles Hersey, 1862.

Lindemann, Erika and Gary Tate, eds. *An Introduction to Composition Studies*. New York: Oxford UP, 1991.

Lloyd-Jones, Richard. "Using the History of Rhetoric." In Enos, 15–25.

Lodge, Henry Cabot. "Memorial Address." *Charles Francis Adams, 1835–1915: An Autobiography*, by Charles Francis Adams Jr. Boston: Houghton, 1916. ix–lx.

Logsdon, Joseph. *Horace White, Nineteenth-Century Liberal*. Westport, CT: Greenwood, 1971.

Lord, Eliot. "A Need of Newspapers." *The Harvard Monthly* 7.4 (January 1889): 127–29.

Lunsford, Andrea A. "The Nature of Composition Studies." In Lindemann and Tate, 3–14.

Lynch, Dennis A., Diana George, and Marilyn M. Cooper. "Moments of Argument: Agonistic Inquiry and Confrontational Cooperation." *College Composition and Communication* 48.1 (1997): 61–85.

Martin, Emily. *Flexible Bodies: Tracking Immunity in American Culture—From the Days of Polio to the Age of AIDS*. Boston: Beacon P, 1995.

Martin, Wanda. "Inquiry and Argument in Writing about Public Policy." *Issues in Writing* 6.1 (1993/1994): 38–50.

Marvin, Abijah P. *History of Worcester in the War of the Rebellion*. Worcester, MA: Abijah P. Marvin, 1870.

Marvin, Carolyn. "Fresh Blood, Public Meat: Rituals of Totem Regeneration in the 1992 Presidential Race." *Communication Research* 21 (June 1994): 264–92.

————. *When Old Technologies Were New: Thinking about Electric Communication in the Late Nineteenth Century.* New York: Oxford UP, 1988.

Marzolf, Marion Tuttle. *Civilizing Voices: American Press Criticism, 1880–1950.* White Plains, NY: Longman, 1991.

McGuire, William J. "The Effectiveness of Supportive and Refutational Defenses in Immunizing and Restoring Beliefs against Persuasion." *Sociometry* 24 (1961): 184–97.

McGerr, Michael E. *The Decline of Popular Politics: The American North, 1865–1928.* New York: Oxford University Press, 1986.

McKeon, Richard. "The Uses of Rhetoric in a Technological Age: Architectonic Productive Arts." *The Prospect of Rhetoric.* Ed. Lloyd F. Bitzer and Edwin Black. Englewood Cliffs, NJ: Prentice Hall, 1971.

Medill, J[oseph]. Letters to Adams Sherman Hill. September 14, 1861 and October 28, 1861. Adams Sherman Hill Papers. Duke University Archives.

Miles, Josephine. *Working Out Ideas: Predication and Other Uses of Language.* Berkeley: Bay Area Writing Project, 1979.

Miller, Richard E. "Making Your Own Skin Crawl: Teaching in the Nervous System." Paper presented at Conference on College Composition and Communication, Phoenix, March 13, 1997.

Miller, Susan. "Composition as Cultural Artifact: Rethinking History as Theory." In Clifford and Schilb, 19–32.

————. *Rescuing the Subject: A Critical Introduction to Rhetoric and the Writer.* Carbondale and Edwardsville: Southern Illinois UP, 1989.

————. *Textual Carnivals: The Politics of Composition.* Carbondale and Edwardsville: Southern Illinois UP, 1991.

Miller, Thomas P. *The Formation of College English: Rhetoric and Belles Lettres in the British Cultural Provinces.* Pittsburgh: U of Pittsburgh P, 1997.

————. "Reinventing Rhetorical Traditions." In Enos, 26–41.

Mohanty, S. P. "Radical Teaching, Radical Theory: The Ambiguous Politics of Meaning." *Theory in the Classroom.* Ed. Cary Nelson. Urbana: U of Illinois P, 1986. 149–76.

Moore, Charles. "Preparation for Newspaper Work." *The Harvard Monthly* 6 (1885): 132–35.

Mott, Frank Luther Mott. *American Journalism: A History, 1690–1960.* 3rd ed. New York: Macmillan, 1960.

————. *A History of American Magazines.* 6 vols. Cambridge: Harvard UP, 1938.

Newkirk, Thomas, ed. *Only Connect: Uniting Reading and Writing.* Portsmouth, NH: Boynton/Cook, 1986.

Nietzsche, Friedrich. "On the Uses and Disadvantages of History for Life." *Untimely Meditations.* Trans. R. J. Hollingdale. Cambridge: Cambridge UP, 1983.

Nord, David Paul. "Newspapers and American Nationhood, 1776–1826." In Hench, 391–406.

North, Stephen M. *The Making of Knowledge in Composition: Portrait of an Emerging Field.* Upper Montclair, NJ: Boynton/Cook, 1987.

Ohmann, Richard. "Afterword." In Fitts and France, 325–332.

———. *Politics of Letters.* Middletown, CT: Wesleyan UP, 1987.

Oleson, Alexandra and John Voss, eds. *The Organization of Knowledge in Modern America, 1860–1920.* Baltimore: Johns Hopkins UP, 1979.

Olson, Gary A. and Sidney I. Dobrin, eds. *Composition Theory for the Postmodern Classroom.* Albany: State U of New York P, 1994.

Ong, Walter J., S.J. *Fighting for Life: Contest, Sexuality, and Consciousness.* Ithaca: Cornell UP, 1981.

———. *Orality and Literacy: The Technologizing of the Word.* London and New York: Routledge, 1982.

———. *The Presence of the Word: Some Prolegomena for Cultural and Religious History.* New Haven: Yale UP, 1967.

Paine, Charles. "The Composition Course and Public Discourse: The Case of Adams Sherman Hill, Popular Culture, and Cultural Inoculation." *Rhetoric Review* 15 (1997): 282–99.

———. "Who Wrote the Harvard Literacy Reports?" Paper presented Conference on College Composition and Communication, Washington, DC, March 22, 1995.

Painter, Nell Irvin. *Standing at Armageddon: The United States, 1877–1919.* New York: Norton, 1987.

Parker, William Riley. "Where Do English Departments Come from?" *College English* 28 (1967): 339–51. Rpt. *The Writing Teacher's Sourcebook.* 2nd ed. Ed. Gary Tate and Edward P. J. Corbett. New York: Oxford UP, 1988. 34–15.

Peirce, Charles S. *Philosophical Writings of Peirce.* Ed. Justus Buchler. New York: Dover, 1955.

Perelman, Chaim, and Lucie Olbrechts-Tyteca. *The New Rhetoric.* Notre Dame: U of Notre Dame P, 1969.

Phelps, Louise Wetherbee. "A Constrained Vision of the Writing Classroom." *ADE Bulletin* 103 (1992): 13–21.

Plato. *The Republic*. Trans. Paul Shorey. *Plato: The Collected Dialogues*. Ed. Edith Hamilton and Huntington Cairns. Princeton: Princeton UP, 1961.

Pfau, Michael, and Allan Louden. "Effectiveness of Adwatch Formats in Deflecting Political Attack Ads." *Communication Research* 21 (1994): 325–41.

Pfau, Michael, Steve Van Bockern, and Jon Geun Kang. "Use of Inoculation to Promote Resistance to Smoking Initiation among Adolescents." *Communication Monographs* 59 (1992): 213–30.

Postman, Neil. *Amusing Ourselves to Death*. New York: Penguin, 1986.

Pratt, Mary Louise. "Arts of the Contact Zone." *Profession 91* (1991): 33–40.

Pred, Allan R. *Urban Growth and the Circulation of Information: The United States System of Cities, 1790–1840*. Cambridge: Harvard UP, 1973.

[Rantoul, Robert Samuel.] "Adams Sherman Hill." In Harvard University, 135–41.

Reid, Ronald F. "The Boylston Professorship of Rhetoric and Oratory, 1806–1904: A Case Study in Changing Concepts of Rhetoric and Pedagogy." *The Quarterly Journal of Speech* 55 (1959): 239–57.

Reid, Whitelaw. Letters to Adams Sherman Hill. December 3 and 9, 1863, and undated [ca. late December] 1863. Adams Sherman Hill Papers. Duke University Archives.

Reilly, Thomas William. "Henry Villard: Civil War Journalist." Masters thesis, University of Oregon, 1970.

"Responsibility 101." Editorial. *Durham Herald-Sun* October 11, 1992: A11.

Ried, Paul E. "The First and Fifth Boylston Professors: A View of Two Worlds." *Quarterly Journal of Speech* 74 (1988): 229–40.

———. "Francis J. Child: The Fourth Boylston Professor of Rhetoric and Oratory." *Quarterly Journal of Speech* 55 (1969): 268–75.

Robinson, Fred N. "Notes in English A, 1887–8." Harvard University Archives.

Robinson, Jay L., and Patricia Stock. "The Politics of Literacy." *Conversations on the Written Word: Essays on Language and Literacy*, by Jay L. Robinson. Portsmouth, NH: Boynton/Cook-Heinemann, 1990. 271–317.

Robison, Lori. "This Could Have Been Me: Composition and the Implications of Cultural Perspective." In Berlin and Vivion, 231–43.

de Romilly, Jacqueline. *Magic and Rhetoric in Ancient Greece*. Cambridge: Harvard UP, 1975.

Rooney, Ellen. *Seductive Reasoning: Pluralism as the Problematic of Contemporary Literary Theory*. Ithaca and London: Cornell UP, 1989.

Rosen, Jay. *Getting the Connections Right: Public Journalism and the Troubles in the Press*. New York: Twentieth Century Fund P, 1996.

Rosewater, Victor. *History of Cooperative News-Gathering in the United States*. New York: Appleton, 1930.

Roskelly, Hephzibah. "The Dialogue of Chaos: An Unthinkable Order." In Louise Smith, 96–106.

Roskelly, Hephzibah and Kate Ronald. "You're Either on the Bus . . . or off the Bus." *Farther Along: Transforming Dichotomies in Rhetoric and Composition*. Ed. Kate Ronald and Hephzibah Roskelly. Portsmouth, NH: Boynton/Cook-Heinemann, 1990. 1–11.

Roszak, Theodore. *The Cult of Information*. Berkeley: U of California P, 1994.

Rudolph, Frederick. *The American College and University: A History*. New York, Vintage, 1962.

Russell, David. *Writing in the Academic Disciplines, 1870–1990: A Curricular History*. Carbondale and Edwardsville: Southern Illinois UP, 1991.

Sacks, Peter. *Generation X Goes to College: An Eye-Opening Account of Teaching in Postmodern America*. Chicago and LaSalle: Open Court, 1996.

Salvatori, Mariolina. "Conversations with Texts: Reading in the Teaching of Composition." *College English* 58 (April 1996): 440–54.

———. "Toward a Hermeneutics of Difficulty." In Louise Smith, 80–95.

Schilb, John. "Comment [on 'Rhetoric and Ideology in the Writing Class' and 'Problem Solving Reconsidered']." *College English* 51 (1989) 769–70.

———. "Cultural Studies, Postmodernism, and Composition." In Harkin and Schilb, 173–88.

Schiller, Dan. *Objectivity and the News: The Public and the Rise of Commercial Journalism*. Philadelphia: U of Pennsylvania P, 1981.

Schneider, Louis, ed. *The Scottish Moralists on Human Nature and Society*. Chicago: U of Chicago P, 1967.

Schriner, Delores K. "One Person, Many Worlds: A Multi-Cultural Composition Curriculum." In Berlin and Vivion, 95–111.

Schudson, Michael. *Discovering the News: A Social History of American Newspapers*. New York: Basic Books, 1978.

———. "Preparing the Minds of the People: Three Hundred Years of the American Newspaper." In Hench, 421–43.

———. "Was There Ever a Public Sphere? If So, When? Reflections on the American Case." *Habermas and the Public Sphere*. Ed. Craig Calhoun. Cambridge: MIT P, 1992. 143–63.

Schwarzlose, Richard A. Schwarzlose. *The Nation's Newsbrokers*. 2 vols. Evanston, IL: Northwestern UP, 1989.

Segerblohm, Wilhelm. "Notes for English A, 1893–94." Harvard University Archives.

Seitz, James. "Roland Barthes, Reading, and Roleplay: Composition's Misguided Rejection of Fragmentary Texts." *College English* 53 (1991): 815–25.

Sellers, Charles. *The Market Revolution: Jacksonian America, 1815–1846*. New York: Oxford UP, 1991.

Shor, Ira. *When Students Have Power: Negotiating Authority in a Critical Pedagogy*. Chicago: U of Chicago P, 1996.

Shor, Ira, ed. *Freire for the Classroom: A Sourcebook for Liberatory Teaching*. Portsmouth, NH: Boynton/Cook, 1987.

Shor, Ira, and Paulo Freire. *A Pedagogy for Liberation: Dialogues on Transforming Education*. New York: Begin & Garvey, 1987.

Shurman, Andrew. Letter to Adams Sherman Hill. January 5, 1864. Adams Sherman Hill Papers. Duke University Archives.

Silverstein, Arthur M. *A History of Immunology*. San Diego: Academic P, 1989.

Smith, Barbara Herrnstein. *Contingencies of Value: Alternative Perspectives for Critical Theory*. Cambridge: Harvard UP, 1988.

Smith, Louise Z., ed. *Audits of Meaning*. Portsmouth, NH: Boynton/Cook, 1988.

Smith, William Henry. "The Press as a News Gatherer." *Century* 42 (1891): 524–36.

Sontag, Susan. *Illness as Metaphor and AIDS and Its Metaphors*. New York and London: Doubleday, 1990.

Spellmeyer, Kurt. "Culture and Agency." *College Composition and Communication* 48 (May 1997): 292–96.

———. "Out of the Fashion Industry: From Cultural Studies to the Anthropology of Knowledge." *College Composition and Communication* 47 (1996): 424–36.

Starr, Louis M. *The Bohemian Brigade: Civil War Newsmen in Action*. New York: Knopf, 1954.

Stedman, Edmund Clarence. *Life and Letters of Edmund Clarence Stedman*. Ed. Laura Stedman and G. M. Gould. 2 vols. New York: Moffat, Yard, and Co., 1910.

Stewart, Donald. "Foreword." *Rhetoric and Reality: Writing Instruction in American Colleges, 1990–1985*. Carbondale and Edwardsville: Southern Illinois UP, 1985.

———. "Harvard's Influence on English Studies: Perceptions from Three Universities in the Early Twentieth Century." *College Composition and Communication* 43 (December 1992): 455–71.

———. "A Model for Our Time: Fred Newton Scott's Rhetoric Program at Michigan." In Enos, 26–41.

————. "The Nineteenth Century." *The Present State of Historical Scholarship in Historical and Contemporary Rhetoric.* 2nd ed. Ed. Winifred Bryan Horner. Columbia: U of Missouri P, 1990. 151–85.

————. "Some History Lessons for Composition Teachers." *Rhetoric Review* 3 (1985): 134–44. Rpt. *The Writing Teacher's Sourcebook.* 2nd ed. Ed. Gary Tate and Edward P. J. Corbett. New York: Oxford UP, 1988. 134–44.

————. "The Status of Composition in American Colleges, 1880–1902." *College English* 47 (1987): 734–46.

————. "Two Model Teachers and the Harvardization of English Departments." *The Rhetorical Tradition and Modern Writing.* Ed. James J. Murphy. New York: MLA, 1982. 118–30.

————. "Which Is Your Job and Which Is Your Strength?" *College English* 40 (1978): 65–69.

Stewart, Kenneth, and John Tebbel. *Makers of Modern Journalism.* New York: Prentice, 1952.

Stone, I. F. *The Trial of Socrates.* Boston: Little Brown, 1988.

Stuckey, J. Elspeth. *The Violence of Literacy.* Portsmouth: Boynton/Cook, 1991.

Swearingen, C. Jan. "Composing Aspasia: What Does the History of Rhetoric Have to Do with Teaching Composition, Anyway?" Paper presented at the Penn State Conference on Rhetoric and Composition, University Park, July 12, 1995.

————. *Rhetoric and Irony: Western Literacy and Western Lies.* New York: Oxford UP, 1991.

Sykes, Charles. *A Nation of Victims: The Decay of American Character.* New York: St. Martin's, 1992.

Tannen, Deborah. *The Argument Culture: Moving from Debate to Dialogue.* New York: Random, 1998.

Tate, Gary. "Empty Pedagogical Space and Silent Students." In Fitts and France, 269–73.

Tebbel, John. *The Media in America.* New York: Crowell, 1974.

Tebbel, John, and Mary Ellen Zuckerman. *The Magazine in America, 1741–1990.* New York: Oxford UP, 1991.

Thoreau, Henry D. *The Illustrated "A Week on the Concord and Merrimack Rivers."* Ed. Carl F. Hovde, William L. Howarth, and Elizabeth Hall Witherall. Princeton: Princeton UP, 1983.

de Tocqueville, Alexis. *Democracy in America.* 2 vols. Trans. Henry Reeve. New York: D. Appleton, 1899.

Townsend, Kim. *Manhood at Harvard: Williams James and Others.* New York: Norton, 1996.

Trachtenberg, Alan. *The Incorporation of America: Culture & Society in the Gilded Age*. New York: Hill and Wang, 1982.

Trimbur, John. "Consensus and Difference in Collaborative Learning." *College English* 51 (October 1989): 602–16.

———. "Cultural Studies and Teaching Writing." *Focuses* 1 (1988): 5–18.

———. "Literacy and the Discourse of Crisis." In Bullock and Trimbur, 277–96.

———. "Response [to Maxine Hairston]." *College Composition and Communication* 44 (May 1993): 248–49.

Tudor, William. [Comment]. *North American Review* 4 (March 1817).

Tuman, Myron. *A Preface to Literacy: An Inquiry into Pedagogy, Practice, and Progress*. Tuscaloosa: U of Alabama P, 1987.

———. *Word Perfect: Literacy in the Computer Age*. Pittsburgh: U of Pittsburgh P, 1992.

Tyack, David. "The Common School and American Society: A Reappraisal." *History of Education Quarterly* 26 (1986): 301–6.

Underwood, F[rancis]. H[enry]. Letter to Adams Sherman Hill. May 26 [1864]. Adams Sherman Hill Papers. Duke University Archives.

Varnum, Robin. *Fencing with Words: A History of Writing Instruction at Amherst College during the Era of Theodore Baird, 1938–1966*. Urbana, IL: National Conference of Teachers of English, 1966.

Veeder, Rex L. "Romantic Rhetoric and the Rhetorical Tradition." *Rhetoric Review* 15 (Spring 1997): 300–21.

Veysey, Lawrence. *The Emergence of the American University*. Chicago: U of Chicago P, 1965.

———. "The Plural Organized Worlds of the Humanities." In Oleson and Voss, 51–106.

Villard, Henry. *Memoirs* I. Boston and New York: Houghton, 1904.

Villard, Oswald Garrison. *Fighting Years: Memoirs of a Liberal Editor*. New York: Harcourt, 1939.

Warner, Michael. *The Letters of the Republic: Publication and the Public Sphere in Eighteenth-Century America*. Cambridge: Harvard UP, 1990.

Watts, Steven. *The Republic Reborn: War and the Making of Liberal America, 1790–1820*. Baltimore: Johns Hopkins UP, 1987.

Wayland, Francis. *Thoughts on the Present Collegiate System in the United States*. Boston: Gould, Kendall & Lincoln, 1842. Rptd. New York: Arno P, 1969.

Webb, Joseph M. "Historical Perspective on the New Journalism." *Journalism History* 1 (1974): 38–42.

Weinstein, Mark. "Critical Thinking and Education for Democracy." *Educational Philosophy and Theory* 23 (1991): 9–29.

Welch, Nancy. "Revising a Writer's Identity: Reading and 'Re-modeling' in a Composition Class." *College Composition and Communication* 47 (1996): 41–61.

Wells, Susan. "Rogue Cops and Health Care: What Do We Want from Public Writing?" *College Composition and Communication* 47 (October 1996): 325–41.

Wendell, Barrett. *Barrett Wendell and His Letters*. Ed. M. A. DeWolfe Howe. Boston: Atlantic Monthly P, 1924.

———. "Recollections of Student Life." Harvard University Archives.

Wiebe, Robert H. *The Search for Order, 1877–1920*. New York: Hill and Wang, 1967.

Wilkerson, Sam[uel] S. Letter to Adams Sherman Hill. n.d. 1859. Adams Sherman Hill Papers. Duke University Archives.

Will, George F. "Disorder in the Schools: Too Many College Students Have Neither the Aptitudes nor the Attitudes Needed in College." *Newsweek* April 13, 1998: 84.

Williams, Raymond. *The Country and the City*. New York: Oxford UP, 1973.

———. *Marxism and Literature*. New York: Oxford UP, 1977.

Young, Richard E. "Paradigms and Problems: Needed Research in Rhetorical Invention." *Research on Composing: Points of Departure*. Ed. Charles R. Cooper and Lee Odell. Urbana, IL: National Council of Teachers of English, 1978. 29–47.

Zebroski, James Thomas. "The Syracuse University Writing Program and Cultural Studies: A Personal View of the Politics of Development." In Berlin and Vivion, 87–94.

Zucker, Steven. "Teaching at the University Level." *Notices of the American Mathematical Society* 43 (August 1996): 863–65.

Index